LLEWELLYN'S

2024

MOON

SIGN

BOOK

*Plan Your Life
by the Cycles of the Moon*

- COMPREHENSIVE GARDENING GUIDE
- WEATHER AND ECONOMIC FORECASTS
- NEW AND FULL MOON HOROSCOPES

Llewellyn's 2024 Moon Sign Book®

ISBN 978-0-7387-6898-4

Cover design by Kevin R. Brown
Editing by Hanna Grimson
Stock photography models used for illustrative purposes only and may not endorse or represent the book's subject.
Interior photographs: Getty Images, except page 266, which is courtesy of Penny Kelly.
Typography owned by Llewellyn Worldwide Ltd.

Weekly tips by Penny Kelly, Lupa, and Shelby Deering.

Any internet references contained in this work are current at publication time, but the publisher cannot guarantee that a specific location will continue to be maintained.

A special thanks to Beth Koch Rosato for astrological proofreading.

Astrological data compiled and programmed by Rique Pottenger, based on the earlier work of Neil F. Michelsen.

You can order Llewellyn annuals and books from *New Worlds*, Llewellyn's catalog. To request a free copy of the catalog, call toll-free 1-877-NEW-WRLD or visit our website at www.llewellyn.com.

Llewellyn Publications is a registered trademark of Llewellyn Worldwide Ltd.
2143 Wooddale Drive, Woodbury, MN 55125-2989 USA
Moon Sign Book® is registered in U.S. Patent and Trademark Office.
Moon Sign Book is a trademark of Llewellyn Worldwide Ltd. (Canada).

Llewellyn Publications
A Division of Llewellyn Worldwide Ltd.
2143 Wooddale Drive
Woodbury, MN 55125-2989
www.llewellyn.com

Printed in China

Table of Contents

The Methods of the
Moon Sign Book

Whether we live in simple, primitive times or a time of high technology and mass communication, we need our connection to Mother Nature and an understanding of how all of her systems work together—soil, sun, wind, water, plants, animals, people, and planets.

The connections among elements of nature become especially relevant when we recognize that many energies—both subtle and obvious—flow through our world and affect all things. Ancient civilizations knew about these changing energies and were much more attuned to the subtle effects that they had on us.

In the world of unseen energies, it has long been accepted in many quarters that the position of the planets makes a difference in the energy flowing around planet Earth. Those who question these energy flows are often sadly divorced from nature.

Imagine placing a large rock in the waters of a flowing stream or creek. Immediately you would notice numerous changes in the flow of the water moving over, around, and past the rock.

It is no different with our solar system. We live on a planet that floats in a solar sea of energies and frequency waves. As the planets move around the sun, the currents of energy flowing through the solar sea change in the same way that flowing water changes around the rock placed in a creek or stream…and we are affected by those changes at every level—physically, mentally, emotionally, and spiritually.

The ability to detect these changes and their effect on us has long been organized into knowledge systems, and the *Moon Sign Book* has always been a stable anchor in maintaining this knowledge and recognizing its importance. We call these organized methods of gaining knowledge *astrology*, and ancient cultures around the globe used this as their science. It was how they found and maintained a sense of prediction, control, and security, something we are still striving for even today as we try to anticipate the cycles and events of our daily lives.

Although there are several ways of organizing and assessing these energy flows based on planetary positions, the *Moon Sign Book* uses the tropical system, which says that spring officially begins when the Sun is directly over the equator at noon, something that occurs around March 20 to 21 every year. Once that moment has been determined, the rest of the zodiac calendar is laid out at thirty-degree intervals. This allows us to be precise, but also flex with the changing nature of all things, including our solar system. We support a knowledge base that upholds the ancient wisdom and teaches it to all who are interested. We invite you to read what we have written here and to celebrate the interactions of these energies with the plants, animals, earth, and stars that share this time and space with us.

Weekly Almanac

**Your Guide to
Lunar Gardening
& Good Timing for Activities**

♑ January

December 31–January 6

*I realize that just living my truth of what I am, there's one
less person to fight me in my own head.* ⁓Raven-Symoné

Date	Qtr.	Sign	Activity
Jan. 5, 7:39 am– Jan. 7, 4:08 pm	4th	Scorpio	Plant biennials, perennials, bulbs and roots. Prune. Irrigate. Fertilize (organic).

Did you know that you can paint your own wall mural in your home? It's surprisingly simple as long as you draw a sketch first (straightforward geometric shapes or stripes are easy to work with and on-trend). Look for matte paint in a hue that matches your palette, draw the design on the wall using a pencil and erase any mistakes, and then paint away.

_____

_____

_____

_____

January 3
10:30 pm EST

JANUARY

S	M	T	W	T	F	S
	1	2	3	4	5	6
7	8	9	10	11	12	13
14	15	16	17	18	19	20
21	22	23	24	25	26	27
28	29	30	31			

January 7–13

I think that to one in sympathy with nature, each season, in its turn, seems the loveliest. ~MARK TWAIN

Date	Qtr.	Sign	Activity
Jan. 7, 4:08 pm– Jan. 9, 8:33 pm	4th	Sagittarius	Cultivate. Destroy weeds and pests. Harvest fruits and root crops for food. Trim to retard growth.
Jan. 9, 8:33 pm– Jan. 11, 6:57 am	4th	Capricorn	Plant potatoes and tubers. Trim to retard growth.
Jan. 11, 6:57 am– Jan. 11, 10:01 pm	1st	Capricorn	Graft or bud plants. Trim to increase growth.
Jan. 13, 10:29 pm– Jan. 15, 11:49 pm	1st	Pisces	Plant grains, leafy annuals. Fertilize (chemical). Graft or bud plants. Irrigate. Trim to increase growth.

Over the winter, the air in your house can become so stale that air freshener and even a diffuser with essential oils do not help. Once a week, open all the doors and windows for five minutes to force a complete air exchange. Then close up and plug in a diffuser with a few drops of lemon or other essential oil in it. You and the house will both feel better.

January 11
6:57 am EST

JANUARY

S	M	T	W	T	F	S
	1	2	3	4	5	6
7	8	9	10	11	12	13
14	15	16	17	18	19	20
21	22	23	24	25	26	27
28	29	30	31			

January 14–20

Even though you and I are in different boats, you in your boat and we in our canoe, we share the same River of Life.

~Oren Lyons

Date	Qtr.	Sign	Activity
Jan. 18, 3:12 am– Jan. 20, 8:58 am	2nd	Taurus	Plant annuals for hardiness. Trim to increase growth.

If your knees are hurting and it's not due to a specific medical condition, you may just need to do some squats! The muscles in your legs, butt, and even your core help to support your knees, and the stronger they are, the happier your knees will be. Don't forget to stretch those muscles too, and always consult a medical professional when making significant changes to your exercise regimen or when dealing with pain.

<hr />
<hr />
<hr />
<hr />

January 17
10:53 pm EST

JANUARY

S	M	T	W	T	F	S
	1	2	3	4	5	6
7	8	9	10	11	12	13
14	15	16	17	18	19	20
21	22	23	24	25	26	27
28	29	30	31			

January 21–27 〰

Being with my friends is like coming home.

~KAREENA KAPOOR KHAN

Date	Qtr.	Sign	Activity
Jan. 22, 4:51 pm– Jan. 25, 2:37 am	2nd	Cancer	Plant grains, leafy annuals. Fertilize (chemical). Graft or bud plants. Irrigate. Trim to increase growth.
Jan. 25, 12:54 pm– Jan. 27, 2:11 pm	3rd	Leo	Cultivate. Destroy weeds and pests. Harvest fruits and root crops for food. Trim to retard growth.
Jan. 27, 2:11 pm– Jan. 30, 3:04 am	3rd	Virgo	Cultivate, especially medicinal plants. Destroy weeds and pests. Trim to retard growth.

For small houseplants, like cacti and succulents, you don't always need to go with traditional planters. Instead, go on a vintage scavenger hunt and see if you can find some unique vessels for them. At thrift stores and garage sales, track down cool coffee mugs, antique vases, and things that weren't originally intended for plants, like sponge holders and figurals, and use them as planters instead.

○

January 25
12:54 pm EST

JANUARY

S	M	T	W	T	F	S
		1	2	3	4	5	6
7	8	9	10	11	12	13
14	15	16	17	18	19	20
21	22	23	24	25	26	27
28	29	30	31			

≈≈ February

January 28–February 3

We can be whatever we have the courage to be.

~Alexandria Ocasio-Cortez

Date	Qtr.	Sign	Activity
Feb. 1, 3:37 pm– Feb. 2, 6:18 pm	3rd	Scorpio	Plant biennials, perennials, bulbs and roots. Prune. Irrigate. Fertilize (organic).
Feb. 2, 6:18 pm– Feb. 4, 1:28 am	4th	Scorpio	Plant biennials, perennials, bulbs and roots. Prune. Irrigate. Fertilize (organic).

A im to try a fruit or vegetable that you've never eaten before. You can improve your nutrition by switching up what's on your plate, and new-to-you produce is a way you can do just that. Mango? Okra? Dragon fruit? Enoki mushrooms? Choose something exotic at the grocery store or farmer's market and challenge yourself to use it in a recipe.

_____

_____

_____

_____

◑

February 2
6:18 pm EST

February

S	M	T	W	T	F	S
				1	2	3
4	5	6	7	8	9	10
11	12	13	14	15	16	17
18	19	20	21	22	23	24
25	26	27	28	29		

February 4–10 〰

In hard times, we are advised by all wise people to look to the margins of a culture, not the center.   ∼ALICE WALKER

Date	Qtr.	Sign	Activity
Feb. 4, 1:28 am– Feb. 6, 7:08 am	4th	Sagittarius	Cultivate. Destroy weeds and pests. Harvest fruits and root crops for food. Trim to retard growth.
Feb. 6, 7:08 am– Feb. 8, 8:59 am	4th	Capricorn	Plant potatoes and tubers. Trim to retard growth.
Feb. 8, 8:59 am– Feb. 9, 5:59 pm	4th	Aquarius	Cultivate. Destroy weeds and pests. Harvest fruits and root crops for food. Trim to retard growth.
Feb. 10, 8:42 am– Feb. 12, 8:26 am	1st	Pisces	Plant grains, leafy annuals. Fertilize (chemical). Graft or bud plants. Irrigate. Trim to increase growth.

Living in the dry climate of a desert or the north in winter can make you feel like a stiff, dried-out sponge. Counter this with a long, warm bath every week. Make sure you're hydrated, and then soak in a tub containing 1 cup of baking soda for 30 minutes. Rinse off with fresh water when you're done relaxing.

February 9
5:59 pm EST

FEBRUARY

S	M	T	W	T	F	S
				1	2	3
4	5	6	7	8	9	10
11	12	13	14	15	16	17
18	19	20	21	22	23	24
25	26	27	28	29		

≋ February 11–17

Black history isn't a separate history. This is all of our history,
this is American history, and we need to understand that.

~Karyn Parsons

Date	Qtr.	Sign	Activity
Feb. 14, 10:02 am–Feb. 16, 10:01 am	1st	Taurus	Plant annuals for hardiness. Trim to increase growth.
Feb. 16, 10:01 am–Feb. 16, 2:39 pm	2nd	Taurus	Plant annuals for hardiness. Trim to increase growth.

Need more kitchen storage? Create a pantry for your kitchen
by cleaning out a couple of cupboards or a closet and getting rid of things you never use. Add shelves that best fit your
storage jars and containers, then stock up with the things that are
most important for your diet and health.

February 16
10:01 am EST

FEBRUARY

S	M	T	W	T	F	S
				1	2	3
4	5	6	7	8	9	10
11	12	13	14	15	16	17
18	19	20	21	22	23	24
25	26	27	28	29		

February 18–24 〜〜〜

When you have a dream you've got to grab on and never let go.   ∼Carol Burnett

Date	Qtr.	Sign	Activity
Feb. 18, 10:25 pm– Feb. 21, 8:40 am	2nd	Cancer	Plant grains, leafy annuals. Fertilize (chemical). Graft or bud plants. Irrigate. Trim to increase growth.
Feb. 24, 7:30 am– Feb. 26, 9:29 am	3rd	Virgo	Cultivate, especially medicinal plants. Destroy weeds and pests. Trim to retard growth.

Is your email inbox currently stuffed? If so, make it a goal this week (or throughout the month) to reach "inbox zero," as people call it—or zero emails in your inbox. File those bills and important documents, answer emails to friends you may have put off, and unsubscribe from newsletters you don't read. Seeing that clear inbox will be a sigh of relief and something you can continue to aspire to in the future.

○

February 24
7:30 am EST

February

S	M	T	W	T	F	S
				1	2	3
4	5	6	7	8	9	10
11	12	13	14	15	16	17
18	19	20	21	22	23	24
25	26	27	28	29		

♓ March

February 25–March 2

We need, in every community, a group of angelic
troublemakers.
~Bayard Rustin

Date	Qtr.	Sign	Activity
Feb. 28, 10:09 pm– Mar. 2, 8:56 am	3rd	Scorpio	Plant biennials, perennials, bulbs and roots. Prune. Irrigate. Fertilize (organic).
Mar. 2, 8:56 am– Mar. 3, 10:23 am	3rd	Sagittarius	Cultivate. Destroy weeds and pests. Harvest fruits and root crops for food. Trim to retard growth.

Before your dog ever needs medication, give them a thin slice (or part of a slice for smaller dogs) of lunchmeat occasionally in the morning before breakfast. Fold it up as though there is a pill in it. After a few weeks, start tucking a pill-sized piece of kibble in the meat. Then in the future if you need to give your dog a pill, just wrap it in the meat instead of the kibble!

March

S	M	T	W	T	F	S
					1	2
3	4	5	6	7	8	9
10	11	12	13	14	15	16
17	18	19	20	21	22	23
24	25	26	27	28	29	30
31						

March 3–9

*It is impossible to care for each other more or differently than
we care for the earth.*   ~WENDELL BERRY

Date	Qtr.	Sign	Activity
Mar. 3, 10:23 am– Mar. 4, 4:15 pm	4th	Sagittarius	Cultivate. Destroy weeds and pests. Harvest fruits and root crops for food. Trim to retard growth.
Mar. 4, 4:15 pm– Mar. 6, 7:38 pm	4th	Capricorn	Plant potatoes and tubers. Trim to retard growth.
Mar. 6, 7:38 pm– Mar. 8, 8:03 pm	4th	Aquarius	Cultivate. Destroy weeds and pests. Harvest fruits and root crops for food. Trim to retard growth.
Mar. 8, 8:03 pm– Mar. 10, 5:00 am	4th	Pisces	Plant biennials, perennials, bulbs and roots. Prune. Irrigate. Fertilize (organic).

One of the best forms of exercise is planting and caring for a garden. Find a small area that gets full sun for at least 8–10 hours a day, till it or add containers that are at least 14 inches deep, and plant your seeds. Mother Nature will do the growing; you just have to weed it and reap.

March 3
10:23 am EST

MARCH

S	M	T	W	T	F	S
					1	2
3	4	5	6	7	8	9
10	11	12	13	14	15	16
17	18	19	20	21	22	23
24	25	26	27	28	29	30
31						

March 10–16

I believe that telling our stories, first to ourselves and then to one another and the world, is a revolutionary act.

~JANET MOCK

Date	Qtr.	Sign	Activity
Mar. 10, 5:00 am– Mar. 10, 8:19 pm	1st	Pisces	Plant grains, leafy annuals. Fertilize (chemical). Graft or bud plants. Irrigate. Trim to increase growth.
Mar. 12, 8:28 pm– Mar. 14, 11:16 pm	1st	Taurus	Plant annuals for hardiness. Trim to increase growth.

Besides the obvious "official" holidays like Christmas, Halloween, and Easter, there are literally thousands of nonofficial holidays or "awareness days," as they're often called, throughout the year. Go online to find a list of holidays for the month and mark a few quirky ones on your calendar. From chocolate to houseplants to sea otters, you can celebrate a unique holiday in small, fun ways to shake up otherwise ordinary days.

---

*Daylight Saving Time
begins March 10, 2:00 am*

*March 10
5:00 am EDT*

MARCH

S	M	T	W	T	F	S
					1	2
3	4	5	6	7	8	9
10	11	12	13	14	15	16
17	18	19	20	21	22	23
24	25	26	27	28	29	30
31						

March 17–23

Whatever it is your heart desires, please go for it. It's yours to
have.   ~GLORIA ESTEFAN

Date	Qtr.	Sign	Activity
Mar. 17, 5:40 am– Mar. 19, 3:33 pm	2nd	Cancer	Plant grains, leafy annuals. Fertilize (chemical). Graft or bud plants. Irrigate. Trim to increase growth.

Macramé was popular back in the 1970s and had many useful applications—plant hangers, beautiful wall hangings, unique purses and bags, stunning curtains and bedcovers. If you like to work with your hands and birdhouses are not your thing, consider learning this ancient art of knot-making.

March 17
12:11 am EDT

MARCH

S	M	T	W	T	F	S
					1	2
3	4	5	6	7	8	9
10	11	12	13	14	15	16
17	18	19	20	21	22	23
24	25	26	27	28	29	30
31						

March 24–30

In recognizing the humanity of our fellow beings, we pay ourselves the highest tribute.   ⌐THURGOOD MARSHALL

Date	Qtr.	Sign	Activity
Mar. 24, 4:37 pm– Mar. 25, 3:00 am	2nd	Libra	Plant annuals for fragrance and beauty. Trim to increase growth.
Mar. 27, 5:03 am– Mar. 29, 3:52 pm	3rd	Scorpio	Plant biennials, perennials, bulbs and roots. Prune. Irrigate. Fertilize (organic).
Mar. 29, 3:52 pm– Apr. 1, 12:05 am	3rd	Sagittarius	Cultivate. Destroy weeds and pests. Harvest fruits and root crops for food. Trim to retard growth.

What's your favorite food from childhood? Whip it up tonight for a taste of nostalgia. Are you longing for comfort food, like your mom's lasagna or your dad's pancakes? Perhaps a Popsicle would make you grin, or that canned soup you always ate after coming in from a chilly day. Give yourself some TLC with a throwback meal.

_____

_____

_____

_____

○
March 25
3:00 am EDT

MARCH

S	M	T	W	T	F	S
					1	2
3	4	5	6	7	8	9
10	11	12	13	14	15	16
17	18	19	20	21	22	23
24	25	26	27	28	29	30
31						

April ♈

March 31–April 6

Art is doing. Art deals directly with life.

~Ruth Asawa

Date	Qtr.	Sign	Activity
Apr. 1, 12:05 am–Apr. 1, 11:15 pm	3rd	Capricorn	Plant potatoes and tubers. Trim to retard growth.
Apr. 1, 11:15 pm–Apr. 3, 5:08 am	4th	Capricorn	Plant potatoes and tubers. Trim to retard growth.
Apr. 3, 5:08 am–Apr. 5, 7:13 am	4th	Aquarius	Cultivate. Destroy weeds and pests. Harvest fruits and root crops for food. Trim to retard growth.
Apr. 5, 7:13 am–Apr. 7, 7:25 am	4th	Pisces	Plant biennials, perennials, bulbs and roots. Prune. Irrigate. Fertilize (organic).

Plant a small herbal medicine garden and tend it with love. Include plants like cilantro, rosemary, chamomile, lemon balm, catnip, marjoram, dill, sage, and echinacea. Do a bit of research on how to use each one, keeping a page of information on each in a handy notebook.

_____

_____

_____

_____

April 1
11:15 pm EDT

April

S	M	T	W	T	F	S
	1	2	3	4	5	6
7	8	9	10	11	12	13
14	15	16	17	18	19	20
21	22	23	24	25	26	27
28	29	30				

♈ **April 7–13**

Nothing ever seems impossible in spring, you know.

~L. M. Montgomery

Date	Qtr.	Sign	Activity
Apr. 7, 7:25 am– Apr. 8, 2:21 pm	4th	Aries	Cultivate. Destroy weeds and pests. Harvest fruits and root crops for food. Trim to retard growth.
Apr. 9, 7:23 am– Apr. 11, 8:59 am	1st	Taurus	Plant annuals for hardiness. Trim to increase growth.
Apr. 13, 1:45 pm– Apr. 15, 3:13 pm	1st	Cancer	Plant grains, leafy annuals. Fertilize (chemical). Graft or bud plants. Irrigate. Trim to increase growth.

Is your home interior needing a lift? Don't hesitate to paint a room, a wall, or even the whole place. Paint is an amazing spirit booster and one of the easiest and cheapest ways to change an atmosphere. Experiment. Go beyond your usual colors even if you limit this to just one wall.

_____

_____

_____

_____

April 8
2:21 pm EDT

APRIL

S	M	T	W	T	F	S
	1	2	3	4	5	6
7	8	9	10	11	12	13
14	15	16	17	18	19	20
21	22	23	24	25	26	27
28	29	30				

April 14–20

But life, as everyone knows, isn't black and white, but shades
and shades and infinite shades of gray. ∼N. J. CAMPBELL

Date	Qtr.	Sign	Activity
Apr. 15, 3:13 pm– Apr. 15, 10:24 pm	2nd	Cancer	Plant grains, leafy annuals. Fertilize (chemical). Graft or bud plants. Irrigate. Trim to increase growth.
Apr. 20, 11:08 pm– Apr. 23, 11:20 am	2nd	Libra	Plant annuals for fragrance and beauty. Trim to increase growth.

Lavender is an incredibly soothing essential oil, but did you know that you can eat it as well? Grow culinary lavender in your garden, dry it, and then look up recipes where you can use it. Cookies, chocolate desserts, and breads lend themselves nicely to lavender buds used as an ingredient. The pleasant taste along with that relaxing aroma might become your new baking go-to.

April 15
3:13 pm EDT

APRIL

S	M	T	W	T	F	S
	1	2	3	4	5	6
7	8	9	10	11	12	13
14	15	16	17	18	19	20
21	22	23	24	25	26	27
28	29	30				

April 21–27

Don't panic.   ∼DOUGLAS ADAMS

Date	Qtr.	Sign	Activity
Apr. 23, 11:20 am– Apr. 23, 7:49 pm	2nd	Scorpio	Plant grains, leafy annuals. Fertilize (chemical). Graft or bud plants. Irrigate. Trim to increase growth.
Apr. 23, 7:49 pm– Apr. 25, 9:37 pm	3rd	Scorpio	Plant biennials, perennials, bulbs and roots. Prune. Irrigate. Fertilize (organic).
Apr. 25, 9:37 pm– Apr. 28, 5:37 am	3rd	Sagittarius	Cultivate. Destroy weeds and pests. Harvest fruits and root crops for food. Trim to retard growth.

If you have difficulty sleeping when you get close to the Full Moon, don't toss and turn in frustration. Put on some relaxing or meditation music and roll onto your back. Give yourself directions to feel completely rested when you get up in the morning, then let your mind wander, think deeply, and use your imagination. You will feel rested and have enough energy to move through the following day.

_____

_____

_____

_____

○
April 23
7:49 pm EDT

APRIL

S	M	T	W	T	F	S
		1	2	3	4	5	6
7	8	9	10	11	12	13
14	15	16	17	18	19	20
21	22	23	24	25	26	27
28	29	30				

May ♉

April 28–May 4

Dreaming, after all, is a form of planning.

~GLORIA STEINEM

Date	Qtr.	Sign	Activity
Apr. 28, 5:37 am–Apr. 30, 11:20 am	3rd	Capricorn	Plant potatoes and tubers. Trim to retard growth.
Apr. 30, 11:20 am–May 1, 7:27 am	3rd	Aquarius	Cultivate. Destroy weeds and pests. Harvest fruits and root crops for food. Trim to retard growth.
May 1, 7:27 am–May 2, 2:52 pm	4th	Aquarius	Cultivate. Destroy weeds and pests. Harvest fruits and root crops for food. Trim to retard growth.
May 2, 2:52 pm–May 4, 4:41 pm	4th	Pisces	Plant biennials, perennials, bulbs and roots. Prune. Irrigate. Fertilize (organic).
May 4, 4:41 pm–May 6, 5:42 pm	4th	Aries	Cultivate. Destroy weeds and pests. Harvest fruits and root crops for food. Trim to retard growth.

Commit to one year of studying the stars and astronomy. Buy a small telescope or at least get some binoculars and spend a little time in the backyard at night looking at the constellations.

May 1
7:27 am EDT

MAY

S	M	T	W	T	F	S
			1	2	3	4
5	6	7	8	9	10	11
12	13	14	15	16	17	18
19	20	21	22	23	24	25
26	27	28	29	30	31	

May 5–11

Blossom by blossom the spring begins.

~Algernon Charles Swinburne

Date	Qtr.	Sign	Activity
May 6, 5:42 pm– May 7, 11:22 pm	4th	Taurus	Plant potatoes and tubers. Trim to retard growth.
May 7, 11:22 pm– May 8, 7:20 pm	1st	Taurus	Plant annuals for hardiness. Trim to increase growth.
May 10, 11:13 pm– May 13, 6:36 am	1st	Cancer	Plant grains, leafy annuals. Fertilize (chemical). Graft or bud plants. Irrigate. Trim to increase growth.

Want to pick up some fresh inspiration for your own garden? Head to a local botanical garden filled with lush blooms and aesthetically pleasing outdoor spaces brimming with art installations and one-of-a-kind planting arrangements. It may stir you to shake up the design of your own backyard garden. Other places for inspiration include university gardens and even greenhouses.

May 7
11:22 pm EDT

			MAY			
S	M	T	W	T	F	S
			1	2	3	4
5	6	7	8	9	10	11
12	13	14	15	16	17	18
19	20	21	22	23	24	25
26	27	28	29	30	31	

May 12–18

Continue to share your heart with people even if it's been broken.   ~AMY POEHLER

Date	Qtr.	Sign	Activity
May 18, 6:23 am– May 20, 6:34 pm	2nd	Libra	Plant annuals for fragrance and beauty. Trim to increase growth.

Start keeping a journal that's dedicated to your mental health. Make it your safe space to get everything down on paper, whether it's the stress from your day or symptoms of anxiety or depression. Getting those feelings out of your mind can feel therapeutic. Just make sure that you're writing on paper and not typing on a computer, since the act of writing your thoughts by hand will be more beneficial to your brain.

_____

_____

_____

_____

May 15
7:48 am EDT

MAY

S	M	T	W	T	F	S
				1	2	3	4
5	6	7	8	9	10	11
12	13	14	15	16	17	18
19	20	21	22	23	24	25
26	27	28	29	30	31	

May 19–25

*At the end of the day, we can endure much more than we
think we can.*   ∼FRIDA KAHLO

Date	Qtr.	Sign	Activity
May 20, 6:34 pm– May 23, 4:24 am	2nd	Scorpio	Plant grains, leafy annuals. Fertilize (chemical). Graft or bud plants. Irrigate. Trim to increase growth.
May 23, 9:53 am– May 25, 11:36 am	3rd	Sagittarius	Cultivate. Destroy weeds and pests. Harvest fruits and root crops for food. Trim to retard growth.
May 25, 11:36 am– May 27, 4:45 pm	3rd	Capricorn	Plant potatoes and tubers. Trim to retard growth.

Take full advantage of strawberry season by picking enough berries to freeze a few quarts, make jam, and indulge in strawberry shortcake. Clean the berries, sprinkle with lime juice and a tablespoon of honey, crush, and spoon over cake or ice cream. Not to be missed!

O

May 23
9:53 am EDT

	MAY					
S	M	T	W	T	F	S
			1	2	3	4
5	6	7	8	9	10	11
12	13	14	15	16	17	18
19	20	21	22	23	24	25
26	27	28	29	30	31	

June ♊

May 26–June 1

In the spring, at the end of the day, you should smell like dirt.
~MARGARET ATWOOD

Date	Qtr.	Sign	Activity
May 27, 4:45 pm–May 29, 8:33 pm	3rd	Aquarius	Cultivate. Destroy weeds and pests. Harvest fruits and root crops for food. Trim to retard growth.
May 29, 8:33 pm–May 30, 1:13 pm	3rd	Pisces	Plant biennials, perennials, bulbs and roots. Prune. Irrigate. Fertilize (organic).
May 30, 1:13 pm–May 31, 11:28 pm	4th	Pisces	Plant biennials, perennials, bulbs and roots. Prune. Irrigate. Fertilize (organic).
May 31, 11:28 pm–Jun. 3, 1:55 am	4th	Aries	Cultivate. Destroy weeds and pests. Harvest fruits and root crops for food. Trim to retard growth.

Guarantee yourself a steady supply of colorful flowers in summer by planting a small flower garden with a variety of cosmos, zinnias, marigolds, asters, bee balm, cleome, daisies, and mums. They will be eye candy for both garden and table.

May 30
1:13 pm EDT

JUNE

S	M	T	W	T	F	S
						1
2	3	4	5	6	7	8
9	10	11	12	13	14	15
16	17	18	19	20	21	22
23	24	25	26	27	28	29
30						

June 2–8

I am lucky that whatever fear I have inside me, my desire to win is always stronger. ∼S<small>ERENA</small> W<small>ILLIAMS</small>

Date	Qtr.	Sign	Activity
Jun. 3, 1:55 am– Jun. 5, 4:36 am	4th	Taurus	Plant potatoes and tubers. Trim to retard growth.
Jun. 5, 4:36 am– Jun. 6, 8:38 am	4th	Gemini	Cultivate. Destroy weeds and pests. Harvest fruits and root crops for food. Trim to retard growth.
Jun. 7, 8:41 am– Jun. 9, 3:29 pm	1st	Cancer	Plant grains, leafy annuals. Fertilize (chemical). Graft or bud plants. Irrigate. Trim to increase growth.

Are you plagued by slugs in your garden? If you have garter snakes in your area, they make great pest control for slugs and more! Make good garter snake habitat by laying down a few wide boards in your yard (don't step on them!). Instead of throwing yard waste in the trash, make a compost heap in one corner, cover it over with a tarp, and voilà—instant garter snake habitat!

_____

_____

_____

_____

June 6
8:38 am EDT

J<small>UNE</small>

S	M	T	W	T	F	S
						1
2	3	4	5	6	7	8
9	10	11	12	13	14	15
16	17	18	19	20	21	22
23	24	25	26	27	28	29
30						

June 9–15

I'm hungry for knowledge. The whole thing is to learn every day, to get brighter and brighter. That's what this world is about.   ~Jay-Z

Date	Qtr.	Sign	Activity
Jun. 14, 2:12 pm–Jun. 17, 2:38 am	2nd	Libra	Plant annuals for fragrance and beauty. Trim to increase growth.

Extend your education by pretending you are a journalist assigned to report on a specific issue. It could be anything from weather to demographics to economics to a public figure. Create a dated and timed journal that tracks what you learn for one year. Assess what has changed in your understanding and why.

_____

_____

_____

_____

June 14
1:18 am EDT

JUNE

S	M	T	W	T	F	S
						1
2	3	4	5	6	7	8
9	10	11	12	13	14	15
16	17	18	19	20	21	22
23	24	25	26	27	28	29
30						

June 16–22

Even in dark times, we not only dream. We do.

~KAMALA HARRIS

Date	Qtr.	Sign	Activity
Jun. 17, 2:38 am– Jun. 19, 12:32 pm	2nd	Scorpio	Plant grains, leafy annuals. Fertilize (chemical). Graft or bud plants. Irrigate. Trim to increase growth.
Jun. 21, 7:08 pm– Jun. 21, 9:08 pm	2nd	Capricorn	Graft or bud plants. Trim to increase growth.
Jun. 21, 9:08 pm– Jun. 23, 11:14 pm	3rd	Capricorn	Plant potatoes and tubers. Trim to retard growth.

Is your wardrobe looking shabby? Go through your clothes and set aside two items from each category—T-shirts, jeans, blouses, shorts, sweatshirts, skirts, dresses, and underwear. Put them in a box or bag to be stored. If you haven't missed them a year later, donate them to charity or recycling.

⎯⎯⎯⎯⎯⎯⎯⎯⎯⎯⎯⎯⎯⎯⎯⎯⎯⎯⎯⎯⎯⎯⎯⎯

⎯⎯⎯⎯⎯⎯⎯⎯⎯⎯⎯⎯⎯⎯⎯⎯⎯⎯⎯⎯⎯⎯⎯⎯

⎯⎯⎯⎯⎯⎯⎯⎯⎯⎯⎯⎯⎯⎯⎯⎯⎯⎯⎯⎯⎯⎯⎯⎯

⎯⎯⎯⎯⎯⎯⎯⎯⎯⎯⎯⎯⎯⎯⎯⎯⎯⎯⎯⎯⎯⎯⎯⎯

○
June 21
9:08 pm EDT

JUNE

S	M	T	W	T	F	S
						1
2	3	4	5	6	7	8
9	10	11	12	13	14	15
16	17	18	19	20	21	22
23	24	25	26	27	28	29
30						

June 23–29

This is what we are doomed to be: to have what we are going through in life show up in what we make.

~RONNIE DEL CARMEN

Date	Qtr.	Sign	Activity
Jun. 23, 11:14 pm– Jun. 26, 2:08 am	3rd	Aquarius	Cultivate. Destroy weeds and pests. Harvest fruits and root crops for food. Trim to retard growth.
Jun. 26, 2:08 am– Jun. 28, 4:52 am	3rd	Pisces	Plant biennials, perennials, bulbs and roots. Prune. Irrigate. Fertilize (organic).
Jun. 28, 4:52 am– Jun. 28, 5:53 pm	3rd	Aries	Cultivate. Destroy weeds and pests. Harvest fruits and root crops for food. Trim to retard growth.
Jun. 28, 5:53 pm– Jun. 30, 8:00 am	4th	Aries	Cultivate. Destroy weeds and pests. Harvest fruits and root crops for food. Trim to retard growth.

Do you have a cat who likes to wander but you're worried about their safety due to cars, coyotes, diseases, and other threats? Build them a catio! This outdoor structure right outside your home gives them a safe place to watch the world go by and get some exercise but keeps them safely contained.

◐

June 28
5:53 pm EDT

JUNE

S	M	T	W	T	F	S
						1
2	3	4	5	6	7	8
9	10	11	12	13	14	15
16	17	18	19	20	21	22
23	24	25	26	27	28	29
30						

♋ July

June 30–July 6

Animals are the bridge between us and the beauty of all that
is natural.   ~TRISHA MCCAGH

Date	Qtr.	Sign	Activity
Jun. 30, 8:00 am– Jul. 2, 11:50 am	4th	Taurus	Plant potatoes and tubers. Trim to retard growth.
Jul. 2, 11:50 am– Jul. 4, 4:51 pm	4th	Gemini	Cultivate. Destroy weeds and pests. Harvest fruits and root crops for food. Trim to retard growth.
Jul. 4, 4:51 pm– Jul. 5, 6:57 pm	4th	Cancer	Plant biennials, perennials, bulbs and roots. Prune. Irrigate. Fertilize (organic).
Jul. 5, 6:57 pm– Jul. 6, 11:56 pm	1st	Cancer	Plant grains, leafy annuals. Fertilize (chemical). Graft or bud plants. Irrigate. Trim to increase growth.

Consider installing an old-fashioned clothesline in your backyard. Once or twice a month, hang your blankets and quilts in the sun to freshen them and kill bacteria in between washings. There is no smell that compares to bedding that's been in the sun!

July 5
6:57 pm EDT

JULY

S	M	T	W	T	F	S
	1	2	3	4	5	6
7	8	9	10	11	12	13
14	15	16	17	18	19	20
21	22	23	24	25	26	27
28	29	30	31			

July 7–13

Watch with glittering eyes the whole world around you
because the greatest secrets are always hidden in the most
unlikely places.   ~ROALD DAHL

Date	Qtr.	Sign	Activity
Jul. 11, 10:06 pm– Jul. 13, 6:49 pm	1st	Libra	Plant annuals for fragrance and beauty. Trim to increase growth.
Jul. 13, 6:49 pm– Jul. 14, 10:53 am	2nd	Libra	Plant annuals for fragrance and beauty. Trim to increase growth.

Enjoy the benefits of learning to sew, knit, or crochet. These are relaxing forms of meditation that produce wonderful gifts to use or share. There is no dishcloth like a dishcloth crocheted using cotton yarn. Ditto for a pair of knitted socks or mittens.

July 13
6:49 pm EDT

		JULY				
S	M	T	W	T	F	S
	1	2	3	4	5	6
7	8	9	10	11	12	13
14	15	16	17	18	19	20
21	22	23	24	25	26	27
28	29	30	31			

July 14–20

Love doesn't just sit there, like a stone, it has to be made, like bread; remade all the time, made new.

~URSULA K. LE GUIN

Date	Qtr.	Sign	Activity
Jul. 14, 10:53 am– Jul. 16, 9:25 pm	2nd	Scorpio	Plant grains, leafy annuals. Fertilize (chemical). Graft or bud plants. Irrigate. Trim to increase growth.
Jul. 19, 4:14 am– Jul. 21, 6:17 am	2nd	Capricorn	Graft or bud plants. Trim to increase growth.

Here's an activity you can do with your little ones or even with adults who want to feel like kids again: Gather several rocks, wash them, allow them to dry, and then draw faces or artwork on them using paints or permanent markers. Drop them around your garden for some instant, can't-help-but-smile charm for your outdoor space.

JULY

S	M	T	W	T	F	S
	1	2	3	4	5	6
7	8	9	10	11	12	13
14	15	16	17	18	19	20
21	22	23	24	25	26	27
28	29	30	31			

July 21–27 ♋

Everyone should listen to me all the time about everything.
~ROSA DIAZ, *BROOKLYN NINE-NINE*

Date	Qtr.	Sign	Activity
Jul. 21, 6:17 am–Jul. 21, 7:43 am	3rd	Capricorn	Plant potatoes and tubers. Trim to retard growth.
Jul. 21, 7:43 am–Jul. 23, 9:23 am	3rd	Aquarius	Cultivate. Destroy weeds and pests. Harvest fruits and root crops for food. Trim to retard growth.
Jul. 23, 9:23 am–Jul. 25, 10:52 am	3rd	Pisces	Plant biennials, perennials, bulbs and roots. Prune. Irrigate. Fertilize (organic).
Jul. 25, 10:52 am–Jul. 27, 1:23 pm	3rd	Aries	Cultivate. Destroy weeds and pests. Harvest fruits and root crops for food. Trim to retard growth.
Jul. 27, 1:23 pm–Jul. 27, 10:52 pm	3rd	Taurus	Plant potatoes and tubers. Trim to retard growth.
Jul. 27, 10:52 pm–Jul. 29, 5:28 pm	4th	Taurus	Plant potatoes and tubers. Trim to retard growth.

If you use a combination lock on your locker at a gym or sports facility, write the combination on the inside of the tongue of one of your athletic shoes. You'll have it in case you forget it.

○
July 21
6:17 am EDT

JULY

S	M	T	W	T	F	S
		1	2	3	4	5	6
7	8	9	10	11	12	13
14	15	16	17	18	19	20
21	22	23	24	25	26	27
28	29	30	31			

♌ August

July 28–August 3

Friendship is a sheltering tree.

~SAMUEL TAYLOR COLERIDGE

Date	Qtr.	Sign	Activity
Jul. 29, 5:28 pm– Jul. 31, 11:19 pm	4th	Gemini	Cultivate. Destroy weeds and pests. Harvest fruits and root crops for food. Trim to retard growth.
Jul. 31, 11:19 pm– Aug. 3, 7:10 am	4th	Cancer	Plant biennials, perennials, bulbs and roots. Prune. Irrigate. Fertilize (organic).
Aug. 3, 7:10 am– Aug. 4, 7:13 am	4th	Leo	Cultivate. Destroy weeds and pests. Harvest fruits and root crops for food. Trim to retard growth.

Find a good book that presents what is happening in the world of technology and read it. It's a good way to keep up with your times, and you will feel younger and more well-informed. Hint: bestsellers are often bestsellers because they're easy for everyone to read and understand!

July 27
10:52 pm EDT

AUGUST

S	M	T	W	T	F	S
				1	2	3
4	5	6	7	8	9	10
11	12	13	14	15	16	17
18	19	20	21	22	23	24
25	26	27	28	29	30	31

August 4–10

Life isn't perfect, any failures you have are actually learning
moments. They teach us how to grow and evolve.

~PHILLIPA SOO

Date	Qtr.	Sign	Activity
Aug. 8, 5:31 am– Aug. 10, 6:34 pm	1st	Libra	Plant annuals for fragrance and beauty. Trim to increase growth.
Aug. 10, 6:34 pm– Aug. 12, 11:19 am	1st	Scorpio	Plant grains, leafy annuals. Fertilize (chemical). Graft or bud plants. Irrigate. Trim to increase growth.

To promote an excellent night's sleep, consider upgrading your bedding. If you're someone who craves softness while sleeping, aim for sheets in a higher thread count (400 or more) and a sumptuous material, like eucalyptus or supple cotton. Do you tend to sleep hot? Look for sheets in bamboo, which is an eco-friendly, naturally cooling fabric. Sleep cold? Seek out a down alternative comforter in a heavy weight and cover it in a cozy duvet.

August 4
7:13 am EDT

AUGUST

S	M	T	W	T	F	S
				1	2	3
4	5	6	7	8	9	10
11	12	13	14	15	16	17
18	19	20	21	22	23	24
25	26	27	28	29	30	31

August 11–17

Like love, pain might trigger compassion—if you're tender with yourself, you can be tender to others."

~GLORIA ANZALDÚA

Date	Qtr.	Sign	Activity
Aug. 12, 11:19 am–Aug. 13, 6:01 am	2nd	Scorpio	Plant grains, leafy annuals. Fertilize (chemical). Graft or bud plants. Irrigate. Trim to increase growth.
Aug. 15, 1:51 pm–Aug. 17, 5:45 pm	2nd	Capricorn	Graft or bud plants. Trim to increase growth.

Are you familiar with the term "forest bathing"? A Japanese practice known as *shinrin-yoku*, which translates to "forest bath," it's the idea that spending time in nature can be restorative to the soul. There are also mental health benefits of forest bathing, and you can do so by taking a walk in a local forest, turning off any music, closing your eyes, focusing on the present, and appreciating the beauty and stillness of nature.

_____

_____

_____

_____

August 12
11:19 am EDT

AUGUST

S	M	T	W	T	F	S
				1	2	3
4	5	6	7	8	9	10
11	12	13	14	15	16	17
18	19	20	21	22	23	24
25	26	27	28	29	30	31

August 18–24

Just don't give up trying to do what you really want to do.
Where there is love and inspiration, I don't think you can go
wrong.   ~ELLA FITZGERALD

Date	Qtr.	Sign	Activity
Aug. 19, 2:26 pm– Aug. 19, 6:52 pm	3rd	Aquarius	Cultivate. Destroy weeds and pests. Harvest fruits and root crops for food. Trim to retard growth.
Aug. 19, 6:52 pm– Aug. 21, 7:02 pm	3rd	Pisces	Plant biennials, perennials, bulbs and roots. Prune. Irrigate. Fertilize (organic).
Aug. 21, 7:02 pm– Aug. 23, 8:00 pm	3rd	Aries	Cultivate. Destroy weeds and pests. Harvest fruits and root crops for food. Trim to retard growth.
Aug. 23, 8:00 pm– Aug. 25, 11:04 pm	3rd	Taurus	Plant potatoes and tubers. Trim to retard growth.

Throw away those fungicides! The presence of mushrooms in your yard is a good sign! These soil-loving fungi are often what your plants (including grass) need to stay healthy, as they can share nutrients the plants couldn't access otherwise. And they're only temporary, so after a few weeks they'll die back down.

○
August 19
2:26 pm EDT

AUGUST

S	M	T	W	T	F	S
				1	2	3
4	5	6	7	8	9	10
11	12	13	14	15	16	17
18	19	20	21	22	23	24
25	26	27	28	29	30	31

♍ August 25–31

That is happiness; to be dissolved into something complete and great.

~WILLA CATHER

Date	Qtr.	Sign	Activity
Aug. 25, 11:04 pm– Aug. 26, 5:26 am	3rd	Gemini	Cultivate. Destroy weeds and pests. Harvest fruits and root crops for food. Trim to retard growth.
Aug. 26, 5:26 am– Aug. 28, 4:47 am	4th	Gemini	Cultivate. Destroy weeds and pests. Harvest fruits and root crops for food. Trim to retard growth.
Aug. 28, 4:47 am– Aug. 30, 1:09 pm	4th	Cancer	Plant biennials, perennials, bulbs and roots. Prune. Irrigate. Fertilize (organic).
Aug. 30, 1:09 pm– Sep. 1, 11:48 pm	4th	Leo	Cultivate. Destroy weeds and pests. Harvest fruits and root crops for food. Trim to retard growth.

Bird feeders are a wonderful way to see local avian life, but they can also spread disease. Hang multiple feeders, each with only one type of food in it (for example, sunflower seeds or thistle seeds) so you have fewer species at each feeder. Clean feeders regularly with a 1:9 bleach solution and soap and water, and if you see a sick bird at your feeder, take all feeders inside for two weeks.

August 26
5:26 am EDT

AUGUST

S	M	T	W	T	F	S
				1	2	3
4	5	6	7	8	9	10
11	12	13	14	15	16	17
18	19	20	21	22	23	24
25	26	27	28	29	30	31

September ♍

September 1–7

Success is a collection of problems solved.   ∼I. M. PEI

Date	Qtr.	Sign	Activity
Sep. 1, 11:48 pm– Sep. 2, 9:56 pm	4th	Virgo	Cultivate, especially medicinal plants. Destroy weeds and pests. Trim to retard growth.
Sep. 4, 12:12 pm– Sep. 7, 1:18 am	1st	Libra	Plant annuals for fragrance and beauty. Trim to increase growth.
Sep. 7, 1:18 am– Sep. 9, 1:26 pm	1st	Scorpio	Plant grains, leafy annuals. Fertilize (chemical). Graft or bud plants. Irrigate. Trim to increase growth.

With friends or family, discover a new area to hike. There must be an impressive local park or even a state park nearby that you've always had on your bucket list. Look for one with a memorable feature that will add plenty of ambiance to your hike, like a waterfall or stunning rock formation, and don't forget to take lots of pictures.

September 2
9:56 pm EDT

SEPTEMBER

S	M	T	W	T	F	S
1	2	3	4	5	6	7
8	9	10	11	12	13	14
15	16	17	18	19	20	21
22	23	24	25	26	27	28
29	30					

♍ September 8–14

I've always believed that if you can possibly make a positive difference in this world, why wouldn't any caring person do so? We have the power of our voices. If not now, when?

~HELEN ZIA

Date	Qtr.	Sign	Activity
Sep. 11, 10:38 pm– Sep. 14, 3:53 am	2nd	Capricorn	Graft or bud plants. Trim to increase growth.

In times of great stress, your hair can become lifeless and even fall out. Nurture yourself and your hair by making a batch of bone broth and then sit quietly by a window, enjoying Mother Nature and a cup of the broth with a bit of salt. The collagen in the broth is excellent for hair, nails, and bones, and the chloride in the salt is necessary for nutrients to get through the cell wall and into your cells.

_____

_____

_____

_____

September 11
2:06 am EDT

SEPTEMBER

S	M	T	W	T	F	S
1	2	3	4	5	6	7
8	9	10	11	12	13	14
15	16	17	18	19	20	21
22	23	24	25	26	27	28
29	30					

September 15–21 ♍

Every noble work is at first impossible.   ∽Thomas Carlyle

Date	Qtr.	Sign	Activity
Sep. 16, 5:39 am–Sep. 17, 10:34 pm	2nd	Pisces	Plant grains, leafy annuals. Fertilize (chemical). Graft or bud plants. Irrigate. Trim to increase growth.
Sep. 17, 10:34 pm–Sep. 18, 5:24 am	3rd	Pisces	Plant biennials, perennials, bulbs and roots. Prune. Irrigate. Fertilize (organic).
Sep. 18, 5:24 am–Sep. 20, 5:03 am	3rd	Aries	Cultivate. Destroy weeds and pests. Harvest fruits and root crops for food. Trim to retard growth.
Sep. 20, 5:03 am–Sep. 22, 6:24 am	3rd	Taurus	Plant potatoes and tubers. Trim to retard growth.

Throw a party right on your front porch. Put out plenty of chairs and even a table if space allows. Make it look magical with strings of fairy lights, garlands, and vases of vibrant flowers. The finishing touch will be the refreshments, like small tea party–inspired snacks and, of course, plenty of lemonade. Spend a breezy afternoon with your best friends on your porch and catch up together.

_____

_____

_____

_____

○
September 17
10:34 pm EDT

SEPTEMBER

S	M	T	W	T	F	S
	1	2	3	4	5	6	7
8	9	10	11	12	13	14
15	16	17	18	19	20	21
22	23	24	25	26	27	28
29	30					

♎ September 22–28

Is not this a true autumn day? Just the still melancholy that I love—that makes life and nature harmonize.

~Geoﬀ Eliot

~George Eliot

Date	Qtr.	Sign	Activity
Sep. 22, 6:24 am– Sep. 24, 10:50 am	3rd	Gemini	Cultivate. Destroy weeds and pests. Harvest fruits and root crops for food. Trim to retard growth.
Sep. 24, 10:50 am– Sep. 24, 2:50 pm	3rd	Cancer	Plant biennials, perennials, bulbs and roots. Prune. Irrigate. Fertilize (organic).
Sep. 24, 2:50 pm– Sep. 26, 6:47 pm	4th	Cancer	Plant biennials, perennials, bulbs and roots. Prune. Irrigate. Fertilize (organic).
Sep. 26, 6:47 pm– Sep. 29, 5:42 am	4th	Leo	Cultivate. Destroy weeds and pests. Harvest fruits and root crops for food. Trim to retard growth.

Want to keep squirrels, raccoons, and even bears out of your bird feeders? If you live in a two-story house, mount a plant hook for each feeder just outside a window, preferably on a perfectly flat wall with no roof or overhang beneath it. The birds will still be able to access them, but other animals will find them to be out of reach.

September 24
2:50 pm EDT

SEPTEMBER

S	M	T	W	T	F	S
	1	2	3	4	5	6	7
8	9	10	11	12	13	14
15	16	17	18	19	20	21
22	23	24	25	26	27	28
29	30					

October ♎

September 29–October 5

*What I preach is: People fall in love with people, not
gender, not looks, not whatever. What I'm in love with
exists on almost a spiritual level.*   ~MILEY CYRUS

Date	Qtr.	Sign	Activity
Sep. 29, 5:42 am–Oct. 1, 6:20 pm	4th	Virgo	Cultivate, especially medicinal plants. Destroy weeds and pests. Trim to retard growth.
Oct. 2, 2:49 pm–Oct. 4, 7:22 am	1st	Libra	Plant annuals for fragrance and beauty. Trim to increase growth.
Oct. 4, 7:22 am–Oct. 6, 7:34 pm	1st	Scorpio	Plant grains, leafy annuals. Fertilize (chemical). Graft or bud plants. Irrigate. Trim to increase growth.

If someone in your family gets seriously ill, don't rush in like
everyone else with tons of advice that tries to tell them how to
get better but often makes them feel inadequate. Instead, bring
them a few flowers, ask them what they need, and try to provide
what they asked for.

October 2
2:49 pm EDT

OCTOBER

S	M	T	W	T	F	S
		1	2	3	4	5
6	7	8	9	10	11	12
13	14	15	16	17	18	19
20	21	22	23	24	25	26
27	28	29	30	31		

October 6–12

October is the fallen leaf, but it is also a wider horizon more clearly seen. It is the distant hills once more in sight, and the enduring constellations above them once again.

~HAL BORLAND

Date	Qtr.	Sign	Activity
Oct. 9, 5:38 am– Oct. 10, 2:55 pm	1st	Capricorn	Graft or bud plants. Trim to increase growth.
Oct. 10, 2:55 pm– Oct. 11, 12:31 pm	2nd	Capricorn	Graft or bud plants. Trim to increase growth.

Instead of sitting in a silent space and meditating, try to capture some zen in a place that has some noise, like your backyard or a nearby park. For this meditation, you'll focus primarily on sound, listening to your breath along with birds chirping, breezes blowing, trees rustling, and children laughing. Your mind will follow the sounds instead of focusing on thoughts, which can put your body and brain at ease.

_____

_____

_____

_____

October 10
2:55 pm EDT

OCTOBER

S	M	T	W	T	F	S
		1	2	3	4	5
6	7	8	9	10	11	12
13	14	15	16	17	18	19
20	21	22	23	24	25	26
27	28	29	30	31		

October 13–19 ♎

A failure is not always a mistake; it may simply be the best
one can do under the circumstances. The real mistake is to
stop trying.   ~B. F. SKINNER

Date	Qtr.	Sign	Activity
Oct. 13, 3:55 pm– Oct. 15, 4:34 pm	2nd	Pisces	Plant grains, leafy annuals. Fertilize (chemical). Graft or bud plants. Irrigate. Trim to increase growth.
Oct. 17, 7:26 am– Oct. 17, 4:00 pm	3rd	Aries	Cultivate. Destroy weeds and pests. Harvest fruits and root crops for food. Trim to retard growth.
Oct. 17, 4:00 pm– Oct. 19, 4:07 pm	3rd	Taurus	Plant potatoes and tubers. Trim to retard growth.
Oct. 19, 4:07 pm– Oct. 21, 6:50 pm	3rd	Gemini	Cultivate. Destroy weeds and pests. Harvest fruits and root crops for food. Trim to retard growth.

Keep your spirits up! Don't take everything so seriously. Give yourself permission to be a little silly at times. Back this up by occasionally watching comedy routines. Some of them will have you flat-out rolling on the floor. Laughter has an extraordinary effect on the psyche.

O
October 17
7:26 am EDT

OCTOBER

S	M	T	W	T	F	S
		1	2	3	4	5
6	7	8	9	10	11	12
13	14	15	16	17	18	19
20	21	22	23	24	25	26
27	28	29	30	31		

October 20–26

Just because we mess up doesn't mean all the lessons we
learned are undone. Healing can be imperfect.

~Jᴏɴᴀᴛʜᴀɴ Vᴀɴ Nᴇss

Date	Qtr.	Sign	Activity
Oct. 21, 6:50 pm– Oct. 24, 1:24 am	3rd	Cancer	Plant biennials, perennials, bulbs and roots. Prune. Irrigate. Fertilize (organic).
Oct. 24, 1:24 am– Oct. 24, 4:03 am	3rd	Leo	Cultivate. Destroy weeds and pests. Harvest fruits and root crops for food. Trim to retard growth.
Oct. 24, 4:03 am– Oct. 26, 11:47 am	4th	Leo	Cultivate. Destroy weeds and pests. Harvest fruits and root crops for food. Trim to retard growth.
Oct. 26, 11:47 am– Oct. 29, 12:30 am	4th	Virgo	Cultivate, especially medicinal plants. Destroy weeds and pests. Trim to retard growth.

Make a smoothie using fruits and vegetables at least once a week. Add a couple dashes of cinnamon and a tablespoon of honey. The cinnamon is antibacterial, antiviral, and antifungal. The honey is full of vitamins and minerals as well as a treat for the tongue.

October 24
4:03 am EDT

Oᴄᴛᴏʙᴇʀ

S	M	T	W	T	F	S
		1	2	3	4	5
6	7	8	9	10	11	12
13	14	15	16	17	18	19
20	21	22	23	24	25	26
27	28	29	30	31		

November ♏

October 27–November 2

When the sun came up, the whole prairie sparkled. Millions of tiny, tiny sparks of color blazed on the grasses.
~LAURA INGALLS WILDER

Date	Qtr.	Sign	Activity
Oct. 31, 1:29 pm–Nov. 1, 8:47 am	4th	Scorpio	Plant biennials, perennials, bulbs and roots. Prune. Irrigate. Fertilize (organic).
Nov. 1, 8:47 am–Nov. 3, 1:19 am	1st	Scorpio	Plant grains, leafy annuals. Fertilize (chemical). Graft or bud plants. Irrigate. Trim to increase growth.

Instead of handing out candy on Halloween, consider making a couple batches of muffins using tiny, bite-sized muffin pans. Wrap each in pretty paper and tie with a ribbon. When the muffins are gone, you are done for the night.

_____

_____

_____

_____

November 1
8:47 am EDT

NOVEMBER

S	M	T	W	T	F	S
					1	2
3	4	5	6	7	8	9
10	11	12	13	14	15	16
17	18	19	20	21	22	23
24	25	26	27	28	29	30

♏ **November 3–9**

Can't rational people create mad work?

~REI KAWAKUBO

Date	Qtr.	Sign	Activity
Nov. 5, 10:17 am– Nov. 7, 5:58 pm	1st	Capricorn	Graft or bud plants. Trim to increase growth.
Nov. 9, 11:00 pm– Nov. 12, 1:26 am	2nd	Pisces	Plant grains, leafy annuals. Fertilize (chemical). Graft or bud plants. Irrigate. Trim to increase growth.

Animal therapy can be an effective way to lift symptoms of anxiety and stress. Many farm animal rescues and emotional support dog groups provide animal therapy programs, which you can check out in your area. Through hugging a cow, participating in a goat yoga class, or simply petting a therapy dog, you can decrease your cortisol levels (the hormone that causes stress). Spending time with a pet, either yours or someone else's, can have a similar effect.

_____

_____

_____

*Daylight Saving Time
ends November 3, 2:00 am*

*November 9
12:55 am EST*

NOVEMBER

S	M	T	W	T	F	S
					1	2
3	4	5	6	7	8	9
10	11	12	13	14	15	16
17	18	19	20	21	22	23
24	25	26	27	28	29	30

November 10–16 ♏

Autumn, that season of peculiar and inexhaustible influence
on the mind of taste and tenderness, that season which has
drawn from every poet worthy of being read, some attempt at
description, or some lines of feeling. ～JANE AUSTEN

Date	Qtr.	Sign	Activity
Nov. 14, 1:59 am– Nov. 15, 4:28 pm	2nd	Taurus	Plant annuals for hardiness. Trim to increase growth.
Nov. 15, 4:28 pm– Nov. 16, 2:09 am	3rd	Taurus	Plant potatoes and tubers. Trim to retard growth.
Nov. 16, 2:09 am– Nov. 18, 3:50 am	3rd	Gemini	Cultivate. Destroy weeds and pests. Harvest fruits and root crops for food. Trim to retard growth.

Explore different decor styles to weave into your home. If the white hues and antique pieces of the farmhouse trend have been your motif, try dipping your toe into another vintage style, like mid-century. Does your home have a coastal feel? Push the free-spirited look further by adding in bohemian pieces, like rattan furniture and macramé wall hangings.

○
November 15
4:28 pm EST

NOVEMBER

S	M	T	W	T	F	S
					1	2
3	4	5	6	7	8	9
10	11	12	13	14	15	16
17	18	19	20	21	22	23
24	25	26	27	28	29	30

♏ November 17–23

There are still so many causes worth sacrificing for. There is still so much history yet to be made.   ∼MICHELLE OBAMA

Date	Qtr.	Sign	Activity
Nov. 18, 3:50 am–Nov. 20, 8:51 am	3rd	Cancer	Plant biennials, perennials, bulbs and roots. Prune. Irrigate. Fertilize (organic).
Nov. 20, 8:51 am–Nov. 22, 6:01 pm	3rd	Leo	Cultivate. Destroy weeds and pests. Harvest fruits and root crops for food. Trim to retard growth.
Nov. 22, 6:01 pm–Nov. 22, 8:28 pm	3rd	Virgo	Cultivate, especially medicinal plants. Destroy weeds and pests. Trim to retard growth.
Nov. 22, 8:28 pm–Nov. 25, 6:20 am	4th	Virgo	Cultivate, especially medicinal plants. Destroy weeds and pests. Trim to retard growth.

Many dog owners have had the upsetting experience of being charged by an off-leash dog. Even if it only wants to play with their dog, it can still lead to accidental injury or a bad scare. Many off-leash dogs can be repelled by a small airhorn, as the loud noise startles them and will give you a chance to get away. Keep a tight hold on your dog in case it gets startled too.

November 22
8:28 pm EST

NOVEMBER

S	M	T	W	T	F	S
					1	2
3	4	5	6	7	8	9
10	11	12	13	14	15	16
17	18	19	20	21	22	23
24	25	26	27	28	29	30

November 24–30

When your dreams are bigger than the places you find yourself in, sometimes you need to seek out your own reminders that there is more. And there is always more waiting for you on the other side of fear.   ~ELAINE WELTEROTH

Date	Qtr.	Sign	Activity
Nov. 27, 7:21 pm– Nov. 30, 6:53 am	4th	Scorpio	Plant biennials, perennials, bulbs and roots. Prune. Irrigate. Fertilize (organic).
Nov. 30, 6:53 am– Dec. 1, 1:21 am	4th	Sagittarius	Cultivate. Destroy weeds and pests. Harvest fruits and root crops for food. Trim to retard growth.

Feeling overwhelmed by everything you feel like you have to get done? You may just need to give yourself more realistic goals, like a few things per day. Remind yourself there will always be a to-do list, so instead of focusing on emptying it, just use it as an organizational tool to keep track of tasks as they come up. Celebrate every time you knock something off your list, even if it's something small.

NOVEMBER

S	M	T	W	T	F	S
					1	2
3	4	5	6	7	8	9
10	11	12	13	14	15	16
17	18	19	20	21	22	23
24	25	26	27	28	29	30

♐ December

December 1–7

People are put into your life for seasons, for different reasons, and to teach you lessons.   ~SELENA GOMEZ

Date	Qtr.	Sign	Activity
Dec. 2, 4:09 pm– Dec. 4, 11:21 pm	1st	Capricorn	Graft or bud plants. Trim to increase growth.
Dec. 7, 4:49 am– Dec. 8, 10:27 am	1st	Pisces	Plant grains, leafy annuals. Fertilize (chemical). Graft or bud plants. Irrigate. Trim to increase growth.

For an aesthetically pleasing way to showcase your favorite artwork in all its glory, create a gallery wall. Inspired by art museum displays, choose five to fifteen pieces of art (or even more if you want to go all-out) to hang on a wall. Create cohesiveness with similar hues in the artwork or by using frames in the same color. Line them up for a streamlined look or place them randomly for a creative feel.

_____

_____

_____

_____

December 1
1:21 am EST

DECEMBER

S	M	T	W	T	F	S
1	2	3	4	5	6	7
8	9	10	11	12	13	14
15	16	17	18	19	20	21
22	23	24	25	26	27	28
29	30	31				

December 8–14

*Only by learning to live in harmony with your contradictions
can you keep it all afloat.*   ∽AUDRE LORDE

Date	Qtr.	Sign	Activity
Dec. 8, 10:27 am– Dec. 9, 8:38 am	2nd	Pisces	Plant grains, leafy annuals. Fertilize (chemical). Graft or bud plants. Irrigate. Trim to increase growth.
Dec. 11, 10:55 am– Dec. 13, 12:22 pm	2nd	Taurus	Plant annuals for hardiness. Trim to increase growth.

Want to improve the energy in your home? If you've recently had a negative experience or the energy is feeling sluggish throughout your spaces, do some things to clear it out. Open the windows. Spritz a favorite scent. Do a smoke cleanse. Weave in pops of colorful decor. Clean out the clutter. Get some good music going. Purchase new houseplants. Light candles and say an intention for how you'd like to feel in your home.

December 8
10:27 am EST

DECEMBER

S	M	T	W	T	F	S
	1	2	3	4	5	6	7
8	9	10	11	12	13	14
15	16	17	18	19	20	21
22	23	24	25	26	27	28
29	30	31				

December 15–21

I prefer winter and fall, when you feel the bone structure in the landscape.   ∼ANDREW WYETH

Date	Qtr.	Sign	Activity
Dec. 15, 4:02 am– Dec. 15, 2:21 pm	3rd	Gemini	Cultivate. Destroy weeds and pests. Harvest fruits and root crops for food. Trim to retard growth.
Dec. 15, 2:21 pm– Dec. 17, 6:39 pm	3rd	Cancer	Plant biennials, perennials, bulbs and roots. Prune. Irrigate. Fertilize (organic).
Dec. 17, 6:39 pm– Dec. 20, 2:37 am	3rd	Leo	Cultivate. Destroy weeds and pests. Harvest fruits and root crops for food. Trim to retard growth.
Dec. 20, 2:37 am– Dec. 22, 2:08 pm	3rd	Virgo	Cultivate, especially medicinal plants. Destroy weeds and pests. Trim to retard growth.

Exercise is essential, but if exercise bores you, put on some music that was popular in your teens and twenties and dance for 20 minutes. You'll be surprised at how renewed you feel.

○
December 15
4:02 am EST

DECEMBER

S	M	T	W	T	F	S
	1	2	3	4	5	6	7
8	9	10	11	12	13	14
15	16	17	18	19	20	21
22	23	24	25	26	27	28
29	30	31				

December 22–28

I felt my lungs inflate with the inrush of scenery—air,
mountains, trees, people. I thought, "This is what it is to be
happy." ～Sylvia Plath

Date	Qtr.	Sign	Activity
Dec. 25, 3:06 am– Dec. 27, 2:46 pm	4th	Scorpio	Plant biennials, perennials, bulbs and roots. Prune. Irrigate. Fertilize (organic).
Dec. 27, 2:46 pm– Dec. 29, 11:37 pm	4th	Sagittarius	Cultivate. Destroy weeds and pests. Harvest fruits and root crops for food. Trim to retard growth.

Meditating has amazing health benefits, and your practice can be even better if you set aside a dedicated spot for meditating in your home. Whether you choose a nook of your bedroom or even an entire small room, make it as tranquil as possible, with a meditation cushion, green plants, decor in soothing colors, crystals, and plenty of candles. Include anything that makes your soul feel at peace.

◑
December 22
5:18 pm EST

DECEMBER

S	M	T	W	T	F	S
1	2	3	4	5	6	7
8	9	10	11	12	13	14
15	16	17	18	19	20	21
22	23	24	25	26	27	28
29	30	31				

December 29–January 4

Real change, enduring change, happens one step at a time.
~RUTH BADER GINSBURG

Date	Qtr.	Sign	Activity
Dec. 29, 11:37 pm– Dec. 30, 5:27 pm	4th	Capricorn	Plant potatoes and tubers. Trim to retard growth.

Consider a decor touch for your home that serves a dual purpose. Coffee table books often display beautiful covers that will only add to your aesthetics, and you can enjoy reading them as well, of course. Stack a large book and a small book on your coffee table for visual interest, or place several throughout your bookshelves and punctuate them with seashells, driftwood, or other decorative objects placed on top of them.

December 30
5:27 pm EST

DECEMBER

S	M	T	W	T	F	S
	1	2	3	4	5	6	7
8	9	10	11	12	13	14
15	16	17	18	19	20	21
22	23	24	25	26	27	28
29	30	31

Gardening by the Moon

Welcome to the world of gardening by the Moon! Unlike most gardening advice, this article is not about how to garden, it's about when to garden. Timing is everything; if you know how to use the Moon, you'll not only be in sync with nature but you can sit back and watch your garden grow beyond your wildest dreams.

Gardening by the Moon is nothing new. It's been around since ancient times when people used both the Sun and the Moon to predict the tides, as well as fertility and growth cycles for plants and animals.

Lunar gardening is simple and the results are immediate. It doesn't matter whether you're a beginner gardener with a single pot or an old hand with years of master gardening experience—your garden will grow bigger and better if you follow the cycles of the Moon and match up the right time with the right garden activity. When the temperature has dropped and the sun is low on the horizon, you can apply what you've learned to your indoor plants as well.

The sky is a celestial clock, with the Sun and the Moon as the "hands" that tell the time. The Sun tells the season, and the light and location of the Moon tell the best times for birth, growth, and death in the garden. The Moon doesn't generate any light by itself, but as it circles the Earth it reflects the light of the Sun, which makes the Moon look like it's getting bigger and smaller. The cyclical increases and decreases in the light of the Moon are phases and tell times of growth.

Moon Phases

The theory behind gardening by the Moon is "as the Moon goes, so goes the garden." The Earth circles around the Sun once a year, but the Moon has a much shorter "life span" of twenty-eight to thirty days. Every month, as the light of the Moon increases and decreases, it mirrors the cycle of birth, growth, and death in the garden. After adjusting your garden activities to the light of the Moon, you'll be amazed to see how well your garden grows.

The **waxing phase** is the growth cycle in the garden. It begins with the New Moon and lasts for two weeks. Each month the Moon is "born" at the New Moon (day one) and grows bigger and brighter until it reaches maturity at the Full Moon (day fourteen). When the light of the Moon is increasing, it's the best time of the month to sow seeds, plant leafy annuals, and cut back or prune plants to encourage bigger growth.

The **waning phase** is the declining cycle in the garden. It begins with the Full Moon (day fourteen) and lasts for two weeks. The Moon grows older after the Full Moon as the light begins to decrease, until it disappears or "dies" at day twenty-eight. The decreasing light of the Moon is the time to plant bulbs, root vegetables, and perennials that store their energy underground. The waning Moon phase is also a good time for garden maintenance, including weeding, raking, deadheading, mowing, working the soil, destroying insects, and burning brush.

How can you tell if the Moon is waxing or waning?

Cup your right hand into a C shape and look up into the sky. If the crescent Moon fits into the closed part of your right hand, it's a waxing Moon.

Cup your left hand into a C shape and look up into the sky. If the crescent Moon fits into the closed part of your left hand, it's a waning Moon.

New Moon and Full Moon

Every month, the Moon takes one day off. This time-out between waning and waxing is called the New Moon. The time-out between waxing and waning is called the Full Moon. When the Moon reaches either of these stopping points, it's time for you to follow its example and take a one-day break from the garden.

Moon Signs

Once you know the Moon phases, the next step is to locate where the Moon is in the zodiac. The Moon hangs out in each of the zodiac signs for two to three days per month.

There's no such thing as a "bad" time in the garden, but there are Moon signs that are better for growth and others that are better for digging and weeding. Growth times alternate every two to three days with maintenance times. The trick is knowing which one is which.

The grow signs are Taurus, Cancer, Libra, Scorpio, Capricorn, and Pisces. When the Moon is in these signs, it's time to seed and plant.

The no-grow/maintenance signs are Aries, Gemini, Leo, Virgo, Sagittarius, and Aquarius. When the Moon is in these signs, it's time for digging, weeding, mowing, and pruning.

Remember: It's always a good time to garden something!

Putting It All Together

In order to get started, you'll need three tools: a calendar with New and Full Moons, the Moon tables (pg. 136), and the Moon phases and signs below.

Then follow these simple steps:

1. Mark your calendar with your time frame for gardening.
2. Figure out when the Moon is waxing (1st and 2nd quarters) and waning (3rd and 4th quarters). Use the tables in the Weekly Almanac section.
3. Locate the Moon by zodiac sign.
4. Check out the gardening advice below, which takes into account the Moon's phase and sign.

Moon Phases and Signs

Note: Can be applied to any calendar year.

Waxing Aries Moon (October–April)

Aries is one of the three fire signs that is hot and barren. Seeds planted under a waxing Aries Moon tend to be bitter or bolt quickly, but if you're feeling lucky, you could try your hand at hot and spicy peppers or herbs that thrive in dry heat.

Waning Aries Moon (April–October)

The decreasing light of the waning Aries Moon makes these two to three days a good time to focus on harvesting, cutting back, mowing the lawn, and getting rid of pests.

Waxing Taurus Moon (November–May)

Taurus is one of the three semi-fruitful earth signs. These days are perfect ones to establish your garden by planting or fertilizing annuals. Annuals with outside seeds like lettuces, cabbage, corn, and broccoli grow faster when planted under a waxing Taurus Moon that is one to seven days old. Vegetables with inside seeds like cucumbers, melons, squash, tomatoes, and beans should be planted when the Moon is seven to twelve days old. Annual flowers can be planted any time during this two-week phase.

Waning Taurus Moon (May–November)

The decreasing light of this semi-fruitful waning Taurus Moon gives you a perfect two- or three-day window for planting perennials or digging in root vegetables and flower bulbs.

Waxing Gemini Moon (December–June)

Gemini is one of the three dry and barren signs. But with the light of the Moon increasing, you can use these two to three days to prune or cut back plants you want to flourish and grow bigger.

Waning Gemini Moon (June–December)

Gemini can be all over the place, so use these couple of dry and barren days when the light is decreasing to weed invasive plants that are out of control.

Waxing Cancer Moon (January–July)

Cancer is one of the three wet and fruitful signs, so when the Moon is waxing in Cancer it's the perfect time to plant seeds or set out seedlings and annual flowers that live for only one season. Annuals with outside seeds grow faster when planted under a Moon that is one to seven days old. Vegetables with inside seeds should be planted when the Moon is seven to twelve days old. Annual flowers can be planted any time during these two weeks.

Waning Cancer Moon (July–January)

Plant perennials, root vegetables, and bulbs to your heart's content under the decreasing light of this fruitful Moon.

Waxing Leo Moon (February–August)

The light of the Moon is increasing, but Leo is one of the three hot and barren fire signs. Use the two or three days of this waxing Leo Moon to cut and prune the plants and shrubs you want to be the king or queen of your garden.

Waning Leo Moon (August–February)
With the light of the Moon decreasing, this Leo Moon is a good period to dig the soil, destroy pests and insects, and burn brush.

Waxing Virgo Moon (March–September)
Virgo is a semi-barren sign, which is good for fertilizing (Virgo is a "greenie" type that loves organics) and for planting woody vines and hardy herbs.

Waning Virgo Moon (September–March)
With the light of this semi-barren Moon decreasing for a couple of days, plan to hoe those rows and get rid of your weeds. Harvest Moon in September.

Waxing Libra Moon (October–April)
Libra is a semi-fruitful sign focused on beauty. Because the Moon is growing brighter in Libra, these two to three days are a great time to give your flower garden some heavy-duty TLC.

Waning Libra Moon (April–October)
If you want to encourage re-blooming, try deadheading your vegetables and flowers under the light of this decreasing Libra Moon. Harvest your flowers.

Waxing Scorpio Moon (November–May)
Scorpio is one of the three wet and fruitful signs. When the Moon is waxing in Scorpio, it's the perfect time for planting annuals that have a bite, like arugula and hot peppers. Annuals with outside seeds grow faster when planted under a Moon that is one to seven days old. Vegetables with inside seeds should be planted when the Moon is seven to twelve days old. Annual flowers can be planted anytime during this two-week phase.

Waning Scorpio Moon (May–November)
With the light of the Moon decreasing in Scorpio, a sign that likes strong and intense flavors, this is the perfect period to plant hardy perennials, garlic bulbs, and onion sets.

Waxing Sagittarius Moon (June–December)

Sagittarius is one of the three hot and barren signs. Because Sagittarius prefers roaming to staying still, this waxing Moon is not a good time for planting. But you can encourage growth during the two or three days when the light is increasing by cutting back, mowing, and pruning.

Waning Sagittarius Moon (December–June)

It's time to discourage growth during the days when the light of the Moon is decreasing in Sagittarius. Cut back, mow the lawn, prune, and destroy pests and insects you never want to darken your garden again.

Waxing Capricorn Moon (July–January)

Capricorn is a semi-fruitful earth sign. The couple of days when the light of the Moon is increasing in Capricorn are good for getting the garden into shape, setting out plants and transplants, and fertilizing.

Waning Capricorn Moon (January–July)

The decreasing light of this fruitful Capricorn Moon is the perfect window for digging and dividing bulbs and pinching back suckers to encourage bigger blooms on your flowers and vegetables.

Waxing Aquarius Moon (August–February)

Aquarius is a dry and barren sign. However, the increasing light of the Aquarian Moon makes this a good opportunity to experiment by pruning or cutting back plants you want to flourish.

Waning Aquarius Moon (February–August)

The light of the Moon is decreasing. Use this time to harvest or to weed, cut back, and prune the shrubs and plants that you want to banish forever from your garden. Harvest vegetables.

Waxing Pisces Moon (September–March)

When the Moon is increasing in fruitful Pisces, it's a perfect period for planting seeds and annuals. Annuals with outside seeds grow faster when planted under a Moon that is one to seven days old.

Vegetables with inside seeds should be planted when the Moon is seven to twelve days old. Annual flowers can be planted any time during these two weeks.

Waning Pisces Moon (March–September)

With the light of the Moon decreasing, it's time to plant all perennials, bulbs, and root vegetables except potatoes. Garden lore has it that potatoes planted under a Pisces Moon tend to grow bumps or "toes" because Pisces is associated with the feet.

Here's hoping that this has inspired you to give gardening by the Moon a try. Not only is it the secret ingredient that will make your garden more abundant, but you can use it as long as the Sun is in the sky and the Moon circles the Earth!

A Guide to Planting

Plant	Quarter	Sign
Annuals	1st or 2nd	
Apple tree	2nd or 3rd	Cancer, Pisces, Virgo
Artichoke	1st	Cancer, Pisces
Asparagus	1st	Cancer, Scorpio, Pisces
Aster	1st or 2nd	Virgo, Libra
Barley	1st or 2nd	Cancer, Pisces, Libra, Capricorn, Virgo
Beans (bush & pole)	2nd	Cancer, Taurus, Pisces, Libra
Beans (kidney, white & navy)	1st or 2nd	Cancer, Pisces
Beech tree	2nd or 3rd	Virgo, Taurus
Beets	3rd	Cancer, Capricorn, Pisces, Libra
Biennials	3rd or 4th	
Broccoli	1st	Cancer, Scorpio, Pisces, Libra
Brussels sprouts	1st	Cancer, Scorpio, Pisces, Libra
Buckwheat	1st or 2nd	Capricorn
Bulbs	3rd	Cancer, Scorpio, Pisces
Bulbs for seed	2nd or 3rd	
Cabbage	1st	Cancer, Scorpio, Pisces, Taurus, Libra
Canes (raspberry, blackberry & gooseberry)	2nd	Cancer, Scorpio, Pisces
Cantaloupe	1st or 2nd	Cancer, Scorpio, Pisces, Taurus, Libra
Carrots	3rd	Cancer, Scorpio, Pisces, Taurus, Libra
Cauliflower	1st	Cancer, Scorpio, Pisces, Libra
Celeriac	3rd	Cancer, Scorpio, Pisces
Celery	1st	Cancer, Scorpio, Pisces
Cereals	1st or 2nd	Cancer, Scorpio, Pisces, Libra
Chard	1st or 2nd	Cancer, Scorpio, Pisces
Chicory	2nd or 3rd	Cancer, Scorpio, Pisces
Chrysanthemum	1st or 2nd	Virgo
Clover	1st or 2nd	Cancer, Scorpio, Pisces

Plant	Quarter	Sign
Coreopsis	2nd or 3rd	Libra
Corn	1st	Cancer, Scorpio, Pisces
Corn for fodder	1st or 2nd	Libra
Cosmos	2nd or 3rd	Libra
Cress	1st	Cancer, Scorpio, Pisces
Crocus	1st or 2nd	Virgo
Cucumber	1st	Cancer, Scorpio, Pisces
Daffodil	1st or 2nd	Libra, Virgo
Dahlia	1st or 2nd	Libra, Virgo
Deciduous trees	2nd or 3rd	Cancer, Scorpio, Pisces, Virgo, Libra
Eggplant	2nd	Cancer, Scorpio, Pisces, Libra
Endive	1st	Cancer, Scorpio, Pisces, Libra
Flowers	1st	Cancer, Scorpio, Pisces, Libra, Taurus, Virgo
Garlic	3rd	Libra, Taurus, Pisces
Gladiola	1st or 2nd	Libra, Virgo
Gourds	1st or 2nd	Cancer, Scorpio, Pisces, Libra
Grapes	2nd or 3rd	Cancer, Scorpio, Pisces, Virgo
Hay	1st or 2nd	Cancer, Scorpio, Pisces, Libra, Taurus
Herbs	1st or 2nd	Cancer, Scorpio, Pisces
Honeysuckle	1st or 2nd	Scorpio, Virgo
Hops	1st or 2nd	Scorpio, Libra
Horseradish	1st or 2nd	Cancer, Scorpio, Pisces
Houseplants	1st	Cancer, Scorpio, Pisces, Libra
Hyacinth	3rd	Cancer, Scorpio, Pisces
Iris	1st or 2nd	Cancer, Virgo
Kohlrabi	1st or 2nd	Cancer, Scorpio, Pisces, Libra
Leek	2nd or 3rd	Sagittarius
Lettuce	1st	Cancer, Scorpio, Pisces, Libra, Taurus
Lily	1st or 2nd	Cancer, Scorpio, Pisces
Maple tree	2nd or 3rd	Taurus, Virgo, Cancer, Pisces
Melon	2nd	Cancer, Scorpio, Pisces
Moon vine	1st or 2nd	Virgo

Plant	Quarter	Sign
Morning glory	1st or 2nd	Cancer, Scorpio, Pisces, Virgo
Oak tree	2nd or 3rd	Taurus, Virgo, Cancer, Pisces
Oats	1st or 2nd	Cancer, Scorpio, Pisces, Libra
Okra	1st or 2nd	Cancer, Scorpio, Pisces, Libra
Onion seed	2nd	Cancer, Scorpio, Sagittarius
Onion set	3rd or 4th	Cancer, Pisces, Taurus, Libra
Pansies	1st or 2nd	Cancer, Scorpio, Pisces
Parsley	1st	Cancer, Scorpio, Pisces, Libra
Parsnip	3rd	Cancer, Scorpio, Taurus, Capricorn
Peach tree	2nd or 3rd	Cancer, Taurus, Virgo, Libra
Peanuts	3rd	Cancer, Scorpio, Pisces
Pear tree	2nd or 3rd	Cancer, Scorpio, Pisces, Libra
Peas	2nd	Cancer, Scorpio, Pisces, Libra
Peony	1st or 2nd	Virgo
Peppers	2nd	Cancer, Scorpio, Pisces
Perennials	3rd	
Petunia	1st or 2nd	Libra, Virgo
Plum tree	2nd or 3rd	Cancer, Pisces, Taurus, Virgo
Poppies	1st or 2nd	Virgo
Portulaca	1st or 2nd	Virgo
Potatoes	3rd	Cancer, Scorpio, Libra, Taurus, Capricorn
Privet	1st or 2nd	Taurus, Libra
Pumpkin	2nd	Cancer, Scorpio, Pisces, Libra
Quince	1st or 2nd	Capricorn
Radishes	3rd	Cancer, Scorpio, Pisces, Libra, Capricorn
Rhubarb	3rd	Cancer, Pisces
Rice	1st or 2nd	Scorpio
Roses	1st or 2nd	Cancer, Virgo
Rutabaga	3rd	Cancer, Scorpio, Pisces, Taurus
Saffron	1st or 2nd	Cancer, Scorpio, Pisces
Sage	3rd	Cancer, Scorpio, Pisces

Plant	Quarter	Sign
Salsify	1st	Cancer, Scorpio, Pisces
Shallot	2nd	Scorpio
Spinach	1st	Cancer, Scorpio, Pisces
Squash	2nd	Cancer, Scorpio, Pisces, Libra
Strawberries	3rd	Cancer, Scorpio, Pisces
String beans	1st or 2nd	Taurus
Sunflowers	1st or 2nd	Libra, Cancer
Sweet peas	1st or 2nd	Any
Tomatoes	2nd	Cancer, Scorpio, Pisces, Capricorn
Trees, shade	3rd	Taurus, Capricorn
Trees, ornamental	2nd	Libra, Taurus
Trumpet vine	1st or 2nd	Cancer, Scorpio, Pisces
Tubers for seed	3rd	Cancer, Scorpio, Pisces, Libra
Tulips	1st or 2nd	Libra, Virgo
Turnips	3rd	Cancer, Scorpio, Pisces, Taurus, Capricorn, Libra
Valerian	1st or 2nd	Virgo, Gemini
Watermelon	1st or 2nd	Cancer, Scorpio, Pisces, Libra
Wheat	1st or 2nd	Cancer, Scorpio, Pisces, Libra

Companion Planting Guide

Plant	Companions	Hindered by
Asparagus	Tomatoes, parsley, basil	None known
Beans	Tomatoes, carrots, cucumbers, garlic, cabbage, beets, corn	Onions, gladiolas
Beets	Onions, cabbage, lettuce, mint, catnip	Pole beans
Broccoli	Beans, celery, potatoes, onions	Tomatoes
Cabbage	Peppermint, sage, thyme, tomatoes	Strawberries, grapes
Carrots	Peas, lettuce, chives, radishes, leeks, onions, sage	Dill, anise
Citrus trees	Guava, live oak, rubber trees, peppers	None known
Corn	Potatoes, beans, peas, melon, squash, pumpkin, sunflowers, soybeans	Quack grass, wheat, straw, mulch
Cucumbers	Beans, cabbage, radishes, sunflowers, lettuce, broccoli, squash	Aromatic herbs
Eggplant	Green beans, lettuce, kale	None known
Grapes	Peas, beans, blackberries	Cabbage, radishes
Melons	Corn, peas	Potatoes, gourds
Onions, leeks	Beets, chamomile, carrots, lettuce	Peas, beans, sage
Parsnip	Peas	None known
Peas	Radishes, carrots, corn, cucumbers, beans, tomatoes, spinach, turnips	Onion, garlic
Potatoes	Beans, corn, peas, cabbage, hemp, cucumbers, eggplant, catnip	Raspberries, pump- kins, tomatoes, sunflowers
Radishes	Peas, lettuce, nasturtiums, cucumbers	Hyssop
Spinach	Strawberries	None known
Squash/ Pumpkin	Nasturtiums, corn, mint, catnip	Potatoes
Tomatoes	Asparagus, parsley, chives, onions, carrots, marigolds, nasturtiums, dill	Black walnut roots, fennel, potatoes
Turnips	Peas, beans, brussels sprouts	Potatoes

Plant	Companions	Uses
Anise	Coriander	Flavor candy, pastry, cheeses, cookies
Basil	Tomatoes	Dislikes rue; repels flies and mosquitoes
Borage	Tomatoes, squash	Use in teas
Buttercup	Clover	Hinders delphinium, peonies, monkshood, columbine
Catnip		Repels flea beetles
Chamomile	Peppermint, wheat, onions, cabbage	Roman chamomile may control damping-off disease; use in herbal sprays
Chervil	Radishes	Good in soups and other dishes
Chives	Carrots	Use in spray to deter black spot on roses
Coriander	Plant anywhere	Hinders seed formation in fennel
Cosmos		Repels corn earworms
Dill	Cabbage	Hinders carrots and tomatoes
Fennel	Plant in borders	Disliked by all garden plants
Horseradish		Repels potato bugs
Horsetail		Makes fungicide spray
Hyssop		Attracts cabbage flies; harmful to radishes
Lavender	Plant anywhere	Use in spray to control insects on cotton, repels clothes moths
Lovage		Lures horn worms away from tomatoes
Marigolds		Pest repellent; use against Mexican bean beetles and nematodes
Mint	Cabbage, tomatoes	Repels ants, flea beetles, cabbage worm butterflies
Morning glory	Corn	Helps melon germination
Nasturtium	Cabbage, cucumbers	Deters aphids, squash bugs, pumpkin beetles
Okra	Eggplant	Attracts leafhopper (lure insects from other plants)
Parsley	Tomatoes, asparagus	Freeze chopped-up leaves to flavor foods
Purslane		Good ground cover
Rosemary		Repels cabbage moths, bean beetles, carrot flies
Savory		Plant with onions for added sweetness
Tansy		Deters Japanese beetles, striped cucumber beetles, squash bugs
Thyme		Repels cabbage worms
Yarrow		Increases essential oils of neighbors

Moon Void-of-Course

Kim Rogers-Gallagher

The Moon circles the Earth in about twenty-eight days, moving through each zodiac sign in two and a half days. As she passes through the thirty degrees of each sign, she "visits" with the planets in numerical order, forming aspects with them. Because she moves one degree in just two to two and a half hours, her influence on each planet lasts only a few hours. She eventually reaches the planet that's in the highest degree of any sign and forms what will be her final aspect before leaving the sign. From this point until she enters the next sign, she is referred to as void-of-course.

Think of it this way: the Moon is the emotional "tone" of the day, carrying feelings with her particular to the sign she's "wearing" at the moment. After she has contacted each of the planets, she symbolically "rests" before changing her costume, so her instinct is temporarily on hold. It's during this time that many people feel "fuzzy" or "vague." Plans or decisions made now often do not pan out. Without the instinctual "knowing" the Moon provides as she touches each planet, we tend to be unrealistic or exercise poor judgment. The traditional definition of the void Moon is that "nothing will come of this." Actions initiated under a void Moon are often wasted, irrelevant, or incorrect—usually because information is hidden, missing, or has been overlooked.

Although it's not a good time to initiate plans, routine tasks seem to go along just fine. This period is ideal for reflection. On the lighter side, remember there are good uses for the void Moon. It is the period when the universe seems to be most open to loopholes. It's a great time to make plans you don't want to fulfill or schedule things you don't want to do. See the tables on pages 76–81 for a schedule of the Moon's void-of-course times.

Last Aspect   **Moon Enters New Sign**

		January		
2	6:36 pm	2	Libra	7:47 pm
5	6:41 am	5	Scorpio	7:39 am
7	3:22 pm	7	Sagittarius	4:08 pm
9	1:24 pm	9	Capricorn	8:33 pm
11	9:33 pm	11	Aquarius	10:01 pm
13	4:59 am	13	Pisces	10:29 pm
15	11:33 pm	15	Aries	11:49 pm
18	3:03 am	18	Taurus	3:12 am
20	8:57 am	20	Gemini	8:58 am
22	3:40 pm	22	Cancer	4:51 pm
24	5:58 pm	25	Leo	2:37 am
26	4:19 pm	27	Virgo	2:11 pm
29	6:20 pm	30	Libra	3:04 am
		February		
1	4:03 am	1	Scorpio	3:37 pm
3	10:24 pm	4	Sagittarius	1:28 am
6	12:06 am	6	Capricorn	7:08 am
8	2:52 am	8	Aquarius	8:59 am
9	5:59 pm	10	Pisces	8:42 am
12	7:32 am	12	Aries	8:26 am
14	5:21 am	14	Taurus	10:02 am
16	10:01 am	16	Gemini	2:39 pm
18	10:21 pm	18	Cancer	10:25 pm
21	1:38 am	21	Leo	8:40 am
22	11:18 pm	23	Virgo	8:38 pm
26	2:35 am	26	Libra	9:29 am
27	1:22 pm	28	Scorpio	10:09 pm

Last Aspect   Moon Enters New Sign

		March		
2	2:47 am	2	Sagittarius	8:56 am
4	10:41 am	4	Capricorn	4:15 pm
6	2:35 pm	6	Aquarius	7:38 pm
8	1:56 pm	8	Pisces	8:03 pm
10	3:45 pm	10	Aries	8:19 pm
12	7:08 am	12	Taurus	8:28 pm
14	6:29 pm	14	Gemini	11:16 pm
17	12:43 am	17	Cancer	5:40 am
19	2:52 pm	19	Leo	3:33 pm
22	2:34 am	22	Virgo	3:42 am
24	11:49 am	24	Libra	4:37 pm
26	7:09 pm	27	Scorpio	5:03 am
29	11:40 am	29	Sagittarius	3:52 pm
31	8:16 pm	1	Capricorn	12:05 am
		April		
3	1:40 am	3	Aquarius	5:08 am
5	1:40 am	5	Pisces	7:13 am
7	4:27 am	7	Aries	7:25 am
8	10:39 pm	9	Taurus	7:23 am
11	6:04 am	11	Gemini	8:59 am
13	10:46 am	13	Cancer	1:45 pm
15	7:22 pm	15	Leo	10:24 pm
18	8:02 am	18	Virgo	10:10 am
20	8:20 pm	20	Libra	11:08 pm
22	7:24 pm	23	Scorpio	11:20 am
25	7:17 pm	25	Sagittarius	9:37 pm
28	3:31 am	28	Capricorn	5:37 am
30	11:19 am	30	Aquarius	11:20 am

Last Aspect   **Moon Enters New Sign**

		May			
2	5:28 am	2	Pisces	2:52 pm
4	3:06 pm	4	Aries	4:41 pm
6	1:57 am	6	Taurus	5:42 pm
8	5:55 pm	8	Gemini	7:20 pm
10	9:49 pm	10	Cancer	11:13 pm
13	5:13 am	13	Leo	6:36 am
15	12:41 pm	15	Virgo	5:33 pm
18	5:09 am	18	Libra	6:23 am
19	11:48 am	20	Scorpio	6:34 pm
23	3:28 am	23	Sagittarius	4:24 am
25	10:47 am	25	Capricorn	11:36 am
27	4:02 pm	27	Aquarius	4:45 pm
29	10:20 am	29	Pisces	8:33 pm
31	10:55 pm	31	Aries	11:28 pm
		June			
2	6:04 pm	3	Taurus	1:55 am
5	4:09 am	5	Gemini	4:36 am
7	8:16 am	7	Cancer	8:41 am
9	3:05 pm	9	Leo	3:29 pm
11	3:16 pm	12	Virgo	1:39 am
14	1:54 pm	14	Libra	2:12 pm
17	2:05 am	17	Scorpio	2:38 am
19	12:19 pm	19	Sagittarius	12:32 pm
21	6:58 pm	21	Capricorn	7:08 pm
23	11:05 pm	23	Aquarius	11:14 pm
25	6:30 pm	26	Pisces	2:08 am
28	4:45 am	28	Aries	4:52 am
30	12:56 am	30	Taurus	8:00 am

Last Aspect   Moon Enters New Sign

		July		
2	11:43 am	2	Gemini	11:50 am
4	4:44 pm	4	Cancer	4:51 pm
6	11:47 pm	6	Leo	11:56 pm
9	2:04 am	9	Virgo	9:48 am
11	9:55 pm	11	Libra	10:06 pm
13	6:49 pm	14	Scorpio	10:53 am
16	9:10 pm	16	Sagittarius	9:25 pm
19	3:58 am	19	Capricorn	4:14 am
21	7:26 am	21	Aquarius	7:43 am
23	5:58 am	23	Pisces	9:23 am
25	10:31 am	25	Aries	10:52 am
26	6:14 pm	27	Taurus	1:23 pm
29	4:59 pm	29	Gemini	5:28 pm
31	10:46 pm	31	Cancer	11:19 pm
		August		
3	6:31 am	3	Leo	7:10 am
5	11:16 am	5	Virgo	5:17 pm
8	4:40 am	8	Libra	5:31 am
9	5:45 pm	10	Scorpio	6:34 pm
13	5:01 am	13	Sagittarius	6:01 am
15	12:52 pm	15	Capricorn	1:51 pm
17	4:43 pm	17	Aquarius	5:45 pm
19	2:26 pm	19	Pisces	6:52 pm
21	5:54 pm	21	Aries	7:02 pm
23	8:44 am	23	Taurus	8:00 pm
25	9:40 pm	25	Gemini	11:04 pm
28	3:14 am	28	Cancer	4:47 am
30	11:24 am	30	Leo	1:09 pm

Last Aspect   Moon Enters New Sign

		September		
1	8:25 pm	1	Virgo	11:48 pm
4	12:06 pm	4	Libra	12:12 pm
7	1:08 am	7	Scorpio	1:18 am
9	1:11 pm	9	Sagittarius	1:26 pm
11	8:21 pm	11	Capricorn	10:38 pm
14	3:35 am	14	Aquarius	3:53 am
16	1:04 am	16	Pisces	5:39 am
18	5:02 am	18	Aries	5:24 am
20	4:39 am	20	Taurus	5:03 am
22	6:14 am	22	Gemini	6:24 am
24	7:59 am	24	Cancer	10:50 am
26	6:12 pm	26	Leo	6:47 pm
28	11:36 pm	29	Virgo	5:42 am
30	5:50 pm	30	Taurus	9:18 pm
		October		
1	5:39 pm	1	Libra	6:20 pm
4	6:40 am	4	Scorpio	7:22 am
6	6:52 pm	6	Sagittarius	7:34 pm
9	1:54 am	9	Capricorn	5:38 am
11	11:53 am	11	Aquarius	12:31 pm
13	10:11 am	13	Pisces	3:55 pm
15	4:00 pm	15	Aries	4:34 pm
17	3:26 pm	17	Taurus	4:00 pm
19	3:33 pm	19	Gemini	4:07 pm
21	5:00 pm	21	Cancer	6:50 pm
24	12:47 am	24	Leo	1:24 am
26	4:04 am	26	Virgo	11:47 am
28	11:54 pm	29	Libra	12:30 am
31	12:57 pm	31	Scorpio	1:29 pm

Last Aspect   **Moon Enters New Sign**

		November		
3	12:51 am	3	Sagittarius	1:19 am
5	5:23 am	5	Capricorn	10:17 am
7	5:38 pm	7	Aquarius	5:58 pm
9	7:23 pm	9	Pisces	11:00 pm
12	1:13 am	12	Aries	1:26 am
14	1:50 am	14	Taurus	1:59 am
16	2:03 am	16	Gemini	2:09 am
17	11:09 pm	18	Cancer	3:50 am
20	6:20 am	20	Leo	8:51 am
22	8:15 am	22	Virgo	6:01 pm
25	12:35 am	25	Libra	6:20 am
27	4:14 am	27	Scorpio	7:21 pm
30	1:19 am	30	Sagittarius	6:53 am
		December		
2	10:47 am	2	Capricorn	4:09 pm
4	6:34 pm	4	Aquarius	11:21 pm
6	7:01 pm	7	Pisces	4:49 am
9	3:45 am	9	Aries	8:38 am
10	5:13 pm	11	Taurus	10:55 am
13	7:39 am	13	Gemini	12:22 pm
15	9:32 am	15	Cancer	2:21 pm
17	1:33 pm	17	Leo	6:39 pm
20	12:19 am	20	Virgo	2:37 am
22	8:27 am	22	Libra	2:08 pm
24	5:44 am	25	Scorpio	3:06 am
27	9:24 am	27	Sagittarius	2:46 pm
29	6:34 pm	29	Capricorn	11:37 pm

The Moon's Rhythm

The Moon journeys around Earth in an elliptical orbit that takes about 27.33 days, which is known as a sidereal month (period of revolution of one body about another). She can move up to 15 degrees or as few as 11 degrees in a day, with the fastest motion occurring when the Moon is at perigee (closest approach to Earth). The Moon is never retrograde, but when her motion is slow, the effect is similar to a retrograde period.

Astrologers have observed that people born on a day when the Moon is fast will process information differently from those who are born when the Moon is slow in motion. People born when the Moon is fast process information quickly and tend to react quickly, while those born during a slow Moon will be more deliberate.

The time from New Moon to New Moon is called the synodic month (involving a conjunction), and the average time span between this Sun-Moon alignment is 29.53 days. Since 29.53 won't divide into 365 evenly, we can have a month with two Full Moons or two New Moons.

Moon Aspects

The aspects the Moon will make during the times you are considering are also important. A trine or sextile, and sometimes a conjunction, are considered favorable aspects. A trine or sextile between the Sun and Moon is an excellent foundation for success. Whether or not a conjunction is considered favorable depends upon the planet the Moon is making a conjunction to. If it's joining the Sun, Venus, Mercury, Jupiter, or even Saturn, the aspect is favorable. If the Moon joins Pluto or Mars, however, that would not be considered favorable. There may be exceptions, but it would depend on what you are electing to do. For example, a trine to Pluto might hasten the end of a relationship you want to be free of.

It is important to avoid times when the Moon makes an aspect to or is conjoining any retrograde planet, unless, of course, you want the thing started to end in failure.

After the Moon has completed an aspect to a planet, that planetary energy has passed. For example, if the Moon squares Saturn at 10:00 am, you can disregard Saturn's influence on your activity if it will occur after that time. You should always look ahead at aspects the Moon will make on the day in question, though, because if the Moon opposes Mars at 11:30 pm on that day, you can expect events that stretch into the evening to be affected by the Moon-Mars aspect. A testy conversation might lead to an argument, or more.

Moon Signs

Much agricultural work is ruled by earth signs—Virgo, Capricorn, and Taurus. The air signs—Gemini, Aquarius, and Libra—rule flying and intellectual pursuits.

Each planet has one or two signs in which its characteristics are enhanced or "dignified," and the planet is said to "rule" that sign. The Sun rules Leo and the Moon rules Cancer, for example. The ruling planet for each sign is listed below. These should not be considered complete lists. We recommend that you purchase a book of planetary rulerships for more complete information.

Aries Moon

The energy of an Aries Moon is masculine, dry, barren, and fiery. Aries provides great start-up energy, but things started at this time may be the result of impulsive action that lacks research or necessary support. Aries lacks staying power.

Use this assertive, outgoing Moon sign to initiate change, but have a plan in place for someone to pick up the reins when you're impatient to move on to the next thing. Work that requires skillful but not necessarily patient use of tools—cutting down trees, hammering, etc.—is appropriate in Aries. Expect things to occur rapidly but to also quickly pass. If you are prone to injury or accidents, exercise caution and good judgment in Aries-related activities.

RULER: Mars
IMPULSE: Action
RULES: Head and face

Taurus Moon

A Taurus Moon's energy is feminine, semi-fruitful, and earthy. The Moon is exalted—very strong—in Taurus. Taurus is known as the farmer's sign because of its associations with farmland and precipitation that is the typical day-long "soaker" variety. Taurus energy is good to incorporate into your plans when patience, practicality, and perseverance are needed. Be aware, though, that you may also experience stubbornness in this sign.

Things started in Taurus tend to be long lasting and to increase in value. This can be very supportive energy in a marriage election. On the downside, the fixed energy of this sign resists change or the letting go of even the most difficult situations. A divorce following a marriage that occurred during a Taurus Moon may be difficult and costly to end. Things begun now tend to become habitual and hard to alter. If you want to make changes in something you started, it would be better to wait for Gemini. This is a good time to get a loan, but expect the people in charge of money to be cautious and slow to make decisions.

RULER: Venus

IMPULSE: Stability

RULES: Neck, throat, and voice

Gemini Moon

A Gemini Moon's energy is masculine, dry, barren, and airy. People are more changeable than usual and may prefer to follow intellectual pursuits and play mental games rather than apply themselves to practical concerns.

This sign is not favored for agricultural matters, but it is an excellent time to prepare for activities, to run errands, and write letters. Plan to use a Gemini Moon to exchange ideas, meet people, go on vacations that include walking or biking, or be in situations that require versatility and quick thinking on your feet.

RULER: Mercury

IMPULSE: Versatility

RULES: Shoulders, hands, arms, lungs, and nervous system

Cancer Moon

A Cancer Moon's energy is feminine, fruitful, moist, and very strong. Use this sign when you want to grow things—flowers, fruits, vegetables, commodities, stocks, or collections—for example. This sensitive sign stimulates rapport between people. Considered the most fertile of the signs, it is often associated with mothering. You can use this moontime to build personal friendships that support mutual growth.

Cancer is associated with emotions and feelings. Prominent Cancer energy promotes growth, but it can also turn people pouty and prone to withdrawing into their shells.

RULER: The Moon

IMPULSE: Tenacity

RULES: Chest area, breasts, and stomach

Leo Moon

A Leo Moon's energy is masculine, hot, dry, fiery, and barren. Use it whenever you need to put on a show, make a presentation, or entertain colleagues or guests. This is a proud yet playful energy that exudes self-confidence and is often associated with romance.

This is an excellent time for fundraisers and ceremonies or to be straightforward, frank, and honest about something. It is advisable not to put yourself in a position of needing public approval or where you might have to cope with underhandedness, as trouble in these areas can bring out the worst Leo traits. There is a tendency in this sign to become arrogant or self-centered.

RULER: The Sun

IMPULSE: I am

RULES: Heart and upper back

Virgo Moon

A Virgo Moon is feminine, dry, barren, earthy energy. It is favorable for anything that needs painstaking attention—especially those things where exactness rather than innovation is preferred.

Use this sign for activities when you must analyze information or when you must determine the value of something. Virgo is the sign of bargain hunting. It's friendly toward agricultural matters with an emphasis on animals and harvesting vegetables. It is an excellent time to care for animals, especially training them and veterinary work.

This sign is most beneficial when decisions have already been made and now need to be carried out. The inclination here is to see details rather than the bigger picture.

There is a tendency in this sign to overdo. Precautions should be taken to avoid becoming too dull from all work and no play. Build relaxation and pleasure into your routine from the beginning.

RULER: Mercury

IMPULSE: Discriminating

RULES: Abdomen and intestines

Libra Moon

A Libra Moon's energy is masculine, semi-fruitful, and airy. This energy will benefit any attempt to bring beauty to a place or thing. Libra is considered good energy for starting things of an intellectual nature. Libra is the sign of partnership and unions, which makes it an excellent time to form partnerships of any kind, to make agreements, and to negotiate. Even though this sign is good for initiating things, it is crucial to work with a partner who will provide incentive and encouragement. A Libra Moon accentuates teamwork (particularly teams of two) and artistic work (especially work that involves color). Make use of this sign when you are decorating your home or shopping for better-quality clothing.

RULER: Venus

IMPULSE: Balance

RULES: Lower back, kidneys, and buttocks

Scorpio Moon

The Scorpio Moon is feminine, fruitful, cold, and moist. It is useful when intensity (that sometimes borders on obsession) is needed. Scorpio is considered a very psychic sign. Use this Moon sign when you must back up something you strongly believe in, such as union or employer relations. There is strong group loyalty here, but a Scorpio Moon is also a good time to end connections thoroughly. This is also a good time to conduct research.

The desire nature is so strong here that there is a tendency to manipulate situations to get what one wants or to not see one's responsibility in an act.

RULER: Pluto, Mars (traditional)

IMPULSE: Transformation

RULES: Reproductive organs, genitals, groin, and pelvis

Sagittarius Moon

The Moon's energy is masculine, dry, barren, and fiery in Sagittarius, encouraging flights of imagination and confidence in the flow of life. Sagittarius is the most philosophical sign. Candor and honesty are enhanced when the Moon is here. This is an excellent time to "get things off your chest" and to deal with institutions of higher learning, publishing companies, and the law. It's also a good time for sport and adventure.

Sagittarians are the crusaders of this world. This is a good time to tackle things that need improvement, but don't try to be the diplomat while influenced by this energy. Opinions can run strong, and the tendency to proselytize is increased.

RULER: Jupiter

IMPULSE: Expansion

RULES: Thighs and hips

Capricorn Moon

In Capricorn the Moon's energy is feminine, semi-fruitful, and earthy. Because Cancer and Capricorn are polar opposites, the Moon's energy is thought to be weakened here. This energy encourages the need for structure, discipline, and organization. This is a good time to set goals and plan for the future, tend to family business, and to take care of details requiring patience or a businesslike manner. Institutional activities are favored. This sign should be avoided if you're seeking favors, as those in authority can be insensitive under this influence.

RULER: Saturn

IMPULSE: Ambitious

RULES: Bones, skin, and knees

Aquarius Moon

An Aquarius Moon's energy is masculine, barren, dry, and airy. Activities that are unique, individualistic, concerned with humanitarian issues, society as a whole, and making improvements are favored under this Moon. It is this quality of making improvements that has caused this sign to be associated with inventors and new inventions.

An Aquarius Moon promotes the gathering of social groups for friendly exchanges. People tend to react and speak from an intellectual rather than emotional viewpoint when the Moon is in this sign.

RULER: Uranus and Saturn
IMPULSE: Reformer
RULES: Calves and ankles

Pisces Moon

A Pisces Moon is feminine, fruitful, cool, and moist. This is an excellent time to retreat, meditate, sleep, pray, or make that dreamed-of escape into a fantasy vacation. However, things are not always what they seem to be with the Moon in Pisces. Personal boundaries tend to be fuzzy, and you may not be seeing things clearly. People tend to be idealistic under this sign, which can prevent them from seeing reality.

There is a live-and-let-live philosophy attached to this sign, which in the idealistic world may work well enough, but chaos is frequently the result. That's why this sign is also associated with alcohol and drug abuse, drug trafficking, and counterfeiting. On the lighter side, many musicians and artists are ruled by Pisces. It's only when they move too far away from reality that the dark side of substance abuse, suicide, or crime takes away life.

RULER: Jupiter and Neptune
IMPULSE: Empathetic
RULES: Feet

More about Zodiac Signs

Element (Triplicity)

Each of the zodiac signs is classified as belonging to an element; these are the four basic elements:

Fire Signs

Aries, Sagittarius, and Leo are action-oriented, outgoing, energetic, and spontaneous.

Earth Signs

Taurus, Capricorn, and Virgo are stable, conservative, practical, and oriented to the physical and material realm.

Air Signs

Gemini, Aquarius, and Libra are sociable and critical, and they tend to represent intellectual responses rather than feelings.

Water Signs

Cancer, Scorpio, and Pisces are emotional, receptive, intuitive, and can be very sensitive.

Quality (Quadruplicity)

Each zodiac sign is further classified as being cardinal, mutable, or fixed. There are four signs in each quadruplicity, one sign from each element.

Cardinal Signs

Aries, Cancer, Libra, and Capricorn represent beginnings and newly initiated action. They initiate each new season in the cycle of the year.

Fixed Signs

Taurus, Leo, Scorpio, and Aquarius want to maintain the status quo through stubbornness and persistence; they represent that "between" time. For example, Leo is the month when summer really feels like summer.

Mutable Signs

Pisces, Gemini, Virgo, and Sagittarius adapt to change and tolerate situations. They represent the last month of each season, when things are changing in preparation for the coming season.

Nature and Fertility

In addition to a sign's element and quality, each sign is further classified as either fruitful, semi-fruitful, or barren. This classification is the most important for readers who use the gardening information in the *Moon Sign Book* because the timing of most events depends on the fertility of the sign occupied by the Moon. The water signs of Cancer, Scorpio, and Pisces are the most fruitful. The semi-fruitful signs are the earth signs Taurus and Capricorn, and the air sign Libra. The barren signs correspond to fire signs Aries, Leo, and Sagittarius; air signs Gemini and Aquarius; and earth sign Virgo.

Good Timing

Sharon Leah

E lectional astrology is the art of electing times to begin any undertaking. Say, for example, you want to start a business. That business will experience ups and downs, as well as reach its potential, according to the promise held in the universe at the time the business was started—its birth time. The horoscope (birth chart) set for the date, time, and place that a business starts would indicate the outcome—its potential to succeed.

So, you might ask yourself the question: If the horoscope for a business start can show success or failure, why not begin at a time that is more favorable to the venture? Well, you can.

While no time is perfect, there are better times and better days to undertake specific activities. There are thousands of examples that prove electional astrology is not only practical, but that it can make a difference in our lives. There are rules for electing times to begin various activities—even shopping. You'll find detailed instructions about how to make elections beginning on page 107.

Personalizing Elections

The election rules in this almanac are based upon the planetary positions at the time for which the election is made. They do not depend on any type of birth chart. However, a birth chart based upon the time, date, and birthplace of an event has advantages. No election is effective for every person. For example, you may leave home to begin a trip at the same time as a friend, but each of you will have a different experience according to whether or not your birth chart favors the trip.

Not all elections require a birth chart, but the timing of very important events—business starts, marriages, etc.—would benefit from the additional accuracy a birth chart provides. To order a birth chart for yourself or a planned event, visit our website at www.llewellyn.com.

Some Things to Consider

You've probably experienced good timing in your life. Maybe you were at the right place at the right time to meet a friend whom you hadn't seen in years. Frequently, when something like that happens, it is the result of following an intuitive impulse—that "gut instinct." Consider for a moment that you were actually responding to planetary energies. Electional astrology is a tool that can help you to align with energies, present and future, that are available to us through planetary placements.

Significators

Decide upon the important significators (planet, sign, and house ruling the matter) for which the election is being made. The Moon is the most important significator in any election, so the Moon should always be fortified (strong by sign and making favorable aspects to other planets).

The Moon's aspects to other planets are more important than the sign the Moon is in.

Other important considerations are the significators of the Ascendant and Midheaven—the house ruling the election matter and the ruler of the sign on that house cusp. Finally, any planet or sign that has a general rulership over the matter in question should be taken into consideration.

Nature and Fertility

Determine the general nature of the sign that is appropriate for your election. For example, much agricultural work is ruled by the earth signs of Virgo, Capricorn, and Taurus; while the air signs—Gemini, Aquarius, and Libra—rule intellectual pursuits.

One Final Comment

Use common sense. If you must do something, like plant your garden or take an airplane trip on a day that doesn't have the best aspects, proceed anyway, but try to minimize problems. For example, leave early for the airport to avoid being left behind due to delays in the security lanes. When you have no other choice, do the best that you can under the circumstances at the time.

If you want to personalize your elections, please turn to page 107 for more information. If you want a quick and easy answer, you can refer to Llewellyn's Astro Almanac on the following pages.

Llewellyn's Astro Almanac

The Astro Almanac tables, beginning on the next page, can help you find the dates best suited to particular activities. The dates provided are determined from the Moon's sign, phase, and aspects to other planets. Please note that the Astro Almanac does not take personal factors, such as your Sun and Moon sign, into account. The dates are general, and they will apply for everyone. Some activities will not have ideal dates during a particular month.

Activity	January
Animals (Neuter or spay)	8–10
Animals (Sell or buy)	13, 14
Automobile (Buy)	1, 10, 11, 29
Brewing	6, 7
Build (Start foundation)	no ideal dates
Business (Conducting for self and others)	1, 6, 15, 20, 31
Business (Start new)	18
Can Fruits and Vegetables	6, 7
Can Preserves	6, 7
Concrete (Pour)	26
Construction (Begin new)	1, 10, 20, 23, 28, 31
Consultants (Begin work with)	4, 9, 10, 13, 14, 18, 23, 28, 29
Contracts (Bid on)	13, 14, 18, 19, 23
Cultivate	no ideal dates
Decorating	12, 13, 20–22
Demolition	7, 8, 25, 26
Electronics (Buy)	4
Entertain Guests	3
Floor Covering (Laying new)	1–5, 26–31
Habits (Break)	10
Hair (Cut to increase growth)	14, 18–21
Hair (Cut to decrease growth)	7–10
Harvest (Grain for storage)	26, 27
Harvest (Root crops)	7–9, 25–27
Investments (New)	1, 20, 31
Loan (Ask for)	18–20
Massage (Relaxing)	3, 13
Mow Lawn (Decrease growth)	1–10, 26–31
Mow Lawn (Increase growth)	12–24
Mushrooms (Pick)	24–26
Negotiate (Business for the elderly)	5, 18
Prune for Better Fruit	5–9
Prune to Promote Healing	10, 11
Wean Children	8–13
Wood Floors (Installing)	10, 11
Write Letters or Contracts	1, 9, 11, 15, 24, 29

Activity	February
Animals (Neuter or spay)	4–7
Animals (Sell or buy)	10, 11, 19
Automobile (Buy)	6, 7, 18, 25
Brewing	2, 29
Build (Start foundation)	14
Business (Conducting for self and others)	5, 14, 18, 29
Business (Start new)	14
Can Fruits and Vegetables	2, 29
Can Preserves	2, 29
Concrete (Pour)	no ideal dates
Construction (Begin new)	5, 6, 14, 18, 19, 24
Consultants (Begin work with)	3, 6, 8, 10, 13, 15, 18, 19, 24, 29
Contracts (Bid on)	10, 13, 15, 18, 19
Cultivate	no ideal dates
Decorating	9, 16–18
Demolition	4, 5
Electronics (Buy)	8, 18
Entertain Guests	16, 27
Floor Covering (Laying new)	1, 8, 9, 25–28
Habits (Break)	6, 7
Hair (Cut to increase growth)	11, 14–17, 21
Hair (Cut to decrease growth)	4–7
Harvest (Grain for storage)	no ideal dates
Harvest (Root crops)	4, 5, 8
Investments (New)	18, 29
Loan (Ask for)	14–16, 21–23
Massage (Relaxing)	27
Mow Lawn (Decrease growth)	1–8, 25–29
Mow Lawn (Increase growth)	10–23
Mushrooms (Pick)	23–25
Negotiate (Business for the elderly)	6, 14, 19, 29
Prune for Better Fruit	1–5, 29
Prune to Promote Healing	6–8
Wean Children	4–9
Wood Floors (Installing)	6–8
Write Letters or Contracts	7, 8, 11, 20, 25

Activity	March
Animals (Neuter or spay)	2–6, 9, 31
Animals (Sell or buy)	12, 18, 23
Automobile (Buy)	5, 6, 15, 23
Brewing	1, 9, 28, 29
Build (Start foundation)	13
Business (Conducting for self and others)	5, 14, 19, 30
Business (Start new)	13, 23
Can Fruits and Vegetables	1, 9, 10, 28, 29
Can Preserves	1, 28, 29
Concrete (Pour)	7, 8
Construction (Begin new)	5, 14, 18, 19, 23, 30
Consultants (Begin work with)	5, 6, 9, 10, 13, 15, 18, 21, 23, 31
Contracts (Bid on)	13, 15, 18, 21, 23
Cultivate	7, 8, 30, 31
Decorating	15–17, 24
Demolition	2, 3, 29–31
Electronics (Buy)	15
Entertain Guests	17
Floor Covering (Laying new)	6–8, 26, 27
Habits (Break)	5, 6, 8
Hair (Cut to increase growth)	12–16, 19
Hair (Cut to decrease growth)	2–5, 9, 29–31
Harvest (Grain for storage)	2, 29–31
Harvest (Root crops)	2–4, 6–8, 29–31
Investments (New)	19, 30
Loan (Ask for)	12–14, 19–22
Massage (Relaxing)	8, 12, 17
Mow Lawn (Decrease growth)	1–9, 26–31
Mow Lawn (Increase growth)	11–24
Mushrooms (Pick)	24–26
Negotiate (Business for the elderly)	5, 13
Prune for Better Fruit	1–3, 27–31
Prune to Promote Healing	5, 6
Wean Children	3–8, 30, 31
Wood Floors (Installing)	5, 6
Write Letters or Contracts	6, 10, 23

Activity	April
Animals (Neuter or spay)	1, 2, 5, 6, 26, 27, 29
Animals (Sell or buy)	11, 17
Automobile (Buy)	2, 12, 20, 29
Brewing	6, 24, 25
Build (Start foundation)	10
Business (Conducting for self and others)	4, 13, 18, 28
Business (Start new)	10, 20
Can Fruits and Vegetables	6, 24, 25
Can Preserves	24, 25
Concrete (Pour)	4
Construction (Begin new)	2, 4, 13, 15, 18, 20, 28, 30
Consultants (Begin work with)	2, 5, 6, 8, 10, 12, 15, 17, 20, 27, 30
Contracts (Bid on)	10, 12, 15, 17, 20
Cultivate	3, 4, 8, 26, 27
Decorating	11–13, 21–23
Demolition	7, 8, 25–27
Electronics (Buy)	5, 12
Entertain Guests	11, 17
Floor Covering (Laying new)	3, 4, 30
Habits (Break)	2, 3, 5, 7
Hair (Cut to increase growth)	9–12, 15
Hair (Cut to decrease growth)	1, 2, 6, 25–29
Harvest (Grain for storage)	25–28, 30
Harvest (Root crops)	3, 4, 7, 25–27, 30
Investments (New)	18, 28
Loan (Ask for)	9–11, 15–18
Massage (Relaxing)	17
Mow Lawn (Decrease growth)	1–7, 24–30
Mow Lawn (Increase growth)	9–22
Mushrooms (Pick)	22–24
Negotiate (Business for the elderly)	14, 24, 29
Prune for Better Fruit	23–27
Prune to Promote Healing	1–3, 28–30
Wean Children	1–5, 26–30
Wood Floors (Installing)	1–3
Write Letters or Contracts	2, 6, 8, 20

Activity	May
Animals (Neuter or spay)	3, 4, 23–25, 27, 30, 31
Animals (Sell or buy)	12, 13, 17, 18
Automobile (Buy)	10, 15, 17, 26, 27
Brewing	3, 4, 30, 31
Build (Start foundation)	no ideal dates
Business (Conducting for self and others)	3, 12, 18, 28
Business (Start new)	18
Can Fruits and Vegetables	3, 4, 30, 31
Can Preserves	7
Concrete (Pour)	1, 28, 29
Construction (Begin new)	12, 13, 18, 27, 28
Consultants (Begin work with)	1, 4, 6, 8, 10, 13, 15, 18, 26, 27, 31
Contracts (Bid on)	8, 10, 13, 15, 18
Cultivate	1, 2, 6, 23, 24
Decorating	8–10, 18–20
Demolition	4, 23, 24
Electronics (Buy)	1, 10
Entertain Guests	7, 12
Floor Covering (Laying new)	1, 2, 7, 27–29
Habits (Break)	4, 6
Hair (Cut to increase growth)	8, 9, 13
Hair (Cut to decrease growth)	3, 6, 7, 24–26, 30
Harvest (Grain for storage)	24, 25, 27–29
Harvest (Root crops)	1, 2, 4, 6, 23, 24, 27–29
Investments (New)	18, 28
Loan (Ask for)	8, 13–15
Massage (Relaxing)	7, 12, 28
Mow Lawn (Decrease growth)	1–4, 6, 24–31
Mow Lawn (Increase growth)	8–22
Mushrooms (Pick)	22–24
Negotiate (Business for the elderly)	7, 26
Prune for Better Fruit	23, 24
Prune to Promote Healing	25–27
Wean Children	1, 2, 23–29
Wood Floors (Installing)	25–27
Write Letters or Contracts	4, 6, 12, 17, 27, 31

Activity	June
Animals (Neuter or spay)	22, 23, 26, 27
Animals (Sell or buy)	11, 17
Automobile (Buy)	5, 14, 23
Brewing	26, 27
Build (Start foundation)	no ideal dates
Business (Conducting for self and others)	1, 11, 16, 26
Business (Start new)	12
Can Fruits and Vegetables	26, 27
Can Preserves	3, 4
Concrete (Pour)	3, 4, 24
Construction (Begin new)	1, 9, 11, 14, 16, 24, 28
Consultants (Begin work with)	1, 5, 9, 10, 14, 17, 24, 27, 28
Contracts (Bid on)	9, 10, 14, 17
Cultivate	1, 2, 5, 29
Decorating	6, 7, 14–17
Demolition	1, 2, 28, 29
Electronics (Buy)	5, 17
Entertain Guests	6, 11
Floor Covering (Laying new)	3–5, 24, 25, 30
Habits (Break)	5, 30
Hair (Cut to increase growth)	6, 9, 19–21
Hair (Cut to decrease growth)	3–5, 22, 27, 30
Harvest (Grain for storage)	23, 24, 28
Harvest (Root crops)	1, 2, 5, 24, 25, 28, 29
Investments (New)	16, 26
Loan (Ask for)	9–12
Massage (Relaxing)	11
Mow Lawn (Decrease growth)	1–5, 22–30
Mow Lawn (Increase growth)	7–20
Mushrooms (Pick)	20–22
Negotiate (Business for the elderly)	4, 8, 18
Prune for Better Fruit	no ideal dates
Prune to Promote Healing	22, 23
Wean Children	20–25
Wood Floors (Installing)	21–23
Write Letters or Contracts	5, 9, 14, 23, 27

Activity	July
Animals (Neuter or spay)	24
Animals (Sell or buy)	7, 11, 12, 17
Automobile (Buy)	11, 20, 21
Brewing	24
Build (Start foundation)	no ideal dates
Business (Conducting for self and others)	1, 11, 16, 25, 30
Business (Start new)	10, 20
Can Fruits and Vegetables	24
Can Preserves	1, 28, 29
Concrete (Pour)	1, 22, 28, 29
Construction (Begin new)	1, 7, 11, 12, 22, 25, 26, 30
Consultants (Begin work with)	2, 3, 7, 12, 13, 18, 22, 26, 27, 30
Contracts (Bid on)	7, 8, 12, 13, 18
Cultivate	3, 4, 30, 31
Decorating	11–14
Demolition	25, 26
Electronics (Buy)	2, 13
Entertain Guests	1, 6, 31
Floor Covering (Laying new)	1–4, 22, 28–31
Habits (Break)	2–4, 29–31
Hair (Cut to increase growth)	6, 16–20
Hair (Cut to decrease growth)	1–3, 24, 27–30
Harvest (Grain for storage)	22, 25, 26
Harvest (Root crops)	2–4, 21, 22, 25–27, 29–31
Investments (New)	16, 25
Loan (Ask for)	6–9
Massage (Relaxing)	1, 6, 11
Mow Lawn (Decrease growth)	1–4, 22–31
Mow Lawn (Increase growth)	6–20
Mushrooms (Pick)	20–22
Negotiate (Business for the elderly)	1, 20, 28
Prune for Better Fruit	no ideal dates
Prune to Promote Healing	21
Wean Children	17–23
Wood Floors (Installing)	21
Write Letters or Contracts	6, 7, 11, 25

Activity	August
Animals (Neuter or spay)	20
Animals (Sell or buy)	9, 11, 16, 18
Automobile (Buy)	6, 7, 16, 17, 27
Brewing	1, 2, 20, 21, 29, 30
Build (Start foundation)	no ideal dates
Business (Conducting for self and others)	9, 15, 23, 28
Business (Start new)	7, 16
Can Fruits and Vegetables	1, 2, 20, 21, 29
Can Preserves	1, 2, 24, 25, 29
Concrete (Pour)	24, 25, 31
Construction (Begin new)	4, 9, 15, 18, 23, 28
Consultants (Begin work with)	1, 4, 6, 9, 10, 15, 18, 23, 27
Contracts (Bid on)	6, 9, 10, 15, 18
Cultivate	26, 27, 31
Decorating	8–10, 17–19
Demolition	3, 4, 21, 22, 30, 31
Electronics (Buy)	27
Entertain Guests	5, 25, 30
Floor Covering (Laying new)	3, 4, 24–27, 31
Habits (Break)	3, 27, 31
Hair (Cut to increase growth)	13–16
Hair (Cut to decrease growth)	3, 20, 23–27, 30
Harvest (Grain for storage)	21–23, 25
Harvest (Root crops)	3, 19, 21–23, 25–27, 30, 31
Investments (New)	15, 23
Loan (Ask for)	4, 5
Massage (Relaxing)	25, 30
Mow Lawn (Decrease growth)	1–3, 20–31
Mow Lawn (Increase growth)	5–18
Mushrooms (Pick)	18–20
Negotiate (Business for the elderly)	2, 16, 29
Prune for Better Fruit	no ideal dates
Prune to Promote Healing	no ideal dates
Wean Children	13–19
Wood Floors (Installing)	no ideal dates
Write Letters or Contracts	3, 6, 7, 17, 21, 30

Activity	September
Animals (Neuter or spay)	no ideal dates
Animals (Sell or buy)	6, 10, 15
Automobile (Buy)	4, 12, 13
Brewing	25, 26
Build (Start foundation)	8
Business (Conducting for self and others)	8, 13, 22, 27
Business (Start new)	3, 13
Can Fruits and Vegetables	25, 26
Can Preserves	21, 25, 26
Concrete (Pour)	1, 21, 27, 28
Construction (Begin new)	1, 6, 13, 15, 19, 22, 27, 28
Consultants (Begin work with)	1, 6, 12, 15, 19, 21, 23, 26, 28
Contracts (Bid on)	6, 12, 15
Cultivate	1, 2, 26–30
Decorating	5–7, 14–16
Demolition	18, 19, 26–28
Electronics (Buy)	6
Entertain Guests	5, 24
Floor Covering (Laying new)	1, 2, 20–23, 27–30
Habits (Break)	1, 27–29
Hair (Cut to increase growth)	9–13, 17
Hair (Cut to decrease growth)	20–23, 26
Harvest (Grain for storage)	18, 19, 22, 23
Harvest (Root crops)	1, 18, 19, 22, 23, 26–28
Investments (New)	13, 22
Loan (Ask for)	no ideal dates
Massage (Relaxing)	5, 15, 24
Mow Lawn (Decrease growth)	1, 18–30
Mow Lawn (Increase growth)	3–16
Mushrooms (Pick)	16–18
Negotiate (Business for the elderly)	8, 25
Prune for Better Fruit	no ideal dates
Prune to Promote Healing	no ideal dates
Wean Children	10–16
Wood Floors (Installing)	no ideal dates
Write Letters or Contracts	4, 13, 18, 26

Activity	October
Animals (Neuter or spay)	no ideal dates
Animals (Sell or buy)	13, 15
Automobile (Buy)	1, 10, 11, 28
Brewing	22
Build (Start foundation)	5
Business (Conducting for self and others)	8, 12, 21, 26
Business (Start new)	10
Can Fruits and Vegetables	22
Can Preserves	18, 19, 22
Concrete (Pour)	18, 19, 24, 25
Construction (Begin new)	3, 8, 12, 13, 17, 21, 25, 26, 30
Consultants (Begin work with)	2, 3, 8, 13, 17, 21, 22, 25, 28, 30
Contracts (Bid on)	3, 8, 13
Cultivate	1, 24–28
Decorating	2–4, 11–13
Demolition	24, 25
Electronics (Buy)	2
Entertain Guests	24, 30
Floor Covering (Laying new)	1, 18–21, 24–31
Habits (Break)	25, 26
Hair (Cut to increase growth)	7–10, 14
Hair (Cut to decrease growth)	18–20
Harvest (Grain for storage)	19–21
Harvest (Root crops)	17, 19, 20, 21, 24, 25
Investments (New)	12, 21
Loan (Ask for)	no ideal dates
Massage (Relaxing)	24, 30
Mow Lawn (Decrease growth)	1, 18–31
Mow Lawn (Increase growth)	3–16
Mushrooms (Pick)	16–18
Negotiate (Business for the elderly)	5, 18, 22
Prune for Better Fruit	no ideal dates
Prune to Promote Healing	no ideal dates
Wean Children	7–13
Wood Floors (Installing)	no ideal dates
Write Letters or Contracts	1, 2, 15, 23, 28

Activity	November
Animals (Neuter or spay)	30
Animals (Sell or buy)	13
Automobile (Buy)	6, 7, 24
Brewing	18, 19, 28, 29
Build (Start foundation)	1
Business (Conducting for self and others)	6, 11, 20, 25
Business (Start new)	6, 14
Can Fruits and Vegetables	1, 18, 19, 28, 29
Can Preserves	1, 18, 19, 28, 29
Concrete (Pour)	21, 22
Construction (Begin new)	6, 9, 13, 20, 21, 25, 26
Consultants (Begin work with)	3, 8, 9, 12, 13, 17, 21, 22, 26, 27
Contracts (Bid on)	3, 8, 9, 12, 13
Cultivate	23, 24
Decorating	7–9
Demolition	20, 21, 30
Electronics (Buy)	8, 27
Entertain Guests	no ideal dates
Floor Covering (Laying new)	16, 17, 20–27
Habits (Break)	no ideal dates
Hair (Cut to increase growth)	3–6, 10–12, 14, 15
Hair (Cut to decrease growth)	16, 17, 20, 30
Harvest (Grain for storage)	16, 17, 20–22
Harvest (Root crops)	16, 17, 20–22
Investments (New)	11, 20
Loan (Ask for)	14
Massage (Relaxing)	9, 14
Mow Lawn (Decrease growth)	16–29
Mow Lawn (Increase growth)	2–14
Mushrooms (Pick)	14–16
Negotiate (Business for the elderly)	1, 6, 14, 28
Prune for Better Fruit	1, 27–30
Prune to Promote Healing	no ideal dates
Wean Children	3–9, 30
Wood Floors (Installing)	no ideal dates
Write Letters or Contracts	3, 7, 11, 19

Activity	December
Animals (Neuter or spay)	28–30
Animals (Sell or buy)	6, 9, 10, 14
Automobile (Buy)	3, 4, 22, 31
Brewing	16, 17, 25–27
Build (Start foundation)	no ideal dates
Business (Conducting for self and others)	6, 10, 20, 25
Business (Start new)	3, 12, 31
Can Fruits and Vegetables	16, 17, 25, 26
Can Preserves	16, 17, 25, 26
Concrete (Pour)	18
Construction (Begin new)	6, 10, 18, 20, 23
Consultants (Begin work with)	1, 6, 10, 14, 18, 23, 28
Contracts (Bid on)	6, 10, 14
Cultivate	no ideal dates
Decorating	4–6, 13, 14
Demolition	17–20, 27, 28
Electronics (Buy)	6, 23
Entertain Guests	14, 24
Floor Covering (Laying new)	18–25
Habits (Break)	no ideal dates
Hair (Cut to increase growth)	1–3, 8, 11–14, 31
Hair (Cut to decrease growth)	17, 27–30
Harvest (Grain for storage)	17–20
Harvest (Root crops)	15, 17–19, 27–29
Investments (New)	10, 20
Loan (Ask for)	11–13
Massage (Relaxing)	24
Mow Lawn (Decrease growth)	16–29
Mow Lawn (Increase growth)	2–14, 31
Mushrooms (Pick)	14–16
Negotiate (Business for the elderly)	3, 12, 16
Prune for Better Fruit	25–29
Prune to Promote Healing	30
Wean Children	1–6, 28–31
Wood Floors (Installing)	30
Write Letters or Contracts	1, 4, 17, 22, 28, 31

Choose the Best Time for Your Activities

When rules or elections refer to "favorable" and "unfavorable" aspects to your Sun or other planets, please refer to the Favorable and Unfavorable Days Tables and Lunar Aspectarian for more information. You'll find instructions beginning on page 129 and the tables beginning on page 136.

The material in this section came from several sources including: *The New A to Z Horoscope Maker and Delineator* by Llewellyn George (Llewellyn, 1999), *Moon Sign Book* (Llewellyn, 1945), and *Electional Astrology* by Vivian Robson (Slingshot Publishing, 2000). Robson's book was originally published in 1937.

Advertise (Internet)

The Moon should be conjunct, sextile, or trine Mercury or Uranus and in the sign of Gemini, Capricorn, or Aquarius.

Advertise (Print)

Write ads on a day favorable to your Sun. The Moon should be conjunct, sextile, or trine Mercury or Venus. Avoid hard aspects to Mars and Saturn. Ad campaigns produce the best results when the Moon is well aspected in Gemini (to enhance communication) or Capricorn (to build business).

Animals

Take home new pets when the day is favorable to your Sun, or when the Moon is trine, sextile, or conjunct Mercury, Jupiter or Venus, or in the sign of Virgo or Pisces. However, avoid days when the Moon is either square or opposing the Sun, Mars, Saturn, Uranus, Neptune, or Pluto. When selecting a pet, have the Moon well aspected by the planet that rules the animal. Cats are ruled by the Sun, dogs by Mercury, birds by Venus, horses by Jupiter, and fish by Neptune. Buy large animals when the Moon is in Sagittarius or Pisces and making favorable aspects to Jupiter or Mercury. Buy animals smaller than sheep when the Moon is in Virgo with favorable aspects to Mercury or Venus.

Animals (Breed)

Animals are easiest to handle when the Moon is in Taurus, Cancer, Libra, or Pisces, but try to avoid the Full Moon. To encourage healthy births, animals should be mated so births occur when the Moon is increasing in Taurus, Cancer, Pisces, or Libra. Those born during a semi-fruitful sign (Taurus and Capricorn) will produce leaner meat. Libra yields beautiful animals for showing and racing.

Animals (Neuter or Spay)

Have livestock and pets neutered or spayed when the Moon is in Sagittarius, Capricorn, or Pisces, after it has passed through Scorpio, the sign that rules reproductive organs. Avoid the week before and after the Full Moon.

Animals (Sell or Buy)

In either buying or selling, it is important to keep the Moon and Mercury free from any aspect to Mars. Aspects to Mars will create discord and increase the likelihood of wrangling over price and quality. The Moon should be passing from the first quarter to full and sextile or trine Venus or Jupiter. When buying racehorses, let the Moon be in an air sign. The Moon should be in air signs when you buy birds. If the birds are to be pets, let the Moon be in good aspect to Venus.

Animals (Train)

Train pets when the Moon is in Virgo or trine to Mercury.

Animals (Train Dogs to Hunt)

Let the Moon be in Aries in conjunction with Mars, which makes them courageous and quick to learn. But let Jupiter also be in aspect to preserve them from danger in hunting.

Automobiles

When buying an automobile, select a time when the Moon is conjunct, sextile, or trine to Mercury, Saturn, or Uranus and in the sign of Gemini or Capricorn. Avoid times when Mercury is in retrograde motion.

Baking Cakes

Your cakes will have a lighter texture if you see that the Moon is in Gemini, Libra, or Aquarius and in good aspect to Venus or Mercury. If you are decorating a cake or confections are being made, have the Moon placed in Libra.

Beauty Treatments (Massage, etc.)

See that the Moon is in Taurus, Cancer, Leo, Libra, or Aquarius and in favorable aspect to Venus. In the case of plastic surgery, aspects to Mars should be avoided, and the Moon should not be in the sign ruling the part to be operated on.

Borrow (Money or Goods)

See that the Moon is not placed between 15 degrees Libra and 15 degrees Scorpio. Let the Moon be waning and in Leo, Scorpio (16 to 30 degrees), Sagittarius, or Pisces. Venus should be in good aspect to the Moon, and the Moon should not be square, opposing, or conjunct either Saturn or Mars.

Brewing

Start brewing during the third or fourth quarter, when the Moon is in Cancer, Scorpio, or Pisces.

Build (Start Foundation)

Turning the first sod for the foundation marks the beginning of the building. For best results, excavate the site when the Moon is in the first quarter of a fixed sign and making favorable aspects to Saturn.

Business (Start New)

When starting a business, have the Moon be in Taurus, Virgo, or Capricorn and increasing. The Moon should be sextile or trine Jupiter or Saturn, but avoid oppositions or squares. The planet ruling the business should be well aspected too.

Buy Goods

Buy during the third quarter, when the Moon is in Taurus for quality or in a mutable sign (Gemini, Sagittarius, Virgo, or Pisces) for savings. Good aspects to Venus or the Sun are desirable. If you are buying for yourself, it is good if the day is favorable for your Sun sign. You may also apply rules for buying specific items.

Canning

Can fruits and vegetables when the Moon is in either the third or fourth quarter and in the water sign Cancer or Pisces. Preserves and jellies use the same quarters and the signs Cancer, Pisces, or Taurus.

Clothing

Buy clothing on a day that is favorable for your Sun sign and when Venus or Mercury is well aspected. Avoid aspects to Mars and Saturn. Buy your clothing when the Moon is in Taurus if you want to remain satisfied. Do not buy clothing or jewelry when the Moon is in Scorpio or Aries. See that the Moon is sextile or trine the Sun during the first or second quarters.

Collections

Try to make collections on days when your natal Sun is well aspected. Avoid days when the Moon is opposing or square Mars or Saturn. If possible, the Moon should be in a cardinal sign (Aries, Cancer, Libra, or Capricorn). It is more difficult to collect when the Moon is in Taurus or Scorpio.

Concrete

Pour concrete when the Moon is in the third quarter of the fixed sign Taurus, Leo, or Aquarius.

Construction (Begin New)

The Moon should be sextile or trine Jupiter. According to Hermes, no building should be begun when the Moon is in Scorpio or Pisces. The best time to begin building is when the Moon is in Aquarius.

Consultants (Work with)

The Moon should be conjunct, sextile, or trine Mercury or Jupiter.

Contracts (Bid On)

The Moon should be in Gemini or Capricorn and either the Moon or Mercury should be conjunct, sextile, or trine Jupiter.

Copyrights/Patents

The Moon should be conjunct, trine, or sextile either Mercury or Jupiter.

Coronations and Installations

Let the Moon be in Leo and in favorable aspect to Venus, Jupiter, or Mercury. The Moon should be applying to these planets.

Cultivate

Cultivate when the Moon is in a barren sign and waning, ideally the fourth quarter in Aries, Gemini, Leo, Virgo, or Aquarius. The third quarter in the sign of Sagittarius will also work.

Cut Timber

Timber cut during the waning Moon does not become worm-eaten; it will season well and not warp, decay, or snap during burning. Cut when the Moon is in Taurus, Gemini, Virgo, or Capricorn—especially in August. Avoid the water signs. Look for favorable aspects to Mars.

Decorating or Home Repairs

Have the Moon waxing and in the sign of Libra, Gemini, or Aquarius. Avoid squares or oppositions to either Mars or Saturn. Venus in good aspect to Mars or Saturn is beneficial.

Demolition

Let the waning Moon be in Leo, Sagittarius, or Aries.

Dental and Dentists

Visit the dentist when the Moon is in Virgo, or pick a day marked favorable for your Sun sign. Mars should be marked sextile, conjunct, or trine; avoid squares or oppositions to Saturn, Uranus, or Jupiter.

Teeth are best removed when the Moon is in Gemini, Virgo, Sagittarius, or Pisces and during the first or second quarter. Avoid the Full Moon! The day should be favorable for your lunar cycle, and Mars and Saturn should be marked conjunct, trine, or sextile. Fillings should be done in the third or fourth quarters in the sign of Taurus, Leo, Scorpio, or Pisces. The same applies for dentures.

Dressmaking

William Lilly wrote in 1676: "Make no new clothes, or first put them on when the Moon is in Scorpio or afflicted by Mars, for they will be apt to be torn and quickly worn out." Design, repair, and sew clothes in the first and second quarters of Taurus, Leo, or Libra on a day marked favorable for your Sun sign. Venus, Jupiter, and Mercury should be favorably aspected, but avoid hard aspects to Mars or Saturn.

Egg-Setting (see p. 161)

Eggs should be set so chicks will hatch during fruitful signs. To set eggs, subtract the number of days given for incubation or gestation from the fruitful dates. Chickens incubate in twenty-one days, turkeys and geese in twenty-eight days.

A freshly laid egg loses quality rapidly if it is not handled properly. Use plenty of clean litter in the nests to reduce the number of dirty or cracked eggs. Gather eggs daily in mild weather and at least two times daily in hot or cold weather. The eggs should be placed in a cooler immediately after gathering and stored at 50 to 55°F. Do not store eggs with foods or products that give off pungent odors since eggs may absorb the odors.

Eggs saved for hatching purposes should not be washed. Only clean and slightly soiled eggs should be saved for hatching. Dirty eggs should not be incubated. Eggs should be stored in a cool place with the large ends up. It is not advisable to store the eggs longer than one week before setting them in an incubator.

Electricity and Gas (Install)

The Moon should be in a fire sign, and there should be no squares, oppositions, or conjunctions with Uranus (ruler of electricity), Neptune (ruler of gas), Saturn, or Mars. Hard aspects to Mars can cause fires.

Electronics (Buying)

Choose a day when the Moon is in an air sign (Gemini, Libra, Aquarius) and well aspected by Mercury and/or Uranus when buying electronics.

Electronics (Repair)

The Moon should be sextile or trine Mars or Uranus and in a fixed sign (Taurus, Leo, Scorpio, Aquarius).

Entertain Friends

Let the Moon be in Leo or Libra and making good aspects to Venus. Avoid squares or oppositions to either Mars or Saturn by the Moon or Venus.

Eyes and Eyeglasses

Have your eyes tested and glasses fitted on a day marked favorable for your Sun sign, and on a day that falls during your favorable lunar cycle. Mars should not be in aspect with the Moon. The same applies for any treatment of the eyes, which should also be started during the Moon's first or second quarter.

Fence Posts

Set posts when the Moon is in the third or fourth quarter of the fixed sign Taurus or Leo.

Fertilize and Compost

Fertilize when the Moon is in a fruitful sign (Cancer, Scorpio, Pisces). Organic fertilizers are best when the Moon is waning. Use chemical fertilizers when the Moon is waxing. Start compost when the Moon is in the fourth quarter in a water sign.

Find Hidden Treasure

Let the Moon be in good aspect to Jupiter or Venus. If you erect a horoscope for this election, place the Moon in the Fourth House.

Find Lost Articles

Search for lost articles during the first quarter and when your Sun sign is marked favorable. Also check to see that the planet ruling the lost item is trine, sextile, or conjunct the Moon. The Moon rules household utensils; Mercury rules letters and books; and Venus rules clothing, jewelry, and money.

Fishing

During the summer months, the best time of the day to fish is from sunrise to three hours after and from two hours before sunset until one hour after. Fish do not bite in cooler months until the air is warm, from noon to three pm. Warm, cloudy days are good. The most favorable winds are from the south and southwest.

Easterly winds are unfavorable. The best days of the month for fishing are when the Moon changes quarters, especially if the change occurs on a day when the Moon is in a water sign (Cancer, Scorpio, Pisces). The best period in any month is the day after the Full Moon.

Friendship

The need for friendship is greater when the Moon is in Aquarius or when Uranus aspects the Moon. Friendship prospers when Venus or Uranus is trine, sextile, or conjunct the Moon. The Moon in Gemini facilitates the chance meeting of acquaintances and friends.

Grafting or Budding

Grafting is the process of introducing new varieties of fruit on less desirable trees. For this process you should use the increasing phase of the Moon in fruitful signs such as Cancer, Scorpio, or Pisces. Capricorn may be used, too. Cut your grafts while trees are dormant, from December to March. Keep them in a cool, dark place, not too dry or too damp. Do the grafting before the sap starts to flow and while the Moon is waxing, preferably while it is in Cancer, Scorpio, or Pisces. The type of plant should determine both cutting and planting times.

Habit (Breaking)

To end an undesirable habit, and this applies to ending everything from a bad relationship to smoking, start on a day when the Moon is in the fourth quarter and in the barren sign of Gemini, Leo, or Aquarius. Aries, Virgo, and Capricorn may be suitable as well, depending on the habit you want to be rid of. Make sure that your lunar cycle is favorable. Avoid lunar aspects to Mars or Jupiter. However, favorable aspects to Pluto are helpful.

Haircuts

Cut hair when the Moon is in Gemini, Sagittarius, Pisces, Taurus, or Capricorn, but not in Virgo. Look for favorable aspects to Venus.

For faster growth, cut hair when the Moon is increasing in Cancer or Pisces. To make hair grow thicker, cut when the Moon is full in the signs of Taurus, Cancer, or Leo. If you want your hair to grow more slowly, have the Moon be decreasing in Aries, Gemini, or Virgo, and have the Moon square or opposing Saturn.

Permanents, straightening, and hair coloring will take well if the Moon is in Taurus or Leo and trine or sextile Venus. Avoid hair treatments if Mars is marked as square or in opposition, especially if heat is to be used. For permanents, a trine to Jupiter is helpful. The Moon also should be in the first quarter. Check the lunar cycle for a favorable day in relation to your Sun sign.

Harvest Crops

Harvest root crops when the Moon is in a dry sign (Aries, Leo, Sagittarius, Gemini, Aquarius) and waning. Harvest grain for storage just after the Full Moon, avoiding Cancer, Scorpio, or Pisces. Harvest in the third and fourth quarters in dry signs. Dry crops in the third quarter in fire signs.

Health

A diagnosis is more likely to be successful when the Moon is in Aries, Cancer, Libra, or Capricorn and less so when in Gemini, Sagittarius, Pisces, or Virgo. Begin a recuperation program or enter a hospital when the Moon is in a cardinal or fixed sign and the day is favorable to your Sun sign. For surgery, see "Surgical Procedures." Buy medicines when the Moon is in Virgo or Scorpio.

Home (Buy New)

If you desire a permanent home, buy when the New Moon is in a fixed sign—Taurus or Leo, for example. Each sign will affect your decision in a different way. A house bought when the Moon is in Taurus is likely to be more practical and have a country look—right down to the split-rail fence. A house purchased when the Moon is in Leo will more likely be a real showplace.

If you're buying for speculation and a quick turnover, be certain that the Moon is in a cardinal sign (Aries, Cancer, Libra, Capricorn). Avoid buying when the Moon is in a fixed sign (Leo, Scorpio, Aquarius, Taurus).

Home (Make Repairs)

In all repairs, avoid squares, oppositions, or conjunctions to the planet ruling the place or thing to be repaired. For example, bathrooms are ruled by Scorpio and Cancer. You would not want to start a project in those rooms when the Moon or Pluto is receiving hard aspects. The front entrance, hall, dining room, and porch are ruled by the Sun So you would want to avoid times when Saturn or Mars are square, opposing, or conjunct the Sun. Also, let the Moon be waxing.

Home (Sell)

Make a strong effort to list your property for sale when the Sun is marked favorable in your sign and in good aspect to Jupiter. Avoid adverse aspects to as many planets as possible.

Home Furnishings (Buy New)

Saturn days (Saturday) are good for buying, and Jupiter days (Thursday) are good for selling. Items bought on days when Saturn is well aspected tend to wear longer and purchases tend to be more conservative.

Job (Start New)

Jupiter and Venus should be sextile, trine, or conjunct the Moon. A day when your Sun is receiving favorable aspects is preferred.

Legal Matters

Good Moon-Jupiter aspects improve the outcome in legal decisions. To gain damages through a lawsuit, begin the process during the increasing Moon. To avoid paying damages, a court date during the decreasing Moon is desirable. Good Moon-Sun aspects strengthen your chance of success. A well-aspected Moon in Cancer or Leo, making good aspects to the Sun, brings the best results in custody cases. In divorce cases, a favorable Moon-Venus aspect is best.

Loan (Ask For)

A first and second quarter phase favors the lender, the third and fourth quarters favor the borrower. Good aspects of Jupiter and Venus to the Moon are favorable to both, as is having the Moon in Leo or Taurus.

Machinery, Appliances, or Tools (Buy)

Tools, machinery, and other implements should be bought on days when your lunar cycle is favorable and when Mars and Uranus are trine, sextile, or conjunct the Moon. Any quarter of the Moon is suitable. When buying gas or electrical appliances, the Moon should be in Aquarius.

Make a Will

Let the Moon be in a fixed sign (Taurus, Leo, Scorpio, or Aquarius) to ensure permanence. If the Moon is in a cardinal sign (Aries, Cancer, Libra, or Capricorn), the will could be altered. Let the Moon be waxing—increasing in light—and in good aspect to Saturn, Venus, or Mercury. In case the will is made in an emergency during illness and the Moon is slow in motion, void-of-course, combust, or under the Sun's beams, the testator will die and the will remain unaltered. There is some danger that it will be lost or stolen, however.

Marriage

The best time for marriage to take place is when the Moon is increasing, but not yet full. Good signs for the Moon to be in are Taurus, Cancer, Leo, or Libra.

The Moon in Taurus produces the most steadfast marriages, but if the partners later want to separate, they may have a difficult time. Make sure that the Moon is well aspected, especially to Venus or Jupiter. Avoid aspects to Mars, Uranus, or Pluto and the signs Aries, Gemini, Virgo, Scorpio, or Aquarius.

The values of the signs are as follows:

- Aries is not favored for marriage
- Taurus from 0 to 19 degrees is good, the remaining degrees are less favorable
- Cancer is unfavorable unless you are marrying a widow
- Leo is favored, but it may cause one party to deceive the other as to his or her money or possessions
- Virgo is not favored except when marrying a widow
- Libra is good for engagements but not for marriage
- Scorpio from 0 to 15 degrees is good, but the last 15 degrees are entirely unfortunate. The woman may be fickle, envious, and quarrelsome

- Sagittarius is neutral
- Capricorn, from 0 to 10 degrees, is difficult for marriage; however, the remaining degrees are favorable, especially when marrying a widow
- Aquarius is not favored
- Pisces is favored, although marriage under this sign can incline a woman to chatter a lot

These effects are strongest when the Moon is in the sign. If the Moon and Venus are in a cardinal sign, happiness between the couple may not continue long.

On no account should the Moon apply to Saturn or Mars, even by good aspect.

Medical Treatment for the Eyes

Let the Moon be increasing in light and motion and making favorable aspects to Venus or Jupiter and be unaspected by Mars. Keep the Moon out of Taurus, Capricorn, or Virgo. If an aspect between the Moon and Mars is unavoidable, let it be separating.

Medical Treatment for the Head

If possible, have Mars and Saturn free of hard aspects. Let the Moon be in Aries or Taurus, decreasing in light, in conjunction or aspect with Venus or Jupiter and free of hard aspects. The Sun should not be in any aspect to the Moon.

Medical Treatment for the Nose

Let the Moon be in Cancer, Leo, or Virgo and not aspecting Mars or Saturn and also not in conjunction with a retrograde or weak planet.

Mining

Saturn rules mining. Begin work when Saturn is marked conjunct, trine, or sextile. Mine for gold when the Sun is marked conjunct, trine, or sextile. Mercury rules quicksilver, Venus rules copper, Jupiter rules tin, Saturn rules lead and coal, Uranus rules radioactive elements, Neptune rules oil, the Moon rules water. Mine for these items when the ruling planet is marked conjunct, trine, or sextile.

Move to New Home

If you have a choice, and sometimes you don't, make sure that Mars is not aspecting the Moon. Move on a day favorable to your Sun sign or when the Moon is conjunct, sextile, or trine the Sun.

Mow Lawn

Mow in the first and second quarters (waxing phase) to increase growth and lushness, and in the third and fourth quarters (waning phase) to decrease growth.

Negotiate

When you are choosing a time to negotiate, consider what the meeting is about and what you want to have happen. If it is agreement or compromise between two parties that you desire, have the Moon be in the sign of Libra. When you are making contracts, it is best to have the Moon in the same element. For example, if

your concern is communication, then elect a time when the Moon is in an air sign. If, on the other hand, your concern is about possessions, an earth sign would be more appropriate. Fixed signs are unfavorable, with the exception of Leo; so are cardinal signs, except for Capricorn. If you are negotiating the end of something, use the rules that apply to ending habits.

Occupational Training

When you begin training, see that your lunar cycle is favorable that day and that the planet ruling your occupation is marked conjunct or trine.

Paint

Paint buildings during the waning Libra or Aquarius Moon. If the weather is hot, paint when the Moon is in Taurus. If the weather is cold, paint when the Moon is in Leo. Schedule the painting to start in the fourth quarter as the wood is drier and paint will penetrate wood better. Avoid painting around the New Moon, though, as the wood is likely to be damp, making the paint subject to scalding when hot weather hits it. If the temperature is below 70°F, it is not advisable to paint while the Moon is in Cancer, Scorpio, or Pisces as the paint is apt to creep, check, or run.

Party (Host or Attend)

A party timed so the Moon is in Gemini, Leo, Libra, or Sagittarius, with good aspects to Venus and Jupiter, will be fun and well attended. There should be no aspects between the Moon and Mars or Saturn.

Pawn

Do not pawn any article when Jupiter is receiving a square or opposition from Saturn or Mars or when Jupiter is within 17 degrees of the Sun, for you will have little chance to redeem the items.

Pick Mushrooms

Mushrooms, one of the most promising traditional medicines in the world, should be gathered at the Full Moon.

Plant

Root crops, like carrots and potatoes, are best if planted in the sign Taurus or Capricorn. Beans, peas, tomatoes, peppers, and other fruit-bearing plants are best if planted in a sign that supports seed growth. Leaf plants, like lettuce, broccoli, or cauliflower, are best planted when the Moon is in a water sign.

It is recommended that you transplant during a decreasing Moon, when forces are streaming into the lower part of the plant. This helps root growth.

Promotion (Ask For)

Choose a day favorable to your Sun sign. Mercury should be marked conjunct, trine, or sextile. Avoid days when Mars or Saturn is aspected.

Prune

Prune during the third and fourth quarter of a Scorpio Moon to retard growth and to promote better fruit. Prune when the Moon is in cardinal Capricorn to promote healing.

Reconcile with People

If the reconciliation is with a woman, let Venus be strong and well aspected. If elders or superiors are involved, see that Saturn is receiving good aspects; if the reconciliation is between young people or between an older and younger person, see that Mercury is well aspected.

Romance

There is less control of when a romance starts, but romances begun under an increasing Moon are more likely to be permanent or satisfying, while those begun during the decreasing Moon tend to transform the participants. The tone of the relationship can be guessed from the sign the Moon is in. Romances begun with the Moon in Aries may be impulsive. Those begun in Capricorn will take greater effort to bring to a desirable conclusion, but they may be very rewarding. Good aspects between the Moon and Venus will have a positive influence on the relationship. Avoid unfavorable aspects to Mars, Uranus, and Pluto. A decreasing Moon, particularly the fourth quarter, facilitates ending a relationship and causes the least pain.

Roof a Building
Begin roofing a building during the third or fourth quarter, when the Moon is in Aries or Aquarius. Shingles laid during the New Moon have a tendency to curl at the edges.

Sauerkraut
The best-tasting sauerkraut is made just after the Full Moon in the fruitful signs of Cancer, Scorpio, or Pisces.

Select a Child's Sex
Count from the last day of menstruation to the first day of the next cycle and divide the interval between the two dates in half. Pregnancy in the first half produces females, but copulation should take place with the Moon in a feminine sign. Pregnancy in the latter half, up to three days before the beginning of menstruation, produces males, but copulation should take place with the Moon in a masculine sign. The three-day period before the next period again produces females.

Sell or Canvass
Begin these activities during a day favorable to your Sun sign. Otherwise, sell on days when Jupiter, Mercury, or Mars is trine, sextile, or conjunct the Moon. Avoid days when Saturn is square or opposing the Moon, for that always hinders business and

causes discord. If the Moon is passing from the first quarter to full, it is best to have the Moon swift in motion and in good aspect with Venus and/or Jupiter.

Sign Papers

Sign contracts or agreements when the Moon is increasing in a fruitful sign and on a day when the Moon is making favorable aspects to Mercury. Avoid days when Mars, Saturn, or Neptune are square or opposite the Moon.

Spray and Weed

Spray pests and weeds during the fourth quarter when the Moon is in the barren sign Leo or Aquarius and making favorable aspects to Pluto. Weed during a waning Moon in a barren sign.

Staff (Fire)

Have the Moon in the third or fourth quarter, but not full. The Moon should not be square any planets.

Staff (Hire)

The Moon should be in the first or second quarter, and preferably in the sign of Gemini or Virgo. The Moon should be conjunct, trine, or sextile Mercury or Jupiter.

Stocks (Buy)

The Moon should be in Taurus or Capricorn, and there should be a sextile or trine to Jupiter or Saturn.

Surgical Procedures

Blood flow, like ocean tides, appears to be related to Moon phases. To reduce hemorrhage after a surgery, schedule it within one week before or after a New Moon. Schedule surgery to occur during the increase of the Moon if possible, as wounds heal better and vitality is greater than during the decrease of the Moon. Avoid surgery within one week before or after the Full Moon. Select a date when the Moon is past the sign governing the part of the body involved in the operation. For example, abdominal operations should be done when the Moon is in Sagittarius, Capricorn, or Aquarius. The further removed the Moon sign is from the sign ruling the afflicted part of the body, the better.

For successful operations, avoid times when the Moon is applying to any aspect of Mars. (This tends to promote inflammation and complications.) See the Lunar Aspectarian on odd pages 137–159 to find days with negative Mars aspects and positive Venus and Jupiter aspects. Never operate with the Moon in the same sign as a person's Sun sign or Ascendant. Let the Moon be in a fixed sign and avoid square or opposing aspects. The Moon should not be void-of-course. Cosmetic surgery should be done in the increase of the Moon, when the Moon is not square or in opposition to Mars. Avoid days when the Moon is square or opposing Saturn or the Sun.

Travel (Air)

Start long trips when the Moon is making favorable aspects to the Sun For enjoyment, aspects to Jupiter are preferable; for visiting, look for favorable aspects to Mercury. To prevent accidents, avoid squares or oppositions to Mars, Saturn, Uranus, or Pluto. Choose a day when the Moon is in Sagittarius or Gemini and well aspected to Mercury, Jupiter, or Uranus. Avoid adverse aspects of Mars, Saturn, or Uranus.

Visit

On setting out to visit a person, let the Moon be in aspect with any retrograde planet, for this ensures that the person you're visiting will be at home. If you desire to stay a long time in a place, let the Moon be in good aspect to Saturn. If you desire to leave the place quickly, let the Moon be in a cardinal sign.

Wean Children

To wean a child successfully, do so when the Moon is in Sagittarius, Capricorn, Aquarius, or Pisces—signs that do not rule vital human organs. By observing this astrological rule, much trouble for parents and child may be avoided.

Weight (Reduce)

If you want to lose weight, the best time to get started is when the Moon is in the third or fourth quarter and in the barren sign of Virgo. Review the section on How to Use the Moon Tables and Lunar Aspectarian beginning on page 136 to help you select a date that is favorable to begin your weight-loss program.

Wine and Drink Other Than Beer

Start brewing when the Moon is in Pisces or Taurus. Sextiles or trines to Venus are favorable, but avoid aspects to Mars or Saturn.

Write

Write for pleasure or publication when the Moon is in Gemini. Mercury should be making favorable aspects to Uranus and Neptune.

How to Use the Moon Tables and Lunar Aspectarian

Timing activities is one of the most important things you can do to ensure success. In many Eastern countries, timing by the planets is so important that practically no event takes place without first setting up a chart for it. Weddings have occurred in the middle of the night because the influences were at the best then. You may not want to take it that far, but you can still make use of the influences of the Moon whenever possible. It's easy and it works!

Llewellyn's Moon Sign Book has information to help you plan just about any activity: weddings, fishing, making purchases, cutting your hair, traveling, and more. We provide the guidelines you need to pick the best day out of the several from which you have to choose. The Moon Tables are the *Moon Sign Book's* primary method for choosing dates. Following are instructions, examples, and directions on how to read the Moon Tables. More advanced information on using the tables containing the Lunar Aspectarian and favorable and unfavorable days (found on odd-numbered pages opposite the Moon Tables), Moon void-of-course and retrograde information to choose the dates best for you is also included.

The Five Basic Steps

Step 1: Directions for Choosing Dates

Look up the directions for choosing dates for the activity that you wish to begin, then go to step 2.

Step 2: Check the Moon Tables

You'll find two tables for each month of the year beginning on page 136. The Moon Tables (on the left-hand pages) include the day, date, and sign the Moon is in; the element and nature of the sign; the Moon's phase; and when it changes sign or phase. If there is a time listed after a date, that time is the time when the Moon moves into that zodiac sign. Until then, the Moon is considered to be in the sign for the previous day.

The abbreviation Full signifies Full Moon and New signifies New Moon. The times listed with dates indicate when the Moon changes sign. The times listed after the phase indicate when the Moon changes phase.

Turn to the month you would like to begin your activity. You will be using the Moon's sign and phase information most often when you begin choosing your own dates. Use the Time Zone Map on page 164 and the Time Zone Conversions table on page 165 to convert time to your own time zone.

When you find dates that meet the criteria for the correct Moon phase and sign for your activity, you may have completed the process. For certain simple activities, such as getting a haircut, the phase and sign information is all that is needed. If the directions for your activity include information on certain lunar aspects, however, you should consult the Lunar Aspectarian. An example of this would be if the directions told you not to perform a certain activity when the Moon is square (Q) Jupiter.

Step 3: Check the Lunar Aspectarian

On the pages opposite the Moon Tables you will find tables containing the Lunar Aspectarian and Favorable and Unfavorable Days. The Lunar Aspectarian gives the aspects (or angles) of the Moon to other planets. Some aspects are favorable, while others are not. To use the Lunar Aspectarian, find the planet that the directions list as favorable for your activity, and run down the column to the date desired. For example, you should avoid aspects to Mars if you are planning surgery. So you would look for Mars across the top and then run down that column looking for days where there are no aspects to Mars (as signified by empty boxes). If you want to find a **favorable** aspect (sextile (X) or trine (T)) to Mercury, run your finger down the column under Mercury until you find an X or T. **Adverse** aspects to planets are squares (Q) or oppositions (O). A conjunction (C) is sometimes beneficial, sometimes not, depending on the activity or planets involved.

Step 4: Favorable and Unfavorable Days

The tables listing favorable and unfavorable days are helpful when you want to choose your personal best dates because your Sun sign is taken into consideration. The twelve Sun signs are listed on the right side of the tables. Once you have determined which days meet your criteria for phase, sign, and aspects, you can determine whether or not those days are positive for you by checking the favorable and unfavorable days for your Sun sign.

To find out if a day is positive for you, find your Sun sign and then look down the column. If it is marked F, it is very favorable. The Moon is in the same sign as your Sun on a favorable day. If it is marked f, it is slightly favorable; U is very unfavorable; and u means slightly unfavorable. A day marked very unfavorable (U) indicates that the Moon is in the sign opposing your Sun

Once you have selected good dates for the activity you are about to begin, you can go straight to "Using What You've Learned," beginning on the next page. To learn how to fine-tune your selections even further, read on.

Step 5: Void-of-Course Moon and Retrogrades

This last step is perhaps the most advanced portion of the procedure. It is generally considered poor timing to make decisions, sign important papers, or start special activities during a Moon void-of-course period or during a Mercury retrograde. Once you have chosen the best date for your activity based on steps one through four, you can check the Void-of-Course tables, beginning on page 76, to find out if any of the dates you have chosen have void periods.

The Moon is said to be void-of-course after it has made its last aspect to a planet within a particular sign, but before it has moved into the next sign. Put simply, the Moon is "resting" during the void-of-course period, so activities initiated at this time generally don't come to fruition. You will notice that there are many void periods during the year, and it is nearly impossible to avoid all of them. Some people choose to ignore these altogether and do not take them into consideration when planning activities.

Next, you can check the Retrograde Planets tables on page 160 to see what planets are retrograde during your chosen date(s).

A planet is said to be retrograde when it appears to move backward in the sky as viewed from Earth. Generally, the farther a planet is away from the Sun, the longer it can stay retrograde. Some planets will retrograde for several months at a time. Avoiding retrogrades is not as important in lunar planning as avoiding the Moon void-of-course, with the exception of the planet Mercury.

Mercury rules thought and communication, so it is advisable not to sign important papers, initiate important business or legal work, or make crucial decisions during these times. As with the Moon void-of-course, it is difficult to avoid all planetary retrogrades when beginning events, and you may choose to ignore this step of the process. Following are some examples using some or all of the steps outlined above.

Using What You've Learned

Let's say it's a new year and you want to have your hair cut. It's thin and you would like it to look fuller, so you find the directions for hair care and you see that for thicker hair you should cut hair while the Moon is Full and in the sign of Taurus, Cancer, or Leo. You should avoid the Moon in Aries, Gemini, or Virgo. Look at the January Moon Table on page 136. You see that the Full Moon is on January 25 at 12:54 pm. The Moon is in Leo on January 25 and moves into Virgo on January 27 at 2:11 pm, so January 25–26 meet both the phase and sign criteria.

Let's move on to a more difficult example using the sign and phase of the Moon. You want to buy a permanent home. After checking the instructions for purchasing a house: "Home (Buy New)" on page 118, you see that you should buy a home when the Moon is in Taurus, Cancer, or Leo. You need to get a loan, so you should also look under "Loan (Ask For)" on page 119. Here it says that the third and fourth quarters favor the borrower (you). You are going to buy the house in October, so go to page 154. The Moon is in the third quarter Oct 17–23 and fourth quarter Oct 1 and Oct 24–31. The Moon is in Leo at 1:24 am on Oct 24 until Oct 26 at 11:47 am; in Taurus from Oct 17 at 4:00 pm until Oct 19 at 4:07 pm; in Cancer from 6:50 pm on Oct 21 to Oct 24 at 1:24 am. The best days for obtaining a loan would be October 17–18 and 21–25.

Just match up the best sign and phase (quarter) to come up with the best date. With all activities, be sure to check the favorable and unfavorable days for your Sun sign in the table adjoining the Lunar Aspectarian. If there is a choice between several dates, pick the one most favorable for you. Because buying a home is an important business decision, you may also wish to see if the Moon is void or if Mercury is retrograde during these dates.

Now let's look at an example that uses signs, phases, and aspects. Our example is starting new home construction. We will use the month of February. Look under "Build (Start Foundation)" on page 110 and you'll see that the Moon should be in the first quarter of a fixed sign—Leo, Taurus, Aquarius, or Scorpio. You should select a time when the Moon is not making unfavorable aspects to Saturn. (Conjunctions are usually considered unfavorable if they are to Mars, Saturn, or Neptune.) Look in the February Moon Table on page 138. You will see that the Moon is in the first quarter Feb 9–15 and in Taurus from 10:02 am on Feb 14 until 2:39 pm on Feb 16. Now, look to the February Lunar Aspectarian. We see that there is a favorable sextile to Saturn the 14; therefore, Feb 14–15 would be the best dates to start a foundation.

A Note about Time and Time Zones

All tables in the Moon Sign Book use Eastern Time. You must calculate the difference between your time zone and the Eastern Time Zone. Please refer to the Time Zone Conversions chart on page 165 for help with time conversions. The sign the Moon is in at midnight is the sign shown in the Aspectarian and Favorable and Unfavorable Days tables.

How Does the Time Matter?

Due to the three-hour time difference between the East and West Coasts of the United States, those of you living on the East Coast may be, for example, under the influence of a Virgo Moon, while those of you living on the West Coast will still have a Leo Moon influence.

We follow a commonly held belief among astrologers: whatever sign the Moon is in at the start of a day—12:00 am Eastern Time— is considered the dominant influence of the day. That sign is indicated in the Moon Tables. If the date you select for an activity shows the Moon changing signs, you can decide how important the sign change may be for your specific election and adjust your election date and time accordingly.

Use Common Sense

Some activities depend on outside factors. Obviously, you can't go out and plant when there is a foot of snow on the ground. You should adjust to the conditions at hand. If the weather was bad during the first quarter, when it was best to plant crops, do it during the second quarter while the Moon is in a fruitful sign. If the Moon is not in a fruitful sign during the first or second quarter, choose a day when it is in a semi-fruitful sign. The best advice is to choose either the sign or phase that is most favorable, when the two don't coincide.

To Summarize

First, look up the activity under the proper heading, then look for the information given in the tables. Choose the best date considering the number of positive factors in effect. If most of the dates are favorable, there is no problem choosing the one that will fit your schedule. However, if there aren't any really good dates, pick the ones with the least number of negative influences. Please keep in mind that the information found here applies in the broadest sense to the events you want to plan or are considering. To be the most effective, when you use electional astrology, you should also consider your own birth chart in relation to a chart drawn for the time or times you have under consideration. The best advice we can offer you is: read the entire introduction to each section.

January Moon Table

Date	Sign	Element	Nature	Phase
1 Mon	Virgo	Earth	Barren	3rd
2 Tue 7:47 pm	Libra	Air	Semi-fruitful	3rd
3 Wed	Libra	Air	Semi-fruitful	4th 10:30 pm
4 Thu	Libra	Air	Semi-fruitful	4th
5 Fri 7:39 am	Scorpio	Water	Fruitful	4th
6 Sat	Scorpio	Water	Fruitful	4th
7 Sun 4:08 pm	Sagittarius	Fire	Barren	4th
8 Mon	Sagittarius	Fire	Barren	4th
9 Tue 8:33 pm	Capricorn	Earth	Semi-fruitful	4th
10 Wed	Capricorn	Earth	Semi-fruitful	4th
11 Thu 10:01 pm	Aquarius	Air	Barren	New 6:57 am
12 Fri	Aquarius	Air	Barren	1st
13 Sat 10:29 pm	Pisces	Water	Fruitful	1st
14 Sun	Pisces	Water	Fruitful	1st
15 Mon 11:49 pm	Aries	Fire	Barren	1st
16 Tue	Aries	Fire	Barren	1st
17 Wed	Aries	Fire	Barren	2nd 10:53 pm
18 Thu 3:12 am	Taurus	Earth	Semi-fruitful	2nd
19 Fri	Taurus	Earth	Semi-fruitful	2nd
20 Sat 8:58 am	Gemini	Air	Barren	2nd
21 Sun	Gemini	Air	Barren	2nd
22 Mon 4:51 pm	Cancer	Water	Fruitful	2nd
23 Tue	Cancer	Water	Fruitful	2nd
24 Wed	Cancer	Water	Fruitful	2nd
25 Thu 2:37 am	Leo	Fire	Barren	Full 12:54 pm
26 Fri	Leo	Fire	Barren	3rd
27 Sat 2:11 pm	Virgo	Earth	Barren	3rd
28 Sun	Virgo	Earth	Barren	3rd
29 Mon	Virgo	Earth	Barren	3rd
30 Tue 3:04 am	Libra	Air	Semi-fruitful	3rd
31 Wed	Libra	Air	Semi-fruitful	3rd

January Aspectarian/Favorable & Unfavorable Days

Date	Sun	Mercury	Venus	Mars	Jupiter	Saturn	Uranus	Neptune	Pluto
1	T						T		
2		Q		Q				O	T
3	Q		X						
4		X							
5				X	O	T			Q
6	X						O		
7						Q		T	X
8			C						
9		C					Q		
10				C	T	X			
11	C						T	X	C
12				Q					
13		X	X				Q		
14				X	X	C			
15	X		Q				X	C	X
16		Q		Q					
17	Q		T						
18		T		T	C	X			Q
19							C		
20	T					Q		X	T
21									
22			O					Q	
23		O		O	X	T			
24								X	T
25	O			Q					O
26							Q		
27									
28			T		T	O			
29		T		T				T	O
30			Q						T
31	T			Q					

Date	Aries	Taurus	Gemini	Cancer	Leo	Virgo	Libra	Scorpio	Sagittarius	Capricorn	Aquarius	Pisces
1		f	u	f		F		f	u	f		U
2		f	u	f		F		f	u	f		U
3	U		f	u	f		F		f	u	f	
4	U		f	u	f		F		f	u	f	
5	U		f	u	f		F		f	u	f	u
6		U		f	u	f		F		f	u	f
7		U		f	u	f		F		f	u	f
8	f		U		f	u	f		F		f	u
9	f		U		f	u	f		F		f	u
10	u	f		U		f	u	f		F		f
11	u	f		U		f	u	f		F		f
12	f	u	f		U		f	u	f		F	
13	f	u	f		U		f	u	f		F	
14		f	u	f		U		f	u	f		F
15		f	u	f		U		f	u	f		F
16	F		f	u	f		U		f	u	f	
17	F		f	u	f		U		f	u	f	
18	F		f	u	f		U		f	u	f	
19		F		f	u	f		U		f	u	f
20		F		f	u	f		U		f	u	f
21	f		F		f	u	f		U		f	u
22	f		F		f	u	f		U		f	u
23	u	f		F		f	u	f		U		f
24	u	f		F		f	u	f		U		f
25	f	u	f		F		f	u	f		U	
26	f	u	f		F		f	u	f		U	
27	f	u	f		F		f	u	f		U	u
28		f	u	f		F		f	u	f		U
29		f	u	f		F		f	u	f		U
30		f	u	f		F		f	u	f		U
31	U		f	u	f		F		f	u	f	

137

February Moon Table

Date	Sign	Element	Nature	Phase
1 Thu 3:37 pm	Scorpio	Water	Fruitful	3rd
2 Fri	Scorpio	Water	Fruitful	4th 6:18 pm
3 Sat	Scorpio	Water	Fruitful	4th
4 Sun 1:28 am	Sagittarius	Fire	Barren	4th
5 Mon	Sagittarius	Fire	Barren	4th
6 Tue 7:08 am	Capricorn	Earth	Semi-fruitful	4th
7 Wed	Capricorn	Earth	Semi-fruitful	4th
8 Thu 8:59 am	Aquarius	Air	Barren	4th
9 Fri	Aquarius	Air	Barren	New 5:59 pm
10 Sat 8:42 am	Pisces	Water	Fruitful	1st
11 Sun	Pisces	Water	Fruitful	1st
12 Mon 8:26 am	Aries	Fire	Barren	1st
13 Tue	Aries	Fire	Barren	1st
14 Wed 10:02 am	Taurus	Earth	Semi-fruitful	1st
15 Thu	Taurus	Earth	Semi-fruitful	1st
16 Fri 2:39 pm	Gemini	Air	Barren	2nd 10:01 am
17 Sat	Gemini	Air	Barren	2nd
18 Sun 10:25 pm	Cancer	Water	Fruitful	2nd
19 Mon	Cancer	Water	Fruitful	2nd
20 Tue	Cancer	Water	Fruitful	2nd
21 Wed 8:40 am	Leo	Fire	Barren	2nd
22 Thu	Leo	Fire	Barren	2nd
23 Fri 8:38 pm	Virgo	Earth	Barren	2nd
24 Sat	Virgo	Earth	Barren	Full 7:30 am
25 Sun	Virgo	Earth	Barren	3rd
26 Mon 9:29 am	Libra	Air	Semi-fruitful	3rd
27 Tue	Libra	Air	Semi-fruitful	3rd
28 Wed 10:09 pm	Scorpio	Water	Fruitful	3rd
29 Thu	Scorpio	Water	Fruitful	3rd

February Aspectarian/Favorable & Unfavorable Days

Date	Sun	Mercury	Venus	Mars	Jupiter	Saturn	Uranus	Neptune	Pluto
1		Q							Q
2	Q		X		O	T			
3		X		X			O	T	
4						Q			X
5	X								
6					T	X		Q	
7			C				T		
8		C		C	Q			X	C
9	C						Q		
10					X	C			
11			X				X		
12				X				C	X
13		X							
14	X		Q	Q		X			Q
15		Q			C		C		
16	Q		T	T				X	T
17						Q			
18	T	T						Q	
19					X	T			
20							X		
21			O	O				T	O
22					Q		Q		
23		O							
24	O				T	O			
25							T		
26								O	T
27			T	T					
28									
29	T	T			O	T			Q

Date	Aries	Taurus	Gemini	Cancer	Leo	Virgo	Libra	Scorpio	Sagittarius	Capricorn	Aquarius	Pisces
1	U		f	u	f		F		f	u	f	
2		U		f	u	f		F		f	u	f
3		U		f	u	f		F		f	u	f
4	f		U		f	u	f		F		f	u
5	f		U		f	u	f		F		f	u
6	f		U		f	u	f		F		f	u
7	u	f		U		f	u	f		F		f
8	u	f		U		f	u	f		F		f
9	f	u	f		U		f	u	f		F	
10	f	u	f		U		f	u	f		F	
11		f	u	f		U		f	u	f		F
12		f	u	f		U		f	u	f		F
13	F		f	u	f		U		f	u	f	
14	F		f	u	f		U		f	u	f	
15		F		f	u	f		U		f	u	f
16		F		f	u	f		U		f	u	f
17	f		F		f	u	f		U		f	u
18	f		F		f	u	f		U		f	u
19	u	f		F		f	u	f		U		f
20	u	f		F		f	u	f		U		f
21	u	f		F		f	u	f		U		f
22	f	u	f		F		f	u	f		U	
23	f	u	f		F		f	u	f		U	
24		f	u	f		F		f	u	f		U
25		f	u	f		F		f	u	f		U
26		f	u	f		F		f	u	f		U
27	U		f	u	f		F		f	u	f	
28	U		f	u	f		F		f	u	f	
29		U		f	u	f		F		f	u	f

March Moon Table

Date	Sign	Element	Nature	Phase
1 Fri	Scorpio	Water	Fruitful	3rd
2 Sat 8:56 am	Sagittarius	Fire	Barren	3rd
3 Sun	Sagittarius	Fire	Barren	4th 10:23 am
4 Mon 4:15 pm	Capricorn	Earth	Semi-fruitful	4th
5 Tue	Capricorn	Earth	Semi-fruitful	4th
6 Wed 7:38 pm	Aquarius	Air	Barren	4th
7 Thu	Aquarius	Air	Barren	4th
8 Fri 8:03 pm	Pisces	Water	Fruitful	4th
9 Sat	Pisces	Water	Fruitful	4th
10 Sun 8:19 pm	Aries	Fire	Barren	New 5:00 am
11 Mon	Aries	Fire	Barren	1st
12 Tue 8:28 pm	Taurus	Earth	Semi-fruitful	1st
13 Wed	Taurus	Earth	Semi-fruitful	1st
14 Thu 11:16 pm	Gemini	Air	Barren	1st
15 Fri	Gemini	Air	Barren	1st
16 Sat	Gemini	Air	Barren	1st
17 Sun 5:40 am	Cancer	Water	Fruitful	2nd 12:11 am
18 Mon	Cancer	Water	Fruitful	2nd
19 Tue 3:33 pm	Leo	Fire	Barren	2nd
20 Wed	Leo	Fire	Barren	2nd
21 Thu	Leo	Fire	Barren	2nd
22 Fri 3:42 am	Virgo	Earth	Barren	2nd
23 Sat	Virgo	Earth	Barren	2nd
24 Sun 4:37 pm	Libra	Air	Semi-fruitful	2nd
25 Mon	Libra	Air	Semi-fruitful	Full 3:00 am
26 Tue	Libra	Air	Semi-fruitful	3rd
27 Wed 5:03 am	Scorpio	Water	Fruitful	3rd
28 Thu	Scorpio	Water	Fruitful	3rd
29 Fri 3:52 pm	Sagittarius	Fire	Barren	3rd
30 Sat	Sagittarius	Fire	Barren	3rd
31 Sun	Sagittarius	Fire	Barren	3rd

March Aspectarian/Favorable & Unfavorable Days

Date	Sun	Mercury	Venus	Mars	Jupiter	Saturn	Uranus	Neptune	Pluto
1			Q	Q			O		
2								T	X
3	Q	Q	X	X		Q			
4								Q	
5	X				T	X			
6		X					T	X	C
7					Q				
8			C	C			Q		
9					X	C			
10	C	C					X	C	X
11									
12			X	X					Q
13					C	X			
14	X			Q			C	X	
15		X	Q			Q			T
16			T						
17	Q		T					Q	
18		Q			X	T	X		
19	T							T	O
20				Q					
21		T				Q			
22			O						
23			O		T	O	T		
24							O		T
25	O								
26		O							
27				T					Q
28			T		O	T	O		
29								T	X
30	T			Q		Q			
31		T	Q					Q	

Date	Aries	Taurus	Gemini	Cancer	Leo	Virgo	Libra	Scorpio	Sagittarius	Capricorn	Aquarius	Pisces
1	U		f	u	f			F		f	u	f
2	U		f	u	f			F		f	u	f
3	f	U		f	u	f			F		f	u
4	f	U		f	u	f			F		f	u
5	u	f	U		f	u	f			F		f
6	u	f	U		f	u	f			F		f
7	f	u	f	U		f	u	f			F	
8	f	u	f	U		f	u	f			F	
9		f	u	f	U		f	u	f			F
10		f	u	f	U		f	u	f			F
11	F		f	u	f	U		f	u	f		
12	F		f	u	f	U		f	u	f		
13		F		f	u	f	U		f	u	f	
14		F		f	u	f	U		f	u	f	
15			F		f	u	f	U		f	u	f
16			F		f	u	f	U		f	u	f
17			F		f	u	f	U		f	u	f
18	f			F		f	u	f	U		f	u
19	f			F		f	u	f	U		f	u
20	u	f			F		f	u	f	U		f
21	u	f			F		f	u	f	U		f
22	u	f			F		f	u	f	U		f
23	f	u	f			F		f	u	f	U	
24	f	u	f			F		f	u	f	U	
25		f	u	f			F		f	u	f	U
26		f	u	f			F		f	u	f	U
27		f	u	f			F		f	u	f	U
28	U		f	u	f			F		f	u	f
29	U		f	u	f			F		f	u	f
30	f	U		f	u	f			F		f	u
31	f	U		f	u	f			F		f	u

141

April Moon Table

Date	Sign	Element	Nature	Phase
1 Mon 12:05 am	Capricorn	Earth	Semi-fruitful	4th 11:15 pm
2 Tue	Capricorn	Earth	Semi-fruitful	4th
3 Wed 5:08 am	Aquarius	Air	Barren	4th
4 Thu	Aquarius	Air	Barren	4th
5 Fri 7:13 am	Pisces	Water	Fruitful	4th
6 Sat	Pisces	Water	Fruitful	4th
7 Sun 7:25 am	Aries	Fire	Barren	4th
8 Mon	Aries	Fire	Barren	New 2:21 pm
9 Tue 7:23 am	Taurus	Earth	Semi-fruitful	1st
10 Wed	Taurus	Earth	Semi-fruitful	1st
11 Thu 8:59 am	Gemini	Air	Barren	1st
12 Fri	Gemini	Air	Barren	1st
13 Sat 1:45 pm	Cancer	Water	Fruitful	1st
14 Sun	Cancer	Water	Fruitful	1st
15 Mon 10:24 pm	Leo	Fire	Barren	2nd 3:13 pm
16 Tue	Leo	Fire	Barren	2nd
17 Wed	Leo	Fire	Barren	2nd
18 Thu 10:10 am	Virgo	Earth	Barren	2nd
19 Fri	Virgo	Earth	Barren	2nd
20 Sat 11:08 pm	Libra	Air	Semi-fruitful	2nd
21 Sun	Libra	Air	Semi-fruitful	2nd
22 Mon	Libra	Air	Semi-fruitful	2nd
23 Tue 11:20 am	Scorpio	Water	Fruitful	Full 7:49 pm
24 Wed	Scorpio	Water	Fruitful	3rd
25 Thu 9:37 pm	Sagittarius	Fire	Barren	3rd
26 Fri	Sagittarius	Fire	Barren	3rd
27 Sat	Sagittarius	Fire	Barren	3rd
28 Sun 5:37 am	Capricorn	Earth	Semi-fruitful	3rd
29 Mon	Capricorn	Earth	Semi-fruitful	3rd
30 Tue 11:20 am	Aquarius	Air	Barren	3rd

April Aspectarian/Favorable & Unfavorable Days

Date	Sun	Mercury	Venus	Mars	Jupiter	Saturn	Uranus	Neptune	Pluto
1	Q			X					
2					T	X	T		
3		Q	X					X	C
4	X				Q		Q		
5		X							
6				C	X	C	X		
7			C					C	X
8	C	C							
9									Q
10				X	C	X	C		
11			X					X	T
12		X		Q		Q			
13	X							Q	
14			Q	T		T			
15	Q	Q			X		X	T	
16									O
17		T	T		Q		Q		
18	T								
19						O			
20				O	T		T	O	
21									T
22		O	O						
23	O								Q
24						T			
25				T	O		O	T	
26									X
27		T				Q			
28	T		T	Q				Q	
29		Q				X	T		
30			Q	X	T			X	C

Date	Aries	Taurus	Gemini	Cancer	Leo	Virgo	Libra	Scorpio	Sagittarius	Capricorn	Aquarius	Pisces
1	u	f		U		f	u	f		F		f
2	u	f		U		f	u	f		F		f
3	u	f		U		f	u	f		F		f
4	f	u	f		U		f	u	f		F	
5	f	u	f		U		f	u	f		F	
6		f	u	f		U		f	u	f		F
7		f	u	f		U		f	u	f		F
8	F		f	u	f		U		f	u	f	
9	F		f	u	f		U		f	u	f	
10		F		f	u	f		U		f	u	f
11		F		f	u	f		U		f	u	f
12	f		F		f	u	f		U		f	u
13	f		F		f	u	f		U		f	u
14	u	f		F		f	u	f		U		f
15	u	f		F		f	u	f		U		f
16	f	u	f		F		f	u	f		U	
17	f	u	f		F		f	u	f		U	
18	f	u	f		F		f	u	f		U	
19		f	u	f		F		f	u	f		U
20		f	u	f		F		f	u	f		U
21	U		f	u	f		F		f	u	f	
22	U		f	u	f		F		f	u	f	
23	U		f	u	f		F		f	u	f	
24		U		f	u	f		F		f	u	f
25		U		f	u	f		F		f	u	f
26	f		U		f	u	f		F		f	u
27	f		U		f	u	f		F		f	u
28	f		U		f	u	f		F		f	u
29	u	f		U		f	u	f		F		f
30	u	f		U		f	u	f		F		f

May Moon Table

Date	Sign	Element	Nature	Phase
1 Wed	Aquarius	Air	Barren	4th 7:27 am
2 Thu 2:52 pm	Pisces	Water	Fruitful	4th
3 Fri	Pisces	Water	Fruitful	4th
4 Sat 4:41 pm	Aries	Fire	Barren	4th
5 Sun	Aries	Fire	Barren	4th
6 Mon 5:42 pm	Taurus	Earth	Semi-fruitful	4th
7 Tue	Taurus	Earth	Semi-fruitful	New 11:22 pm
8 Wed 7:20 pm	Gemini	Air	Barren	1st
9 Thu	Gemini	Air	Barren	1st
10 Fri 11:13 pm	Cancer	Water	Fruitful	1st
11 Sat	Cancer	Water	Fruitful	1st
12 Sun	Cancer	Water	Fruitful	1st
13 Mon 6:36 am	Leo	Fire	Barren	1st
14 Tue	Leo	Fire	Barren	1st
15 Wed 5:33 pm	Virgo	Earth	Barren	2nd 7:48 am
16 Thu	Virgo	Earth	Barren	2nd
17 Fri	Virgo	Earth	Barren	2nd
18 Sat 6:23 am	Libra	Air	Semi-fruitful	2nd
19 Sun	Libra	Air	Semi-fruitful	2nd
20 Mon 6:34 pm	Scorpio	Water	Fruitful	2nd
21 Tue	Scorpio	Water	Fruitful	2nd
22 Wed	Scorpio	Water	Fruitful	2nd
23 Thu 4:24 am	Sagittarius	Fire	Barren	Full 9:53 am
24 Fri	Sagittarius	Fire	Barren	3rd
25 Sat 11:36 am	Capricorn	Earth	Semi-fruitful	3rd
26 Sun	Capricorn	Earth	Semi-fruitful	3rd
27 Mon 4:45 pm	Aquarius	Air	Barren	3rd
28 Tue	Aquarius	Air	Barren	3rd
29 Wed 8:33 pm	Pisces	Water	Fruitful	3rd
30 Thu	Pisces	Water	Fruitful	4th 1:13 pm
31 Fri 11:28 pm	Aries	Fire	Barren	4th

May Aspectarian/Favorable & Unfavorable Days

Date	Sun	Mercury	Venus	Mars	Jupiter	Saturn	Uranus	Neptune	Pluto
1	Q	X							
2			X		Q		Q		
3	X					C			
4				C	X		X	C	X
5									
6		C							Q
7	C		C			X			
8					C		C	X	T
9				X					
10		X				Q		Q	
11				Q					
12	X		X			T	X		
13		Q			X			T	O
14			Q	T					
15	Q	T			Q		Q		
16									
17			T			O	T		
18	T				T			O	T
19				O					
20									Q
21		O							
22						T	O		
23	O		O		O			T	X
24				T		Q			
25								Q	
26		T		Q		X			
27					T		T	X	C
28	T		T						
29		Q		X	Q		Q		
30	Q		Q						
31		X				C	X	C	

Date	Aries	Taurus	Gemini	Cancer	Leo	Virgo	Libra	Scorpio	Sagittarius	Capricorn	Aquarius	Pisces
1	f	u	f		U		f	u	f		F	
2	f	u	f		U		f	u	f		F	
3		f	u	f		U		f	u	f		F
4		f	u	f		U		f	u	f		F
5	F		f	u	f		U		f	u	f	
6	F		f	u	f		U		f	u	f	
7		F		f	u	f		U		f	u	f
8		F		f	u	f		U		f	u	f
9	f		F		f	u	f		U		f	u
10	f		F		f	u	f		U		f	u
11	u	f		F		f	u	f		U		f
12	u	f		F		f	u	f		U		f
13	u	f		F		f	u	f		U		f
14	f	u	f		F		f	u	f		U	
15	f	u	f		F		f	u	f		U	
16		f	u	f		F		f	u	f		U
17		f	u	f		F		f	u	f		U
18		f	u	f		F		f	u	f		U
19	U		f	u	f		F		f	u	f	
20	U		f	u	f		F		f	u	f	
21		U		f	u	f		F		f	u	f
22		U		f	u	f		F		f	u	f
23		U		f	u	f		F		f	u	f
24	f		U		f	u	f		F		f	u
25	f		U		f	u	f		F		f	u
26	u	f		U		f	u	f		F		f
27	u	f		U		f	u	f		F		f
28	f	u	f		U		f	u	f		F	
29	f	u	f		U		f	u	f		F	
30		f	u	f		U		f	u	f		F
31		f	u	f		U		f	u	f		F

June Moon Table

Date	Sign	Element	Nature	Phase
1 Sat	Aries	Fire	Barren	4th
2 Sun	Aries	Fire	Barren	4th
3 Mon 1:55 am	Taurus	Earth	Semi-fruitful	4th
4 Tue	Taurus	Earth	Semi-fruitful	4th
5 Wed 4:36 am	Gemini	Air	Barren	4th
6 Thu	Gemini	Air	Barren	New 8:38 am
7 Fri 8:41 am	Cancer	Water	Fruitful	1st
8 Sat	Cancer	Water	Fruitful	1st
9 Sun 3:29 pm	Leo	Fire	Barren	1st
10 Mon	Leo	Fire	Barren	1st
11 Tue	Leo	Fire	Barren	1st
12 Wed 1:39 am	Virgo	Earth	Barren	1st
13 Thu	Virgo	Earth	Barren	1st
14 Fri 2:12 pm	Libra	Air	Semi-fruitful	2nd 1:18 am
15 Sat	Libra	Air	Semi-fruitful	2nd
16 Sun	Libra	Air	Semi-fruitful	2nd
17 Mon 2:38 am	Scorpio	Water	Fruitful	2nd
18 Tue	Scorpio	Water	Fruitful	2nd
19 Wed 12:32 pm	Sagittarius	Fire	Barren	2nd
20 Thu	Sagittarius	Fire	Barren	2nd
21 Fri 7:08 pm	Capricorn	Earth	Semi-fruitful	Full 9:08 pm
22 Sat	Capricorn	Earth	Semi-fruitful	3rd
23 Sun 11:14 pm	Aquarius	Air	Barren	3rd
24 Mon	Aquarius	Air	Barren	3rd
25 Tue	Aquarius	Air	Barren	3rd
26 Wed 2:08 am	Pisces	Water	Fruitful	3rd
27 Thu	Pisces	Water	Fruitful	3rd
28 Fri 4:52 am	Aries	Fire	Barren	4th 5:53 pm
29 Sat	Aries	Fire	Barren	4th
30 Sun 8:00 am	Taurus	Earth	Semi-fruitful	4th

June Aspectarian/Favorable & Unfavorable Days

Date	Sun	Mercury	Venus	Mars	Jupiter	Saturn	Uranus	Neptune	Pluto
1	X		X		X				X
2				C					
3									Q
4						X	C		
5		C			C			X	T
6	C		C			Q			
7					X			Q	
8							T		
9				Q	X		X	T	O
10		X							
11	X		X					Q	
12				T	Q				
13		Q					O		
14	Q		Q		T		T	O	T
15									
16	T								
17		T	T	O					Q
18							T		
19					O		O	T	X
20									
21	O					Q		Q	
22		O	O	T					
23						X	T	X	
24				Q	T				C
25							Q		
26	T		T		Q				
27		T		X		C	X		
28	Q				X			C	X
29			Q						
30		Q							Q

Date	Aries	Taurus	Gemini	Cancer	Leo	Virgo	Libra	Scorpio	Sagittarius	Capricorn	Aquarius	Pisces
1	F		f	u	f		U		f	u	f	
2	F		f	u	f		U		f	u	f	
3		F		f	u	f		U		f	u	f
4		F		f	u	f		U		f	u	f
5		F		f	u	f		U		f	u	f
6	f		F		f	u	f		U		f	u
7	f		F		f	u	f		U		f	u
8	u	f		F		f	u	f		U		f
9	u	f		F		f	u	f		U		f
10	f	u	f		F		f	u	f		U	
11	f	u	f		F		f	u	f		U	
12		f	u	f		F		f	u	f		U
13		f	u	f		F		f	u	f		U
14		f	u	f		F		f	u	f		U
15	U		f	u	f		F		f	u	f	
16	U		f	u	f		F		f	u	f	
17		U		f	u	f		F		f	u	f
18		U		f	u	f		F		f	u	f
19		U		f	u	f		F		f	u	f
20	f		U		f	u	f		F		f	u
21	f		U		f	u	f		F		f	u
22	u	f		U		f	u	f		F		f
23	u	f		U		f	u	f		F		f
24	f	u	f		U		f	u	f		F	
25	f	u	f		U		f	u	f		F	
26		f	u	f		U		f	u	f		F
27		f	u	f		U		f	u	f		F
28		f	u	f		U		f	u	f		F
29	F		f	u	f		U		f	u	f	
30	F		f	u	f		U		f	u	f	

July Moon Table

Date	Sign	Element	Nature	Phase
1 Mon	Taurus	Earth	Semi-fruitful	4th
2 Tue 11:50 am	Gemini	Air	Barren	4th
3 Wed	Gemini	Air	Barren	4th
4 Thu 4:51 pm	Cancer	Water	Fruitful	4th
5 Fri	Cancer	Water	Fruitful	New 6:57 pm
6 Sat 11:56 pm	Leo	Fire	Barren	1st
7 Sun	Leo	Fire	Barren	1st
8 Mon	Leo	Fire	Barren	1st
9 Tue 9:48 am	Virgo	Earth	Barren	1st
10 Wed	Virgo	Earth	Barren	1st
11 Thu 10:06 pm	Libra	Air	Semi-fruitful	1st
12 Fri	Libra	Air	Semi-fruitful	1st
13 Sat	Libra	Air	Semi-fruitful	2nd 6:49 pm
14 Sun 10:53 am	Scorpio	Water	Fruitful	2nd
15 Mon	Scorpio	Water	Fruitful	2nd
16 Tue 9:25 pm	Sagittarius	Fire	Barren	2nd
17 Wed	Sagittarius	Fire	Barren	2nd
18 Thu	Sagittarius	Fire	Barren	2nd
19 Fri 4:14 am	Capricorn	Earth	Semi-fruitful	2nd
20 Sat	Capricorn	Earth	Semi-fruitful	2nd
21 Sun 7:43 am	Aquarius	Air	Barren	Full 6:17 am
22 Mon	Aquarius	Air	Barren	3rd
23 Tue 9:23 am	Pisces	Water	Fruitful	3rd
24 Wed	Pisces	Water	Fruitful	3rd
25 Thu 10:52 am	Aries	Fire	Barren	3rd
26 Fri	Aries	Fire	Barren	3rd
27 Sat 1:23 pm	Taurus	Earth	Semi-fruitful	4th 10:52 pm
28 Sun	Taurus	Earth	Semi-fruitful	4th
29 Mon 5:28 pm	Gemini	Air	Barren	4th
30 Tue	Gemini	Air	Barren	4th
31 Wed 11:19 pm	Cancer	Water	Fruitful	4th

July Aspectarian/Favorable & Unfavorable Days

Date	Sun	Mercury	Venus	Mars	Jupiter	Saturn	Uranus	Neptune	Pluto
1	X		X	C		X			
2		X					C	X	T
3					C	Q			
4						Q			
5	C								
6			C	X		T	X	T	
7		C			X				O
8			Q						
9								Q	
10						Q			
11	X		X	T		O	T	O	
12					T				T
13	Q	X							
14			Q						Q
15									
16	T	Q		O		T	O	T	X
17			T		O				
18		T				Q			
19								Q	
20						X			
21	O			T			T	X	C
22			O		T				
23		O		Q		Q			
24					Q	C			
25	T			X			X	C	X
26			T		X				
27	Q	T							Q
28						X			
29		Q	Q				C	X	T
30	X			C	C				
31			X			Q		Q	

Date	Aries	Taurus	Gemini	Cancer	Leo	Virgo	Libra	Scorpio	Sagittarius	Capricorn	Aquarius	Pisces
1		F		f	u	f		U		f	u	f
2		F		f	u	f		U		f	u	f
3	f		F		f	u	f		U		f	u
4	f		F		f	u	f		U		f	u
5	u	f		F		f	u	f		U		f
6	u	f		F		f	u	f		U		f
7	f	u	f		F		f	u	f		U	
8	f	u	f		F		f	u	f		U	
9	f	u	f		F		f	u	f		U	
10		f	u	f		F		f	u	f		U
11		f	u	f		F		f	u	f		U
12	U		f	u	f		F		f	u	f	
13	U		f	u	f		F		f	u	f	
14	U		f	u	f		F		f	u	f	
15		U		f	u	f		F		f	u	f
16		U		f	u	f		F		f	u	f
17	f		U		f	u	f		F		f	u
18	f		U		f	u	f		F		f	u
19	f		U		f	u	f		F		f	u
20	u	f		U		f	u	f		F		f
21	u	f		U		f	u	f		F		f
22	f	u	f		U		f	u	f		F	
23	f	u	f		U		f	u	f		F	
24		f	u	f		U		f	u	f		F
25		f	u	f		U		f	u	f		F
26	F		f	u	f		U		f	u	f	
27	F		f	u	f		U		f	u	f	
28		F		f	u	f		U		f	u	f
29		F		f	u	f		U		f	u	f
30	f		F		f	u	f		U		f	u
31	f		F		f	u	f		U		f	u

August Moon Table

Date	Sign	Element	Nature	Phase
1 Thu	Cancer	Water	Fruitful	4th
2 Fri	Cancer	Water	Fruitful	4th
3 Sat 7:10 am	Leo	Fire	Barren	4th
4 Sun	Leo	Fire	Barren	New 7:13 am
5 Mon 5:17 pm	Virgo	Earth	Barren	1st
6 Tue	Virgo	Earth	Barren	1st
7 Wed	Virgo	Earth	Barren	1st
8 Thu 5:31 am	Libra	Air	Semi-fruitful	1st
9 Fri	Libra	Air	Semi-fruitful	1st
10 Sat 6:34 pm	Scorpio	Water	Fruitful	1st
11 Sun	Scorpio	Water	Fruitful	1st
12 Mon	Scorpio	Water	Fruitful	2nd 11:19 am
13 Tue 6:01 am	Sagittarius	Fire	Barren	2nd
14 Wed	Sagittarius	Fire	Barren	2nd
15 Thu 1:51 pm	Capricorn	Earth	Semi-fruitful	2nd
16 Fri	Capricorn	Earth	Semi-fruitful	2nd
17 Sat 5:45 pm	Aquarius	Air	Barren	2nd
18 Sun	Aquarius	Air	Barren	2nd
19 Mon 6:52 pm	Pisces	Water	Fruitful	Full 2:26 pm
20 Tue	Pisces	Water	Fruitful	3rd
21 Wed 7:02 pm	Aries	Fire	Barren	3rd
22 Thu	Aries	Fire	Barren	3rd
23 Fri 8:00 pm	Taurus	Earth	Semi-fruitful	3rd
24 Sat	Taurus	Earth	Semi-fruitful	3rd
25 Sun 11:04 pm	Gemini	Air	Barren	3rd
26 Mon	Gemini	Air	Barren	4th 5:26 am
27 Tue	Gemini	Air	Barren	4th
28 Wed 4:47 am	Cancer	Water	Fruitful	4th
29 Thu	Cancer	Water	Fruitful	4th
30 Fri 1:09 pm	Leo	Fire	Barren	4th
31 Sat	Leo	Fire	Barren	4th

August Aspectarian/Favorable & Unfavorable Days

Date	Sun	Mercury	Venus	Mars	Jupiter	Saturn	Uranus	Neptune	Pluto
1		X							
2						T			
3							X	T	O
4	C			X	X				
5			C				Q		
6		C		Q					
7					Q	O	T		
8								O	T
9	X			T	T				
10		X							Q
11			X						
12	Q					T			
13		Q					O	T	X
14			Q	O	O	O	Q		
15	T	T						Q	
16			T			X			
17							T	X	C
18						T			
19	O	O		T			Q		
20					Q	C			
21			O	Q			X	C	X
22									
23	T	T		X	X				Q
24									
25		Q	T			X	C	X	T
26	Q								
27		X			C	C	Q		
28	X		Q					Q	
29						T			
30			X				X	T	O
31									

Date	Aries	Taurus	Gemini	Cancer	Leo	Virgo	Libra	Scorpio	Sagittarius	Capricorn	Aquarius	Pisces
1	u	f		F		f	u	f		U		f
2	u	f		F		f	u	f		U		f
3	u	f		F		f	u	f		U		f
4	f	u	f		F		f	u	f		U	
5	f	u	f		F		f	u	f		U	
6		f	u	f		F		f	u	f		U
7		f	u	f		F		f	u	f		U
8		f	u	f		F		f	u	f		U
9	U		f	u	f		F		f	u	f	
10	U		f	u	f		F		f	u	f	
11		U		f	u	f		F		f	u	f
12		U		f	u	f		F		f	u	f
13		U		f	u	f		F		f	u	f
14	f		U		f	u	f		F		f	u
15	f		U		f	u	f		F		f	u
16	u	f		U		f	u	f		F		f
17	u	f		U		f	u	f		F		f
18	f	u	f		U		f	u	f		F	
19	f	u	f		U		f	u	f		F	
20		f	u	f		U		f	u	f		F
21		f	u	f		U		f	u	f		F
22	F		f	u	f		U		f	u	f	
23	F		f	u	f		U		f	u	f	
24		F		f	u	f		U		f	u	f
25		F		f	u	f		U		f	u	f
26	f		F		f	u	f		U		f	u
27	f		F		f	u	f		U		f	u
28	f		F		f	u	f		U		f	u
29	u	f		F		f	u	f		U		f
30	u	f		F		f	u	f		U		f
31	f	u	f		F		f	u	f		U	

151

September Moon Table

Date	Sign	Element	Nature	Phase
1 Sun 11:48 pm	Virgo	Earth	Barren	4th
2 Mon	Virgo	Earth	Barren	New 9:56 pm
3 Tue	Virgo	Earth	Barren	1st
4 Wed 12:12 pm	Libra	Air	Semi-fruitful	1st
5 Thu	Libra	Air	Semi-fruitful	1st
6 Fri	Libra	Air	Semi-fruitful	1st
7 Sat 1:18 am	Scorpio	Water	Fruitful	1st
8 Sun	Scorpio	Water	Fruitful	1st
9 Mon 1:26 pm	Sagittarius	Fire	Barren	1st
10 Tue	Sagittarius	Fire	Barren	1st
11 Wed 10:38 pm	Capricorn	Earth	Semi-fruitful	2nd 2:06 am
12 Thu	Capricorn	Earth	Semi-fruitful	2nd
13 Fri	Capricorn	Earth	Semi-fruitful	2nd
14 Sat 3:53 am	Aquarius	Air	Barren	2nd
15 Sun	Aquarius	Air	Barren	2nd
16 Mon 5:39 am	Pisces	Water	Fruitful	2nd
17 Tue	Pisces	Water	Fruitful	Full 10:34 pm
18 Wed 5:24 am	Aries	Fire	Barren	3rd
19 Thu	Aries	Fire	Barren	3rd
20 Fri 5:03 am	Taurus	Earth	Semi-fruitful	3rd
21 Sat	Taurus	Earth	Semi-fruitful	3rd
22 Sun 6:24 am	Gemini	Air	Barren	3rd
23 Mon	Gemini	Air	Barren	3rd
24 Tue 10:50 am	Cancer	Water	Fruitful	4th 2:50 pm
25 Wed	Cancer	Water	Fruitful	4th
26 Thu 6:47 pm	Leo	Fire	Barren	4th
27 Fri	Leo	Fire	Barren	4th
28 Sat	Leo	Fire	Barren	4th
29 Sun 5:42 am	Virgo	Earth	Barren	4th
30 Mon	Virgo	Earth	Barren	4th

September Aspectarian/Favorable & Unfavorable Days

Date	Sun	Mercury	Venus	Mars	Jupiter	Saturn	Uranus	Neptune	Pluto
1		C		X	X		Q		
2	C								
3					Q	O			
4				Q			T	O	T
5			C						
6		X				T			
7			T						Q
8	X					T			
9		Q					O	T	X
10			X			Q			
11	Q				O		Q		
12		T		O					
13	T		Q			X	T		
14								X	C
15			T		T				
16			T				Q		
17	O	O			Q	C			
18				Q			X	C	X
19			O	X					
20				X					Q
21		T				X			
22	T					C		X	T
23					C	Q			
24	Q	Q	T					Q	
25					C		T		
26		X					X	T	O
27	X		Q						
28					X		Q		
29			X						
30				X		O			

Date	Aries	Taurus	Gemini	Cancer	Leo	Virgo	Libra	Scorpio	Sagittarius	Capricorn	Aquarius	Pisces
1	f	u	f		F		f	u	f		U	
2		f	u	f		F		f	u	f		U
3		f	u	f		F		f	u	f		U
4		f	u	f		F		f	u	f		U
5	U		f	u	f		F		f	u	f	
6	U		f	u	f		F		f	u	f	
7		U		f	u	f		F		f	u	f
8		U		f	u	f		F		f	u	f
9		U		f	u	f		F		f	u	f
10	f		U		f	u	f		F		f	u
11	f		U		f	u	f		F		f	u
12	u	f		U		f	u	f		F		f
13	u	f		U		f	u	f		F		f
14	u	f		U		f	u	f		F		f
15	f	u	f		U		f	u	f		F	
16	f	u	f		U		f	u	f		F	
17		f	u	f		U		f	u	f		F
18		f	u	f		U		f	u	f		F
19	F		f	u	f		U		f	u	f	
20	F		f	u	f		U		f	u	f	
21		F		f	u	f		U		f	u	f
22		F		f	u	f		U		f	u	f
23	f		F		f	u	f		U		f	u
24	f		F		f	u	f		U		f	u
25	u	f		F		f	u	f		U		f
26	u	f		F		f	u	f		U		f
27	f	u	f		F		f	u	f		U	
28	f	u	f		F		f	u	f		U	
29	f	u	f		F		f	u	f		U	
30		f	u	f		F		f	u	f		U

October Moon Table

Date	Sign	Element	Nature	Phase
1 Tue 6:20 pm	Libra	Air	Semi-fruitful	4th
2 Wed	Libra	Air	Semi-fruitful	New 2:49 pm
3 Thu	Libra	Air	Semi-fruitful	1st
4 Fri 7:22 am	Scorpio	Water	Fruitful	1st
5 Sat	Scorpio	Water	Fruitful	1st
6 Sun 7:34 pm	Sagittarius	Fire	Barren	1st
7 Mon	Sagittarius	Fire	Barren	1st
8 Tue	Sagittarius	Fire	Barren	1st
9 Wed 5:38 am	Capricorn	Earth	Semi-fruitful	1st
10 Thu	Capricorn	Earth	Semi-fruitful	2nd 2:55 pm
11 Fri 12:31 pm	Aquarius	Air	Barren	2nd
12 Sat	Aquarius	Air	Barren	2nd
13 Sun 3:55 pm	Pisces	Water	Fruitful	2nd
14 Mon	Pisces	Water	Fruitful	2nd
15 Tue 4:34 pm	Aries	Fire	Barren	2nd
16 Wed	Aries	Fire	Barren	2nd
17 Thu 4:00 pm	Taurus	Earth	Semi-fruitful	Full 7:26 am
18 Fri	Taurus	Earth	Semi-fruitful	3rd
19 Sat 4:07 pm	Gemini	Air	Barren	3rd
20 Sun	Gemini	Air	Barren	3rd
21 Mon 6:50 pm	Cancer	Water	Fruitful	3rd
22 Tue	Cancer	Water	Fruitful	3rd
23 Wed	Cancer	Water	Fruitful	3rd
24 Thu 1:24 am	Leo	Fire	Barren	4th 4:03 am
25 Fri	Leo	Fire	Barren	4th
26 Sat 11:47 am	Virgo	Earth	Barren	4th
27 Sun	Virgo	Earth	Barren	4th
28 Mon	Virgo	Earth	Barren	4th
29 Tue 12:30 am	Libra	Air	Semi-fruitful	4th
30 Wed	Libra	Air	Semi-fruitful	4th
31 Thu 1:29 pm	Scorpio	Water	Fruitful	4th

October Aspectarian/Favorable & Unfavorable Days

Date	Sun	Mercury	Venus	Mars	Jupiter	Saturn	Uranus	Neptune	Pluto
1					Q		T	O	T
2	C	C							
3				Q	T				
4									Q
5			C	T			T		
6							O	T	X
7					Q				
8	X	X			O				
9								Q	
10	Q		X	O		X			
11		Q					T	X	C
12	T								
13		T	Q		T			Q	
14						C			
15		T		T	Q		X	C	X
16									
17	O				Q	X			Q
18		O					X		
19			O	X			C	X	T
20					Q				
21	T				C			Q	
22		T				T			
23				C				X	T
24	Q			T					O
25		Q			X				
26	X							Q	
27			Q			O			
28		X		X	Q		T	O	T
29									
30				X	T				
31					Q				Q

Date	Aries	Taurus	Gemini	Cancer	Leo	Virgo	Libra	Scorpio	Sagittarius	Capricorn	Aquarius	Pisces
1		f	u	f		F		f	u	f		U
2	U		f	u	f		F		f	u	f	
3	U		f	u	f		F		f	u	f	
4	U		f	u	f		F		f	u	f	
5		U		f	u	f		F		f	u	f
6		U		f	u	f		F		f	u	f
7	f		U		f	u	f		F		f	u
8	f		U		f	u	f		F		f	u
9	f		U		f	u	f		F		f	u
10	u	f		U		f	u	f		F		f
11	u	f		U		f	u	f		F		f
12	f	u	f		U		f	u	f		F	
13	f	u	f		U		f	u	f		F	
14		f	u	f		U		f	u	f		F
15		f	u	f		U		f	u	f		F
16	F		f	u	f		U		f	u	f	
17	F		f	u	f		U		f	u	f	
18		F		f	u	f		U		f	u	f
19		F		f	u	f		U		f	u	f
20	f		F		f	u	f		U		f	u
21	f		F		f	u	f		U		f	u
22	u	f		F		f	u	f		U		f
23	u	f		F		f	u	f		U		f
24	f	u	f		F		f	u	f		U	
25	f	u	f		F		f	u	f		U	
26	f	u	f		F		f	u	f		U	
27		f	u	f		F		f	u	f		U
28		f	u	f		F		f	u	f		U
29	U		f	u	f		F		f	u	f	
30	U		f	u	f		F		f	u	f	
31	U		f	u	f		F		f	u	f	

November Moon Table

Date	Sign	Element	Nature	Phase
1 Fri	Scorpio	Water	Fruitful	New 8:47 am
2 Sat	Scorpio	Water	Fruitful	1st
3 Sun 1:19 am	Sagittarius	Fire	Barren	1st
4 Mon	Sagittarius	Fire	Barren	1st
5 Tue 10:17 am	Capricorn	Earth	Semi-fruitful	1st
6 Wed	Capricorn	Earth	Semi-fruitful	1st
7 Thu 5:58 pm	Aquarius	Air	Barren	1st
8 Fri	Aquarius	Air	Barren	1st
9 Sat 11:00 pm	Pisces	Water	Fruitful	2nd 12:55 am
10 Sun	Pisces	Water	Fruitful	2nd
11 Mon	Pisces	Water	Fruitful	2nd
12 Tue 1:26 am	Aries	Fire	Barren	2nd
13 Wed	Aries	Fire	Barren	2nd
14 Thu 1:59 am	Taurus	Earth	Semi-fruitful	2nd
15 Fri	Taurus	Earth	Semi-fruitful	Full 4:28 pm
16 Sat 2:09 am	Gemini	Air	Barren	3rd
17 Sun	Gemini	Air	Barren	3rd
18 Mon 3:50 am	Cancer	Water	Fruitful	3rd
19 Tue	Cancer	Water	Fruitful	3rd
20 Wed 8:51 am	Leo	Fire	Barren	3rd
21 Thu	Leo	Fire	Barren	3rd
22 Fri 6:01 pm	Virgo	Earth	Barren	4th 8:28 pm
23 Sat	Virgo	Earth	Barren	4th
24 Sun	Virgo	Earth	Barren	4th
25 Mon 6:20 am	Libra	Air	Semi-fruitful	4th
26 Tue	Libra	Air	Semi-fruitful	4th
27 Wed 7:21 pm	Scorpio	Water	Fruitful	4th
28 Thu	Scorpio	Water	Fruitful	4th
29 Fri	Scorpio	Water	Fruitful	4th
30 Sat 6:53 am	Sagittarius	Fire	Barren	4th

November Aspectarian/Favorable & Unfavorable Days

Date	Sun	Mercury	Venus	Mars	Jupiter	Saturn	Uranus	Neptune	Pluto
1	C					T			
2							O	T	
3		C		T					X
4			C		O	Q			
5						Q			
6	X				X				
7				O			T	X	C
8		X							
9	Q		X		T		Q		
10		Q				C			
11	T				Q		X	C	
12		T	Q	T					X
13				X					
14			T	Q		X			Q
15	O						C	X	
16				X		Q			T
17		O			C			Q	
18		O							
19							T	X	
20	T			C				T	O
21				X					
22	Q	T						Q	
23			T			O			
24		Q			Q		T		
25	X			X				O	T
26			Q		T				
27		X							Q
28			Q		T				
29			X				O		
30				T				T	X

Date	Aries	Taurus	Gemini	Cancer	Leo	Virgo	Libra	Scorpio	Sagittarius	Capricorn	Aquarius	Pisces
1		U		f	u	f		F		f	u	f
2		U		f	u	f		F		f	u	f
3	f		U		f	u	f		F		f	u
4	f		U		f	u	f		F		f	u
5	f		U		f	u	f		F		f	u
6	u	f		U		f	u	f		F		f
7	u	f		U		f	u	f		F		f
8	f	u	f		U		f	u	f		F	
9	f	u	f		U		f	u	f		F	
10		f	u	f		U		f	u	f		F
11		f	u	f		U		f	u	f		F
12	F		f	u	f		U		f	u	f	
13	F		f	u	f		U		f	u	f	
14		F		f	u	f		U		f	u	f
15		F		f	u	f		U		f	u	f
16	f		F		f	u	f		U		f	u
17	f		F		f	u	f		U		f	u
18	f		F		f	u	f		U		f	u
19	u	f		F		f	u	f		U		f
20	u	f		F		f	u	f		U		f
21	f	u	f		F		f	u	f		U	
22	f	u	f		F		f	u	f		U	
23		f	u	f		F		f	u	f		U
24		f	u	f		F		f	u	f		U
25		f	u	f		F		f	u	f		U
26	U		f	u	f		F		f	u	f	
27	U		f	u	f		F		f	u	f	
28		U		f	u	f		F		f	u	f
29		U		f	u	f		F		f	u	f
30		U		f	u	f		F		f	u	f

December Moon Table

Date	Sign	Element	Nature	Phase
1 Sun	Sagittarius	Fire	Barren	New 1:21 am
2 Mon 4:09 pm	Capricorn	Earth	Semi-fruitful	1st
3 Tue	Capricorn	Earth	Semi-fruitful	1st
4 Wed 11:21 pm	Aquarius	Air	Barren	1st
5 Thu	Aquarius	Air	Barren	1st
6 Fri	Aquarius	Air	Barren	1st
7 Sat 4:49 am	Pisces	Water	Fruitful	1st
8 Sun	Pisces	Water	Fruitful	2nd 10:27 am
9 Mon 8:38 am	Aries	Fire	Barren	2nd
10 Tue	Aries	Fire	Barren	2nd
11 Wed 10:55 am	Taurus	Earth	Semi-fruitful	2nd
12 Thu	Taurus	Earth	Semi-fruitful	2nd
13 Fri 12:22 pm	Gemini	Air	Barren	2nd
14 Sat	Gemini	Air	Barren	2nd
15 Sun 2:21 pm	Cancer	Water	Fruitful	Full 4:02 am
16 Mon	Cancer	Water	Fruitful	3rd
17 Tue 6:39 pm	Leo	Fire	Barren	3rd
18 Wed	Leo	Fire	Barren	3rd
19 Thu	Leo	Fire	Barren	3rd
20 Fri 2:37 am	Virgo	Earth	Barren	3rd
21 Sat	Virgo	Earth	Barren	3rd
22 Sun 2:08 pm	Libra	Air	Semi-fruitful	4th 5:18 pm
23 Mon	Libra	Air	Semi-fruitful	4th
24 Tue	Libra	Air	Semi-fruitful	4th
25 Wed 3:06 am	Scorpio	Water	Fruitful	4th
26 Thu	Scorpio	Water	Fruitful	4th
27 Fri 2:46 pm	Sagittarius	Fire	Barren	4th
28 Sat	Sagittarius	Fire	Barren	4th
29 Sun 11:37 pm	Capricorn	Earth	Semi-fruitful	4th
30 Mon	Capricorn	Earth	Semi-fruitful	New 5:27 pm
31 Sat 12:08 pm	Taurus	Earth	Semi-fruitful	2nd

December Aspectarian/Favorable & Unfavorable Days

Date	Sun	Mercury	Venus	Mars	Jupiter	Saturn	Uranus	Neptune	Pluto
1	C	C			O	Q			
2								Q	
3							X		
4			C				T	X	C
5				O					
6	X	X			T	Q			
7									
8	Q	Q			Q	C	X		
9			X	T				C	X
10	T	T			X				
11			Q	Q					Q
12						X			
13		O		X			C	X	T
14			T		C	Q			
15	O							Q	
16						T			
17							X	T	O
18		T	O	C	X				
19								Q	
20	T	Q							
21					Q	O			
22	Q			X			T	O	T
23		X			T				
24			T						
25	X			Q					Q
26						T			
27			Q	T			O	T	X
28		C			O	Q			
29			X					Q	
30	C								
31							X	T	

Date	Aries	Taurus	Gemini	Cancer	Leo	Virgo	Libra	Scorpio	Sagittarius	Capricorn	Aquarius	Pisces
1	f		U		f	u	f		F		f	u
2	f		U		f	u	f		F		f	u
3	u	f		U		f	u	f		F		f
4	u	f		U		f	u	f		F		f
5	f	u	f		U		f	u	f		F	
6	f	u	f		U		f	u	f		F	
7	f	u	f		U		f	u	f		F	
8		f	u	f		U		f	u	f		F
9		f	u	f		U		f	u	f		F
10	F		f	u	f		U		f	u	f	
11	F		f	u	f		U		f	u	f	
12		F		f	u	f		U		f	u	f
13		F		f	u	f		U		f	u	f
14	f		F		f	u	f		U		f	u
15	f		F		f	u	f		U		f	u
16	u	f		F		f	u	f		U		f
17	u	f		F		f	u	f		U		f
18	f	u	f		F		f	u	f		U	
19	f	u	f		F		f	u	f		U	
20		f	u	f		F		f	u	f		U
21		f	u	f		F		f	u	f		U
22		f	u	f		F		f	u	f		U
23	U		f	u	f		F		f	u	f	
24	U		f	u	f		F		f	u	f	
25	U		f	u	f		F		f	u	f	
26		U		f	u	f		F		f	u	f
27		U		f	u	f		F		f	u	f
28	f		U		f	u	f		F		f	u
29	f		U		f	u	f		F		f	u
30	u	f		U		f	u	f		F		f
31	u	f		U		f	u	f		F		f

2024 Retrograde Planets

Planet	Begin	Eastern	Pacific	End	Eastern	Pacific
Uranus	8/28/23	10:39 pm	**7:39 pm**	1/26		**11:35 pm**
Uranus	8/28/23	10:39 pm	**7:39 pm**	1/27	2:35 am	
Mercury	12/12/23		**11:09 pm**	1/1	10:08 pm	**7:08 pm**
Mercury	12/13/23	2:09 am		1/1	10:08 pm	**7:08 pm**
Mercury	4/1	6:14 pm	**3:14 pm**	4/25	8:54 am	**5:54 am**
Pluto	5/2	1:46 pm	**10:46 am**	10/11	8:34 pm	**5:34 pm**
Saturn	6/29	3:07 pm	**12:07 pm**	11/15	9:20 am	**6:20 am**
Neptune	7/2	6:40 am	**3:40 am**	12/7	6:43 pm	**3:43 pm**
Mercury	8/4		**9:56 pm**	8/28	5:14 pm	**2:14 pm**
Mercury	8/5	12:56 am		8/28	5:14 pm	**2:14 pm**
Uranus	9/1	11:18 am	**8:18 am**	1/30/25	11:22 am	**8:22 am**
Jupiter	10/9	3:05 am	**12:05 am**	2/4/25	4:40 am	**1:40 am**
Mercury	11/25	9:42 pm	**6:42 pm**	12/15	3:56 pm	**12:56 pm**
Mars	12/6	6:33 pm	**3:33 pm**	2/23/25	9:00 pm	**6:00 pm**

Eastern Time in plain type, **Pacific Time in bold type**

	Dec 23	Jan 24	Feb	Mar	Apr	May	Jun	Jul	Aug	Sep	Oct	Nov	Dec	Jan 25
☿	■				■				■				■	
♃											■	■	■	■
♀														
♄							■	■	■	■	■	■		
♇						■	■	■	■	■	■			
♆								■	■	■	■	■	■	
♅	■	■								■	■	■	■	■
♂													■	■

Egg-Setting Dates

To Have Eggs by this Date	Sign	Qtr.	Date to Set Eggs
Jan 13, 10:29 pm–Jan 15, 11:49 pm	Pisces	1st	Dec 23, 2023
Jan 18, 3:12 am–Jan 20, 8:58 am	Taurus	2nd	Dec 28, 2023
Jan 22, 4:51 pm–Jan 25, 2:37 am	Cancer	2nd	Jan 01, 2024
Feb 10, 8:42 am–Feb 12, 8:26 am	Pisces	1st	Jan 20
Feb 14, 10:02 am–Feb 16, 2:39 pm	Taurus	1st	Jan 24
Feb 18, 10:25 pm–Feb 21, 8:40 am	Cancer	2nd	Jan 28
Mar 10, 5:00 am–Mar 10, 8:19 pm	Pisces	1st	Feb 18
Mar 12, 8:28 pm–Mar 14, 11:16 pm	Taurus	1st	Feb 20
Mar 17, 5:40 am–Mar 19, 3:33 pm	Cancer	2nd	Feb 25
Mar 24, 4:37 pm–Mar 25, 3:00 am	Libra	2nd	Mar 03
Apr 9, 7:23 am–Apr 11, 8:59 am	Taurus	1st	Mar 19
Apr 13, 1:45 pm–Apr 15, 10:24 pm	Cancer	1st	Mar 23
Apr 20, 11:08 pm–Apr 23, 11:20 am	Libra	2nd	Mar 30
May 7, 11:22 pm–May 8, 7:20 pm	Taurus	1st	Apr 16
May 10, 11:13 pm–May 13, 6:36 am	Cancer	1st	Apr 19
May 18, 6:23 am–May 20, 6:34 pm	Libra	2nd	Apr 27
Jun 7, 8:41 am–Jun 9, 3:29 pm	Cancer	1st	May 17
Jun 14, 2:12 pm–Jun 17, 2:38 am	Libra	2nd	May 24
Jul 5, 6:57 pm–Jul 6, 11:56 pm	Cancer	1st	Jun 14
Jul 11, 10:06 pm–Jul 14, 10:53 am	Libra	1st	Jun 20
Aug 8, 5:31 am–Aug 10, 6:34 pm	Libra	1st	Jul 18
Sep 4, 12:12 pm–Sep 7, 1:18 am	Libra	1st	Aug 14
Sep 16, 5:39 am–Sep 17, 10:34 pm	Pisces	2nd	Aug 26
Oct 2, 2:49 pm–Oct 4, 7:22 am	Libra	1st	Sep 11
Oct 13, 3:55 pm–Oct 15, 4:34 pm	Pisces	2nd	Sep 22
Nov 9, 11:00 pm–Nov 12, 1:26 am	Pisces	2nd	Oct 19
Nov 14, 1:59 am–Nov 15, 4:28 pm	Taurus	2nd	Oct 24
Dec 7, 4:49 am–Dec 9, 8:38 am	Pisces	1st	Nov 16
Dec 11, 10:55 am–Dec 13, 12:22 pm	Taurus	2nd	Nov 20

Dates to Hunt and Fish

Date	Quarter	Sign
Jan 5, 7:39 am–Jan 7, 4:08 pm	4th	Scorpio
Jan 13, 10:29 pm–Jan 15, 11:49 pm	1st	Pisces
Jan 22, 4:51 pm–Jan 25, 2:37 am	2nd	Cancer
Feb 1, 3:37 pm–Feb 4, 1:28 am	3rd	Scorpio
Feb 10, 8:42 am–Feb 12, 8:26 am	1st	Pisces
Feb 18, 10:25 pm–Feb 21, 8:40 am	2nd	Cancer
Feb 28, 10:09 pm–Mar 2, 8:56 am	3rd	Scorpio
Mar 2, 8:56 am–Mar 4, 4:15 pm	3rd	Sagittarius
Mar 8, 8:03 pm–Mar 10, 8:19 pm	4th	Pisces
Mar 17, 5:40 am–Mar 19, 3:33 pm	2nd	Cancer
Mar 27, 5:03 am–Mar 29, 3:52 pm	3rd	Scorpio
Mar 29, 3:52 pm–Apr 1, 12:05 am	3rd	Sagittarius
Apr 5, 7:13 am–Apr 7, 7:25 am	4th	Pisces
Apr 13, 1:45 pm–Apr 15, 10:24 pm	1st	Cancer
Apr 23, 11:20 am–Apr 25, 9:37 pm	2nd	Scorpio
Apr 25, 9:37 pm–Apr 28, 5:37 am	3rd	Sagittarius
May 2, 2:52 pm–May 4, 4:41 pm	4th	Pisces
May 10, 11:13 pm–May 13, 6:36 am	1st	Cancer
May 20, 6:34 pm–May 23, 4:24 am	2nd	Scorpio
May 23, 4:24 am–May 25, 11:36 am	2nd	Sagittarius
May 29, 8:33 pm–May 31, 11:28 pm	3rd	Pisces
Jun 7, 8:41 am–Jun 9, 3:29 pm	1st	Cancer
Jun 17, 2:38 am–Jun 19, 12:32 pm	2nd	Scorpio
Jun 19, 12:32 pm–Jun 21, 7:08 pm	2nd	Sagittarius
Jun 26, 2:08 am–Jun 28, 4:52 am	3rd	Pisces
Jun 28, 4:52 am–Jun 30, 8:00 am	3rd	Aries
Jul 4, 4:51 pm–Jul 6, 11:56 pm	4th	Cancer
Jul 14, 10:53 am–Jul 16, 9:25 pm	2nd	Scorpio
Jul 16, 9:25 pm–Jul 19, 4:14 am	2nd	Sagittarius
Jul 23, 9:23 am–Jul 25, 10:52 am	3rd	Pisces
Jul 25, 10:52 am–Jul 27, 1:23 pm	3rd	Aries
Jul 31, 11:19 pm–Aug 3, 7:10 am	4th	Cancer
Aug 10, 6:34 pm–Aug 13, 6:01 am	1st	Scorpio
Aug 13, 6:01 am–Aug 15, 1:51 pm	2nd	Sagittarius
Aug 19, 6:52 pm–Aug 21, 7:02 pm	3rd	Pisces
Aug 21, 7:02 pm–Aug 23, 8:00 pm	3rd	Aries
Aug 28, 4:47 am–Aug 30, 1:09 pm	4th	Cancer
Sep 7, 1:18 am–Sep 9, 1:26 pm	1st	Scorpio
Sep 16, 5:39 am–Sep 18, 5:24 am	2nd	Pisces
Sep 18, 5:24 am–Sep 20, 5:03 am	3rd	Aries
Sep 24, 10:50 am–Sep 26, 6:47 pm	3rd	Cancer
Oct 4, 7:22 am–Oct 6, 7:34 pm	1st	Scorpio
Oct 13, 3:55 pm–Oct 15, 4:34 pm	2nd	Pisces
Oct 15, 4:34 pm–Oct 17, 4:00 pm	2nd	Aries
Oct 21, 6:50 pm–Oct 24, 1:24 am	3rd	Cancer
Oct 31, 1:29 pm–Nov 3, 1:19 am	4th	Scorpio
Nov 9, 11:00 pm–Nov 12, 1:26 am	2nd	Pisces
Nov 12, 1:26 am–Nov 14, 1:59 am	2nd	Aries
Nov 18, 3:50 am–Nov 20, 8:51 am	3rd	Cancer
Nov 27, 7:21 pm–Nov 30, 6:53 am	4th	Scorpio
Dec 7, 4:49 am–Dec 9, 8:38 am	1st	Pisces
Dec 9, 8:38 am–Dec 11, 10:55 am	2nd	Aries
Dec 15, 2:21 pm–Dec 17, 6:39 pm	3rd	Cancer
Dec 25, 3:06 am–Dec 27, 2:46 pm	4th	Scorpio

Dates to Destroy Weeds and Pests

Date	Sign	Qtr.
Jan 7, 4:08 pm–Jan 9, 8:33 pm	Sagittarius	4th
Jan 25, 12:54 pm–Jan 27, 2:11 pm	Leo	3rd
Jan 27, 2:11 pm–Jan 30, 3:04 am	Virgo	3rd
Feb 4, 1:28 am–Feb 6, 7:08 am	Sagittarius	4th
Feb 8, 8:59 am–Feb 9, 5:59 pm	Aquarius	4th
Feb 24, 7:30 am–Feb 26, 9:29 am	Virgo	3rd
Mar 2, 8:56 am–Mar 3, 10:23 am	Sagittarius	3rd
Mar 3, 10:23 am–Mar 4, 4:15 pm	Sagittarius	4th
Mar 6, 7:38 pm–Mar 8, 8:03 pm	Aquarius	4th
Mar 29, 3:52 pm–Apr 1, 12:05 am	Sagittarius	3rd
Apr 3, 5:08 am–Apr 5, 7:13 am	Aquarius	4th
Apr 7, 7:25 am–Apr 8, 2:21 pm	Aries	4th
Apr 25, 9:37 pm–Apr 28, 5:37 am	Sagittarius	3rd
Apr 30, 11:20 am–May 1, 7:27 am	Aquarius	3rd
May 1, 7:27 am–May 2, 2:52 pm	Aquarius	4th
May 4, 4:41 pm–May 6, 5:42 pm	Aries	4th
May 23, 9:53 am–May 25, 11:36 am	Sagittarius	3rd
May 27, 4:45 pm–May 29, 8:33 pm	Aquarius	3rd
May 31, 11:28 pm–Jun 3, 1:55 am	Aries	4th
Jun 5, 4:36 am–Jun 6, 8:38 am	Gemini	4th
Jun 23, 11:14 pm–Jun 26, 2:08 am	Aquarius	3rd
Jun 28, 4:52 am–Jun 28, 5:53 pm	Aries	3rd
Jun 28, 5:53 pm–Jun 30, 8:00 am	Aries	4th
Jul 2, 11:50 am–Jul 4, 4:51 pm	Gemini	4th
Jul 21, 7:43 am–Jul 23, 9:23 am	Aquarius	3rd
Jul 25, 10:52 am–Jul 27, 1:23 pm	Aries	3rd
Jul 29, 5:28 pm–Jul 31, 11:19 pm	Gemini	4th
Aug 3, 7:10 am–Aug 4, 7:13 am	Leo	4th
Aug 19, 2:26 pm–Aug 19, 6:52 pm	Aquarius	3rd
Aug 21, 7:02 pm–Aug 23, 8:00 pm	Aries	3rd
Aug 25, 11:04 pm–Aug 26, 5:26 am	Gemini	3rd
Aug 26, 5:26 am–Aug 28, 4:47 am	Gemini	4th
Aug 30, 1:09 pm–Sep 1, 11:48 pm	Leo	4th
Sep 1, 11:48 pm–Sep 2, 9:56 pm	Virgo	4th
Sep 18, 5:24 am–Sep 20, 5:03 am	Aries	3rd
Sep 22, 6:24 am–Sep 24, 10:50 am	Gemini	3rd
Sep 26, 6:47 pm–Sep 29, 5:42 am	Leo	4th
Sep 29, 5:42 am–Oct 1, 6:20 pm	Virgo	4th
Oct 17, 7:26 am–Oct 17, 4:00 pm	Aries	3rd
Oct 19, 4:07 pm–Oct 21, 6:50 pm	Gemini	3rd
Oct 24, 1:24 am–Oct 24, 4:03 am	Leo	3rd
Oct 24, 4:03 am–Oct 26, 11:47 am	Leo	4th
Oct 26, 11:47 am–Oct 29, 12:30 am	Virgo	4th
Nov 16, 2:09 am–Nov 18, 3:50 am	Gemini	3rd
Nov 20, 8:51 am–Nov 22, 6:01 pm	Leo	3rd
Nov 22, 6:01 pm–Nov 22, 8:28 pm	Virgo	3rd
Nov 22, 8:28 pm–Nov 25, 6:20 am	Virgo	4th
Nov 30, 6:53 am–Dec 1, 1:21 am	Sagittarius	4th
Dec 15, 4:02 am–Dec 15, 2:21 pm	Gemini	3rd
Dec 17, 6:39 pm–Dec 20, 2:37 am	Leo	3rd
Dec 20, 2:37 am–Dec 22, 2:08 pm	Virgo	3rd
Dec 27, 2:46 pm–Dec 29, 11:37 pm	Sagittarius	4th

Time Zone Map

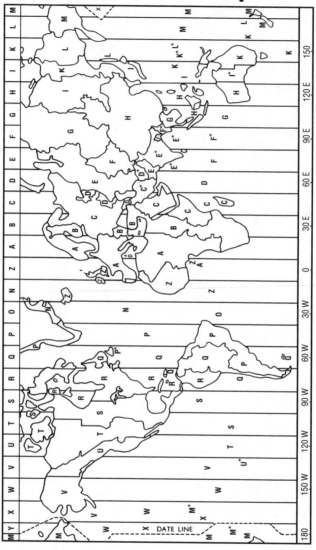

Time Zone Conversions

(R) EST—Used in book
(S) CST—Subtract 1 hour
(T) MST—Subtract 2 hours
(U) PST—Subtract 3 hours
(V) Subtract 4 hours
(V*) Subtract 4½ hours
(U*) Subtract 3½ hours
(W) Subtract 5 hours
(X) Subtract 6 hours
(Y) Subtract 7 hours
(Q) Add 1 hour
(P) Add 2 hours
(P*) Add 2½ hours
(O) Add 3 hours
(N) Add 4 hours
(Z) Add 5 hours
(A) Add 6 hours
(B) Add 7 hours
(C) Add 8 hours
(C*) Add 8½ hours

(D) Add 9 hours
(D*) Add 9½ hours
(E) Add 10 hours
(E*) Add 10½ hours
(F) Add 11 hours
(F*) Add 11½ hours
(G) Add 12 hours
(H) Add 13 hours
(I) Add 14 hours
(I*) Add 14½ hours
(K) Add 15 hours
(K*) Add 15½ hours
(L) Add 16 hours
(L*) Add 16½ hours
(M) Add 17 hours
(M*) Add 18 hours
(P*) Add 2½ hours

Important!

All times given in the *Moon Sign Book* are set in Eastern Time. The conversions shown here are for standard times only. Use the time zone conversions map and table to calculate the difference in your time zone. You must make the adjustment for your time zone and adjust for Daylight Saving Time where applicable.

Weather, Economic
& Lunar Forecasts

An Introduction to Long-Range Weather Forecasting

Vincent Decker

Long-range weather forecasting based on planetary cycles, also known as astrometeorology, has been a field of study for centuries. The basic premise underlying the field is that the main heavenly bodies of our solar system exercise an influence over weather conditions on Earth.

Planets

The heat of summer and the chill of winter can be traced back to the Sun's apparent movement north and south of our terrestrial equator. The Moon, while mostly known for its effect on the oceans' tides, in astrometeorology also affects air tides in its circuit around the earth and serves as a triggering influence on solar and planetary configurations as they form. Under Mercury's domain, we find high pressure or fair weather as well as gentle breezes to hurricane-force winds. Venus is known for gentle showers, moderate temperatures, and snowfall or freezing rain in winter. Mars, the red planet, brings hot summers, mild winters, dry conditions, and fierce storms. Jupiter's trademark is a temperate and invigorating atmosphere under benign configurations. The traditional malefic Saturn engenders cold, damp conditions, and when aggravated by certain configurations, low-pressure systems. Like Mercury, the power of Uranus brings high-barometer and erratic wind velocities. Neptune is the pluvial planet *par excellence* capable of torrential downpours, flooding conditions, and warming trends. Pluto is held by some to be a warm influence while for others it is considered cold. In the forecasts included here, Pluto is considered a warm influence.

Aspects and Influences

The foregoing effects of the Sun, Moon, and planets are modified depending on the aspect that each one makes in relation to the other heavenly bodies. The traditional astrological aspects are employed: the conjunction, sextile, square, trine, opposition, and parallel of declination. Fair weather aspects are the sextile and trine. Disturbed weather is induced by the square and opposition. The kind of weather produced by the conjunction and parallel of declination vary depending on if the celestial bodies involved are of similar or contrary natures.

The signs of the zodiac in which the members of the solar system reside at any given moment also affect the manifestation of weather conditions. Heat and dryness are associated with the fire signs Aries, Leo, and Sagittarius. The water signs of Cancer, Scorpio, and Pisces enhance precipitation. Air signs such as Gemini, Libra, and Aquarius relate to lower temperatures and wind, while the earth signs Taurus, Virgo, and Capricorn are generally wet and cold.

Forecasting

Although the aspects involved in the planetary configurations determine the time that weather processes will be at work (do keep in mind to allow a day or two leeway in all forecasting), it is by the use of key charts that the geographical locations of weather systems are ascertained. When a planet in a key chart is angular, that is to say it is on the cusp of the first, fourth, seventh, or tenth house, the influence associated with that planet will be strongest at that locale. The monthly alignments of the Sun and Moon such as New Moon, Full Moon, and Quarter Moons are examples of key charts. Other important charts include the cardinal solar ingresses and solar and lunar eclipses to name a few. Through setting up these key charts, noting the angular planets, the signs they tenant, and their aspects, as well as the kind of weather typical at the location in question, the long-range weather forecaster makes a judgment as to the type of weather to be expected. By faithfully comparing the forecasts with the actual ensuing weather, the forecaster has an opportunity to improve on method and results.

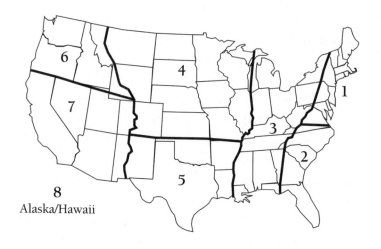

Weather Forecast for 2024

Vincent Decker

Winter

Weather conditions for Zone 1 start with a warm influence more on the dry side in January. A cold, cloudy, and wet influence moves in from the west as February progresses into March.

Zone 2 experiences an increasingly cold and wet winter pattern. Zone 3 and central through eastern portions of Zones 4 and 5 are slated to see a combination of descending, cold air and high barometric pressure interspersed with a few storms packing gusty winds. Western extremes of Zones 4 and 5 generally see more benign weather with higher temperatures.

Western areas of Zones 6 and 7 are warmer than average with periods of windy storms. Eastern portions of these zones see higher-than-average temperatures and conditions generally more on the pleasant side.

Western Alaska mostly sees lower temperatures and precipitation while central and eastern areas are under a warmer influence that can lead to foggy conditions and winter thaws with occasional bouts of precipitation. Hawaii is warmer with spells of stormy weather. As March approaches, a cold and damp influence increases.

4th Quarter January 1–11

Zone 1: The mid-Atlantic area starts out cloudy, rainy, and chilly. Temperatures rise over the zone after the 4th. By the 8th, New England sees an increasing chance of precipitation.

Zone 2: Cooler with possible heavy precipitation. Then temperatures rise. Central and southern areas become cloudy and windy the 7th–9th.

Zone 3: Cooler with possible heavy precipitation, then becoming cloudy and windy the 7th–9th.

Zone 4: Western areas are fair. Temperatures decline the 8th. Central portions start with thunderstorm potential, then see declining temperatures. Cloudy and windy the 9th. Eastern areas see increasing moisture. Cold front the 6th brings precipitation, then cool and fair conditions the 10th.

Zone 5: Western areas are fair. Temperatures decline the 8th. Central portions start with thunderstorm potential, then see declining temperatures. Cloudy and windy the 9th. Eastern areas see increasing moisture. Cold front the 6th brings precipitation, then cool and fair conditions the 10th.

Zone 6: Fair conditions for western sections. Eastern sections are fair with increasing temperatures around the 4th.

Zone 7: Fair conditions for western sections. Eastern sections are fair with increasing temperatures around the 4th.

Zone 8: Alaska: Western areas begin with precipitation, some possibly heavy over southwest. Cloudy, windy with potential low pressure the 7th. Central and eastern areas potentially windy, then see possible precipitation, fog, or thaws. Hawaii: Initially windy conditions likely. Temperatures increase with a chance of storms the 4th. More precipitation likely after the 8th.

New Moon January 11–17

Zone 1: Generally warm and dry.

Zone 2: Generally warm and dry.

Zone 3: The Great Lakes region sees increased wind velocities. Increasing temperatures and dry conditions are indicated for the rest of the zone.

Zone 4: Western portions are warm and dry. Central areas see increasing temperatures and humidity with a chance of precipitation. Eastern regions are mild and fair with some wind.

Zone 5: Temperatures increase over the west. Central and eastern regions see windy conditions.

Zone 6: Period begins with storm potential for western areas. Fair conditions for eastern portions.

Zone 7: Period begins with storm potential for western areas. Fair conditions for eastern portions.

Zone 8: Alaska: The zone begins with storm potential, then becomes more pleasant as the period progresses. Hawaii: Increased wind velocities likely with some thunderstorm potential around the 15th.

2nd Quarter January 17–25

Zone 1: Warm and dry conditions prevail. The mid-Atlantic sees a chance of thunderstorms the 21st.

Zone 2: Fair conditions prevail. Southern areas are initially cloudy and cooler. Northern areas have a chance of thunderstorms the 21st.

Zone 3: Cloudy with lower ranges of temperatures. A cold front triggers storms over western areas the 19th.

Zone 4: Western regions experience fair conditions, especially at first. Central and eastern portions are fair. A cold front triggers storms the 19th.

Zone 5: Western regions experience fair conditions, especially at first. A cold front triggers storms the 19th.

Zone 6: The west shows potential for stormy weather. Eastern portions see higher temperatures and fair conditions.

Zone 7: The west shows potential for stormy weather. Eastern portions see higher temperatures and fair conditions.

Zone 8: Alaska: The west starts with cloudy skies and lower temperatures, which then give way to stormy conditions. Central areas experience an increase in storm potential. The east sees potentially heavy precipitation the 19th and remains somewhat stormy. Hawaii: Increasing temperatures and humidity with a chance of rain, possibly heavy, around the 19th.

Full Moon January 25–February 2

Zone 1: Windy and stormy throughout the region as the period begins, then calm conditions.

Zone 2: Windy and stormy conditions likely along coastal areas the 27th, then calm weather.

Zone 3: Western areas see lower ranges of temperatures, windy weather, and possible thunderstorms. Fair conditions with lower temperatures for central and eastern portions.

Zone 4: At first, increasing wind velocities and stormy conditions from west to east. Cool and fair afterward, then windy and stormy the 30th.

Zone 5: At first, increasing wind velocities and stormy conditions from west to east. Cool and fair afterward, then windy and stormy the 30th.

Zone 6: Coastal areas may be affected by windy and stormy conditions. Chance of thunderstorms the 31st. Eastern areas are fair with cool to mild temperatures.

Zone 7: Coastal areas may be affected by windy and stormy conditions. Chance of thunderstorms the 31st. Eastern areas are fair with cool to mild temperatures.

Zone 8: Alaska: Cold and windy over western sections. Southern coast is windy and stormy. Central and eastern areas see wind and storms, then become fair with increasing temperatures. Hawaii: The period starts with a front that may generate showers. Around the 1st, thunderstorms with wind gusts.

4th Quarter February 2–9

Zone 1: Expect lower-than-average temperatures and gusty winds. Fair conditions likely until the 8th when cold, windy weather is accompanied by precipitation.

Zone 2: Expect lower-than-average temperatures and gusty winds. Fair conditions likely until the 8th when cold, windy weather is accompanied by precipitation.

Zone 3: Expect lower ranges of temperatures and fair conditions with some breezy weather likely around the 8th.

Zone 4: Western areas are fair and breezy. Windy and stormy with lower temperatures the 5th. Central portion ends cooler, windy, and stormy. Eastern areas receive precipitation the 3rd. Stronger storms the 8th.

Zone 5: Western areas are fair and breezy. Windy and stormy with lower temperatures the 5th. Central portion ends cooler, windy, and stormy. Eastern areas receive precipitation the 3rd. Stronger storms the 8th.

Zone 6: Western precipitation the 4th. Eastern sections see lower temperatures with windy conditions. Increasing temperatures the 7th.

Zone 7: Western precipitation the 4th. Eastern sections see lower temperatures with windy conditions. Increasing temperatures the 7th.

Zone 8: Alaska: Northwest initially cold and windy; southwest warm and fair. Thunderstorms the 4th, then fair. Storm potential the 8th, then fair. Central and eastern areas stormy the 4th. Fair the 7th. Ending cloudy and breezy. Hawaii: Fair with potential thunderstorms the 8th, then period ends fair with increasing temperatures.

New Moon February 9–16

Zone 1: Lower-than-average temperatures and windy. A chance of rain at first. Mild and breezy mid-Atlantic the 13th. Period ends with lower temperatures, gusty winds, and wintry precipitation.

Zone 2: Lower-than-average temperatures and windy. A chance of rain at first. Northern area mild and breezy the 13th. Period ends with lower temperatures, gusty winds, and wintry precipitation.

Zone 3: Mild and pleasant zone wide. Breezy conditions the 13th. Lower temperatures, gusty winds, and wintry precipitation the 16th.

Zone 4: Fair, mild, and breezy conditions affect the zone. Lower temperatures, gusty winds, and wintry conditions the 15th.

Zone 5: Fair, mild, and breezy conditions affect the zone. Lower temperatures, gusty winds, and wintry conditions the 15th.

Zone 6: Fair and mild. Low pressure pushes onshore the 14th and crosses the zone.

Zone 7: Fair and mild. Low pressure pushes onshore the 14th and crosses the zone.

Zone 8: Alaska: The zone sees a windy and stormy period. Hawaii: The period likely begins with some shower potential, which then gives way to fair and breezy conditions.

2nd Quarter February 16–24

Zone 1: Stormy and windy with lower temperatures for New England. Mid-Atlantic sees higher temperatures with some precipitation. A cold wave ends the period with rain or snow.

Zone 2: Northern areas see higher temperatures with some precipitation. A cold wave ends the period with rain or snow zone wide.

Zone 3: Colder with storms and occasionally heavier precipitation. Western storms the 16th, then calm. Afterward, colder with storms.

Zone 4: The zone begins stormy, then becomes mild, partly cloudy, and breezy. Thunderstorms for west and central areas the 16th. Afterward, zone is partly cloudy with moderate winds.

Zone 5: The zone begins stormy, then becomes mild, partly cloudy, and breezy. Thunderstorms for west and central areas the 16th. Afterward, zone is partly cloudy with moderate winds.

Zone 6: Initially a strong onshore front brings windy and stormy conditions. More western storms the 21st. East is fair. Then thunderstorms the 20th. Period ends with cooler temperatures.

Zone 7: Initially a strong onshore front brings windy and stormy conditions. More western storms the 21st. East is fair. Then thunderstorms the 20th. Period ends with cooler temperatures.

Zone 8: Alaska: From the 21st on, western and central areas see cold and precipitation. Eastern portions are cold, windy, and stormy. Another blast of cold hits around the 22nd. Hawaii: Fair conditions with a chance of precipitation around the 17th and 22nd.

Full Moon February 24–March 3

Zone 1: A major winter storm affects the zone with lower temperatures, windy conditions, and wintry precipitation the 28th. Clearing, rising temperatures, and fair weather follow.

Zone 2: A major winter storm affects the zone with lower temperatures, windy conditions, and wintry precipitation the 28th. Clearing, rising temperatures, and fair weather follow.

Zone 3: The zone experiences a major winter storm with lower temperatures, windy conditions, and wintry precipitation around the 28th. Lower temperatures will likely continue afterward.

Zone 4: Initially milder temperatures with some precipitation, especially through central areas. Strong storms zone wide the 27th. Fair conditions the 29th and 1st. More storms the 3rd.

Zone 5: Initially milder temperatures with some precipitation, especially through central areas. Strong storms zone wide the 27th. Fair conditions the 29th and 1st. More storms the 3rd.

Zone 6: The west is warmer with some precipitation. Strong thunderstorms and lower temperatures zone wide the 27th.

Zone 7: The west is warmer with some precipitation. Strong thunderstorms and lower temperatures zone wide the 27th.

Zone 8: Alaska: Initially western areas see low pressure and colder temperatures. Stronger storms the 27th. Fair conditions the 29th. Northern sections of central zone are stormy through the 27th. Central areas end windy. Eastern sections start stormy and end windy. Hawaii: A cold front lowers temperatures and brings rainy weather to the area for the first half of the period. Fair conditions return afterward.

4th Quarter March 3–10

Zone 1: Several factors point to an active weather pattern over the region bringing increased wind velocities and thunderstorms.

Zone 2: Northern areas are stormy and cool. Thunderstorms affect the Florida Panhandle. Central regions are cool with a chance of thunderstorms.

Zone 3: Western areas experience windy and stormy conditions. Central and eastern portions see an increase in temperature and humidity, leading to some precipitation.

Zone 4: Western and central areas are initially stormy, then calm. Storms bring gusty winds and precipitation the 8th. Eastern areas begin cool, fair, and breezy. Stormy and windy the 9th.

Zone 5: Western and central areas are initially stormy, then calm. Storms bring gusty winds and precipitation the 8th. Eastern areas begin cool, fair, and breezy. Stormy and windy the 9th.

Zone 6: Rising temperatures and moderate breezes push inland from coastal areas. Eastern areas are cooler with strong thunderstorms around the 8th.

Zone 7: Rising temperatures and moderate breezes push inland from coastal areas. Eastern areas are cooler with strong thunderstorms around the 8th.

Zone 8: Alaska: Western showers the 6th. Stronger storms after the 8th. Central areas are initially fair, then showers the 6th. Stronger storms the 9th. Eastern portions begin fair, then cloudy or foggy the 7th. The period ends windy. Hawaii: A stormy period for the area. Expect wind and thunderstorms as the period begins and toward the end.

New Moon March 10–17

Zone 1: Fair conditions begin the period. A chance of precipitation develops around the 12th onward.

Zone 2: Fair conditions begin the period for northern sections. A chance of precipitation develops around the 12th onward. Southern areas are warmer and partly cloudy. A chance of rain the 13th.

Zone 3: Western areas start warmer and partly cloudy. Heavy rain and lower temperatures zone wide the 13th. Afterward, fair and warmer.

Zone 4: Scattered showers and thunderstorms zone wide. West and central areas end fair and warm but rainy for eastern sections.

Zone 5: Scattered showers and thunderstorms zone wide. West and central areas end fair and warm but rainy for eastern sections.

Zone 6: Coastal areas begin fair. Western temperatures rise, rain and wind increase after the 12th. Eastern portions fair and warm.

Zone 7: Coastal areas begin fair. Western temperatures rise, rain and wind increase after the 12th. Eastern portions fair and warm.

Zone 8: Alaska: Lower-than-average temperatures for western areas and rising temperatures for eastern portions. Chance of heavy precipitation and windy conditions for the zone the 13th. Hawaii: Warm and fair conditions start the period. Strong thunderstorms the 13th. The period ends with showers.

Spring

Western portions of Zone 1 will see generally warm and fair conditions in March, April, and the first half of May. The potential for hotter and stormier weather takes hold until the beginning of June, after which fair conditions resume. Cooler temperatures and breezy conditions are shown for the New England area.

Generally fair conditions are indicated for Zones 2 and 3 with increased storm potential during the month of May. Warm, fair, and dry conditions predominate throughout Zones 4 and 5. Heat may be excessive at times. Toward the end of April, more moisture is drawn up over the region, resulting in showers. When disruptive planetary alignments affect these zones, excessive rainfall and gusty winds will result.

Zones 6 and 7 show a tendency to below-average temperatures with winds of varying velocities and frequency. Mid-April shows some increasing temperatures. Temperatures begin a rising trend the second week of May and push eastward.

When benign planetary aspects affect Alaska, fair but cooler and partly cloudy conditions affect the zone. Under adverse aspects, overcast, humid, and cooler conditions impact the area with easterly winds and, at times, heavy precipitation. April sees a modifying warm and dry influence moving from west to east. The Hawaiian Islands will see fair conditions with lower ranges of temperatures under good planetary alignments and heavy precipitation under adverse aspects along with easterly winds.

2nd Quarter March 17–25

Zone 1: Lower temperatures with cloudy and wet conditions zone wide. Becoming fair the 24th.

Zone 2: Temperatures rise along with humidity, leading to showers.

Zone 3: The period starts with coastal thunderstorms. Increasing temperatures and dry conditions progress eastward. Increased humidity after the 22nd. Period ends with gusty thunderstorms.

Zone 4: Fair conditions for the zone. Western and central areas end with the likelihood of gusty thunderstorms.

Zone 5: Fair conditions for the zone. Western and central areas end with the likelihood of gusty thunderstorms.

Zone 6: Warm and fair conditions west. Eastern areas see increasing cloudiness and cooler temperatures with a chance of precipitation.

Zone 7: Warm and fair conditions west. Eastern areas see increasing cloudiness and cooler temperatures with a chance of precipitation.

Zone 8: Alaska: Increasing cloudiness, cooler temperatures, and possibly heavy precipitation for western regions. Central areas see increasing temperatures and possibly heavy rain around the 21st. Precipitation likely for eastern areas toward the close of the period. Hawaii: Increasing chance of rain from the 21st on.

Full Moon March 25–April 1

Zone 1: The zone sees the potential for some windy conditions as well as thunderstorms throughout the period. Around the 28th, a brief period of cool, clear weather.

Zone 2: Windy weather is indicated during the period along with thunderstorm potential.

Zone 3: Thunderstorms are likely throughout the period in addition to windy conditions.

Zone 4: Temperatures begin to rise, bringing variable weather conditions. The potential for increased wind velocities and thunderstorm activity remains strong.

Zone 5: Temperatures begin to rise, bringing variable weather conditions. The potential for increased wind velocities and thunderstorm activity remains strong.

Zone 6: Western areas see cool and clear conditions the 28th. A warm, humid air mass brings shower potential. The period ends windy. The eastern zone is warm with variable conditions. Cool and clear weather around the 28th.

Zone 7: Western areas see cool and clear conditions the 28th. A warm, humid air mass brings shower potential. The period ends windy. The eastern zone is warm with variable conditions. Cool and clear weather around the 28th.

Zone 8: Alaska: Western portions see thunderstorms and wind. Central areas become clear and cool the 28th. Afterward, warmer with shower potential. Eastern sections may start foggy, then warmer with showers. Hawaii: Temperatures somewhat below average with an increasing chance of showers and thunderstorms around the 30th.

4th Quarter April 1–8

Zone 1: Temperatures increase. Windy conditions and possible thunderstorms as the period progresses. The period ends with severe thunderstorms and gusty winds.

Zone 2: Temperatures increase. Windy conditions and possible thunderstorms as the period progresses. The period ends with severe thunderstorms and gusty winds, especially over northern areas.

Zone 3: Dry and breezy conditions over the area. Windy with increasing thunderstorm potential the 4th.

Zone 4: Western and central areas are subject to increasing wind velocities. Thunderstorm potential increases as the period progresses. Destructive windy storms likely toward the end of the period, initiating a cooldown. Eastern areas warm and breezy.

Zone 5: Western and central areas subject to increasing wind velocities. Thunderstorm potential increases as the period progresses.

Destructive windy storms likely toward the end of the period, initiating a cooldown. Eastern areas warm and breezy.

Zone 6: Cooler and cloudy along the coast. Thunderstorms and windy conditions for inland areas. Severe storms likely zone wide the 8th.

Zone 7: Cooler and cloudy along the coast. Thunderstorms and windy conditions for inland areas. Severe storms likely zone wide the 8th.

Zone 8: Alaska: Western areas are warmer with showery weather. Severe thunderstorms increase after the 6th. Potentially heavy rain for central and eastern areas the 3rd. Destructive storms the 6th. Afterward, a decrease in temperatures. Hawaii: Temperatures increase during the period. Possible heavy rain the 3rd. Stronger storms likely toward the end of the period.

New Moon April 8–15

Zone 1: Initially warm and dry. Afterward, temperatures decline a bit. The period finishes with a cool and windy pattern.

Zone 2: Initially fair and warm before turning a bit cooler and windy with a chance of precipitation.

Zone 3: The southwest area sees thunderstorms and windy conditions. Warm, dry, and fair conditions are indicated for most of the remaining zone. The chance of precipitation increases. Eastern portions are cooler with some wind toward the end.

Zone 4: Western areas start with severe thunderstorm potential. High winds likely during the period. Increasing temperatures, strong thunderstorms, and gusty winds for central and eastern areas.

Zone 5: Western areas start with severe thunderstorm potential. High winds likely during the period. Increasing temperatures, strong thunderstorms, and gusty winds for central and eastern areas.

Zone 6: Coastal wind and rain. High winds over eastern portions. Increasing temperatures and moisture feed thunderstorm activity.

Zone 7: Coastal wind and rain. High winds over eastern portions. Increasing temperatures and moisture feed thunderstorm activity.

Zone 8: Alaska: Western and central storms will be strong to severe. Eastern portions see increasing temperatures and moisture that lead to precipitation. Hawaii: Thunderstorm potential is strong as the period begins. Afterward, declining temperatures and possible precipitation is likely.

2nd Quarter April 15–23

Zone 1: Initially warm and dry. Winds and thunderstorm probability intensify. Cooler temperatures likely.

Zone 2: Cooler and breezy. Wind velocities increase. Thunderstorm formation is favored throughout the region.

Zone 3: Fair and breezy conditions are indicated. Wind velocities progressively strengthen along with the chance of showers and thunderstorms.

Zone 4: Shower and thunderstorm development is favored over western areas. Central and eastern zones are warm and dry. Changing conditions encourage shower and thunderstorm formation.

Zone 5: Shower and thunderstorm development is favored over western areas. Central and eastern zones are warm and dry. Changing conditions encourage shower and thunderstorm formation.

Zone 6: Western and eastern zones are ripe for showers and thunderstorms, which center over the Pacific Northwest and the Great Basin area.

Zone 7: Western and eastern zones are ripe for showers and thunderstorms, which center over south-central California and the Great Basin area.

Zone 8: Alaska: Western areas see thunderstorm activity. Central portions begin dry, warm, partly cloudy, and breezy. Thunderstorm development ensues but is strongest over coastal areas of central and eastern portions. Hawaii: Initially conditions are fair. Thunderstorms develop between the 17th and 19th. Afterward, fair conditions return.

Full Moon April 23–May 1

Zone 1: Cool and fair with increasing winds and storminess. Mid-period, conditions are warm and fair.

Zone 2: Fair through mid-period. Cool and windy with possible heavy precipitation around the 30th.

Zone 3: Showers transit west to east. Windy and stormy conditions with possible heavy rain around the 30th.

Zone 4: Initially dry, warm, and windy zone wide. Stormy weather develops with potential for heavy precipitation.

Zone 5: Initially dry, warm, and windy zone wide. Stormy weather develops with potential for heavy precipitation.

Zone 6: Western areas are warm with increasing windiness. Storms with heavy rain the 28th. The east is dry, warm, and windy with thunderstorm development.

Zone 7: Western areas are warm with increasing windiness. Storms with heavy rain the 28th. The east is dry, warm, and windy with thunderstorm development.

Zone 8: Alaska: Cool, windy, and stormy over western and central areas. Low pressure and easterly winds over eastern areas. Possible squally storms east the 27th–29th. Hawaii: Cool and windy. Possible showers mid-period. Mild and fair conditions develop toward the end.

4th Quarter May 1–7

Zone 1: Mostly cooler temperatures, increased wind velocities, and possible thunderstorms.

Zone 2: Mostly cooler temperatures, increased wind velocities, and possible thunderstorms.

Zone 3: Partly cloudy and cooler. Strong storms, hail, and wind, especially for the western Great Lakes states of Wisconsin, Illinois, and Indiana.

Zone 4: The zone sees southerly breezes and temperate showers. However, a severe weather outbreak is likely bringing hail and possible tornadoes the 2nd.

Zone 5: The zone sees southerly breezes and temperate showers. However, a severe weather outbreak is likely bringing hail and possible tornadoes the 2nd.

Zone 6: Initially western areas are dry and windy. Temperatures increase along with strong thunderstorms the 2nd. Thunderstorms and breezy conditions over eastern areas.

Zone 7: Initially western areas are dry and windy. Temperatures increase along with strong thunderstorms the 2nd. Thunderstorms and breezy conditions over eastern areas.

Zone 8: Alaska: Cooler with increasing wind velocities over western and central portions. Thunderstorm formation is favored throughout the zone the 2nd. Hawaii: The islands experience cooler temperatures, windy conditions, and possible thunderstorms.

New Moon May 7–15

Zone 1: Mid-Atlantic is breezy with variable winds. Chance of rain the 10th. The New England area sees a sudden lowering of temperatures, windy weather, and a chance of rain the 10th. Temperatures remain below average.

Zone 2: Fair conditions, partly cloudy skies, and breezy for northern sections the 13th. Average temperatures.

Zone 3: Initially western portions see rising temperatures and possible thunderstorms. Central and eastern areas see mild temperatures and temperate showers. Becoming cool and fair the 13th.

Zone 4: Western areas are cloudy with a chance of rain, lower temperatures, and easterly winds. Central and eastern portions see rising temperatures and possible thunderstorms. Showers likely the 13th.

Zone 5: Western areas are cloudy with a chance of rain, lower temperatures, and easterly winds. Central and eastern portions see rising temperatures and possible thunderstorms. Showers likely the 13th.

Zone 6: Coastal areas see precipitation around the 9th. The zone sees rapidly falling temperatures, gusty winds, and high pressure.

Zone 7: Coastal areas see precipitation around the 9th. The zone sees rapidly falling temperatures, gusty winds, and high pressure.

Zone 8: Western areas are cloudy and cooler with a chance of rain the 10th. The west ends mild, sunny, and pleasant. South-central coastal areas see stormy conditions. Fair and cool as the period ends. Eastern portions are breezy with a chance of rain the 10th. Hawaii: Initially partly cloudy, fair, and cooler. A chance of rain the 10th, then breezy and cooler with a chance of rain the 12th.

2nd Quarter May 15–23

Zone 1: The mid-Atlantic opens with thunderstorms and increasing temperatures. The chance of precipitation continues through the 21st. New England begins with a period of cooler, windy, and possibly rainy weather. A time of thunderstorm potential.

Zone 2: Increasing temperatures and thunderstorm potential for northern areas through the 21st. Southern areas are fair.

Zone 3: An unsettled period for the zone with showers and thunderstorms.

Zone 4: Western areas at first see strong storms with hail potential. Cooler conditions with precipitation. Central and eastern sections initially see strong storms with hail potential. Continues stormy.

Zone 5: Western areas at first see strong storms with hail potential. Cooler conditions with precipitation. Central and eastern sections initially see strong storms with hail potential. Continues stormy.

Zone 6: The west is mostly warm and dry, but breezy along coastal areas. Strong chance of wind and rain the 17th. Eastern portions see thunderstorms the 19th with warming and gusty winds the 23rd.

Zone 7: The west is mostly warm and dry, but breezy along coastal areas. Strong chance of wind and rain the 17th. Eastern portions see thunderstorms the 19th with warming and gusty winds the 23rd.

Zone 8: Alaska: Thunderstorm development over far western areas through the 17th. Becoming warm and fair through the

23rd. Thunderstorm potential for central and eastern areas the 17th. Hawaii: Showers likely as the period begins. Becoming warm and fair the 22nd with a chance of showers afterward.

Full Moon May 23–30

Zone 1: A fair and warm beginning to the period with moderate winds, then partly cloudy and cooler. Thunderstorm development the 25th. The zone experiences increasing wind velocities, storm potential, and lower ranges of temperature the 28th.

Zone 2: Partly cloudy and cooler. Fair and warm with moderate winds the 25th, then partly cloudy and cooler. The zone experiences increasing wind velocities, storm potential, and lower ranges of temperature the 28th.

Zone 3: Partly cloudy and cooler. The zone experiences increasing wind velocities, storm potential, and lower ranges of temperature the 28th.

Zone 4: Warm and breezy throughout the zone. Western and central areas see potential thunderstorms the 25th. Thunderstorms zone wide the 27th, then partly cloudy and cooler.

Zone 5: Warm and breezy throughout the zone. Western and central areas see potential thunderstorms the 25th. Thunderstorms zone wide the 27th, then partly cloudy and cooler.

Zone 6: Western areas are warm and dry. A low-pressure area generates stormy conditions, which intensify over eastern areas the 25th.

Zone 7: Western areas are warm and dry. A low-pressure area generates stormy conditions, which intensify over eastern areas the 25th.

Zone 8: Alaska: Western areas begin breezy, fair, and mild. A low-pressure area generates stormy conditions over central and eastern portions the 24th, then becoming partly cloudy and cooler. Western regions end with shower potential. Hawaii: Initially breezy with fair conditions and mild temperatures. Potential thunderstorms the 25th. The lunar phase ends with shower potential.

4th Quarter May 30–June 6

Zone 1: Severe thunderstorms and gusty winds start the period. Cloudy, lower temperatures, and rain. Possible showers around the 4th.

Zone 2: Initially severe thunderstorms and gusty winds over northern sections. Cold front, possible showers the 4th. Southern areas see rising temperatures and shower potential.

Zone 3: Western areas see lower temperatures, windy weather, possible storms. Central areas are fair. Eastern portions are warmer and showery.

Zone 4: Initially warm and dry over western areas. Passing front on the 3rd, then continuing fair through the 5th. Eastern portions see cooler, potentially windy weather and thunderstorms.

Zone 5: Initially warm and dry over western areas. Passing front on the 3rd, then continuing fair through the 5th. Eastern portions see cooler, potentially windy weather and thunderstorms.

Zone 6: Increasing temperatures and dryness over coastal areas push eastward.

Zone 7: Increasing temperatures and dryness over coastal areas push eastward.

Zone 8: Alaska: Temperatures warm over western and central areas with a chance of showers. West continues warm and dry. Showers over central and eastern areas the 31st. Colder west and central with possible heavy rain after the 2nd. Western regions fair with variable winds the 3rd–5th. Central showers the 4th. Hawaii: Increasing temperatures with a chance of showers the 31st, then potentially heavy rain the 2nd. Afterward cloudy, cooler with showers.

New Moon June 6–14

Zone 1: Lower temperatures and possible thunderstorms over the mid-Atlantic the 11th. New England sees thunderstorms throughout the period—most intense around the 11th.

Zone 2: Cold front and thunderstorms around the 11th.

Zone 3: Rising temperatures and humidity. Low pressure with occasionally heavy precipitation as storm systems push eastward through the zone.

Zone 4: West is initially fair and somewhat breezy. Continuing fair through the 11th. The western zone is caught between fair conditions to their west and windy, stormy weather to the east. Central is mostly windy and stormy throughout the period. Strong thunderstorms on the 9th intensify around the 11th. East is mostly windy, stormy, and cloudy with lower temperatures. Strong thunderstorms on the 9th intensify around the 11th.

Zone 5: West is initially fair and somewhat breezy. Continuing fair through the 11th. The western zone is caught between fair conditions to their west and windy, stormy weather to the east. Central is mostly windy and stormy throughout the period. Strong thunderstorms on the 9th intensify around the 11th. East is mostly windy, stormy, and cloudy with lower temperatures. Strong thunderstorms on the 9th intensify around the 11th.

Zone 6: Clashing atmospheric conditions lead to showers and thunderstorms in the west, which push eastward. East is initially fair and somewhat breezy. Low pressure and precipitation develop as the period progresses.

Zone 7: Clashing atmospheric conditions lead to showers and thunderstorms in the west, which push eastward. East is initially fair and somewhat breezy. Low pressure and precipitation develop as the period progresses.

Zone 8: Alaska: Western areas see cloudiness and precipitation the 8th, then fair conditions by the 11th. Thunderstorms for central and eastern portions. Stronger storms the 8th and 11th with windy conditions. The period ends with windy thunderstorms. Areas east of Anchorage and Fairbanks see strong thunderstorms throughout the period, but especially around the 10th–12th. Hawaii: Initially fair and somewhat breezy. Cloudy and rainy around the 8th. Fair and breezy the 11th.

Summer

As the season begins, warm and dry conditions affect Zones 1 and 2. July brings breezy to windy conditions and as August begins, increasing temperatures, humidity, and temperate showers. Weather tends toward windy and stormy conditions as August leads into September.

Zone 3 will see rising temperatures and dry conditions that give way to windier and stormy conditions in July. Eastern areas of the zone will see warm and dry conditions with a breezy to windy atmosphere.

Higher ranges of temperatures are in store for Zones 4 and 5. This warmth provides the necessary ingredients to trigger thunderstorm activity, especially the first half of July, or drought conditions throughout the season.

Eastern sections of Zones 6 and 7 experience southerly airflows, increased humidity, and warmer temperatures. Depending on planetary configurations, weather conditions can range from cloudy weather, variable winds, and showers to thunderstorms unleashing excessive precipitation and localized flooding. Conditions over coastal areas are warm, breezy, and partly cloudy. From mid-August through September, the chances of frontal activity bringing heavy rain increases.

Far western portions of Alaska will see high barometric pressure and lower ranges of temperatures when benefic planetary aspects are in play. Under adverse planetary configurations, the atmosphere is cold and overcast with increasing wind velocities. West central areas tend more toward temperate conditions. Central and eastern areas incline more toward easterly winds, low pressure, cloudy skies, and lower temperatures. The Hawaiian Islands see generally fine weather and temperatures interspersed with local thunderstorms.

2nd Quarter June 14–21
Zone 1: Initially warm and fair, then continuing windy and rainy throughout the period. There is strong potential for a tropical system or influx of tropical moisture to affect the zone.

Zone 2: Initially warm and fair, then continuing windy and rainy throughout the period. This may be due to a tropical system traveling up the coast or tropical moisture penetrating the area.

Zone 3: Thunderstorms around the 17th. The period ends with rising temperatures and windy conditions.

Zone 4: Initially strong thunderstorms through central and eastern areas. Possible heavy rain over eastern areas the 20th. Otherwise, fair with north winds. Western areas see cooler and windy conditions.

Zone 5: Initially strong thunderstorms through central and eastern areas. Possible heavy rain over eastern areas the 20th. Otherwise, fair with north winds. Western areas see cooler and windy conditions.

Zone 6: West: The period begins with windy and rainy weather and ends dry and breezy. East: Pressure gradient brings windy conditions and fluctuating temperatures.

Zone 7: West: The period begins with windy and rainy weather and ends dry and breezy. East: Pressure gradient brings windy conditions and fluctuating temperatures.

Zone 8: Alaska: Western areas see potential for heavy rain and windy conditions throughout the period. Central areas see windy thunderstorms at first. Lower temperatures, cloudy, and rainy around the 20th. East is initially warm and windy. Heavy precipitation may bring potential flooding. Lower temperatures, cloudy, and rainy the 20th. Hawaii: Mostly a rainy and windy period for the islands.

Full Moon June 21–28

Zone 1: Initially warm, dry, and breezy. Showers around the 24th and 26th.

Zone 2: Initially warm, dry, and breezy. Showers around the 24th and 26th.

Zone 3: Initially dry and breezy. Warm and fair conditions predominately.

Zone 4: Storms over the Montana-North Dakota area the 25th. Western areas fair and partly cloudy the 26th. Temperatures rise, giving way to showers. Showers over central and eastern sections the 24th and 26th.

Zone 5: Western areas fair and partly cloudy the 26th. Temperatures rise, giving way to showers. Showers over central and eastern sections the 24th and 26th.

Zone 6: Coastal areas see partly cloudy skies, warm temperatures, and possible showers throughout the period. Eastern areas are fair and partly cloudy the 26th and remain warm with moderate humidity.

Zone 7: Coastal areas see partly cloudy skies, warm temperatures, and possible showers throughout the period. Low pressure, cloudy, and rainy conditions over Southern California and Nevada during the period. Eastern areas are fair and partly cloudy the 26th and remain warm with moderate humidity.

Zone 8: Alaska: Western areas see higher ranges of temperatures. Central and eastern areas become cool and partly cloudy, leading to showers the 26th—possibly heavy over the south-central coastal area. Hawaii: Rising temperatures and dry conditions. A slight chance of showers on the 26th.

4th Quarter June 28–July 5

Zone 1: Cooler, cloudy, and wet weather with thunderstorms and increasing wind velocities at the period's end.

Zone 2: After starting warm and dry, cooler, wet, and cloudy conditions develop. Possibly a tropical system threatens the area the 2nd. Heavy rain over Florida.

Zone 3: Warm and dry over the zone. Low pressure affects the Great Lakes. Northeastern portions see heavy tropical moisture. Strong storms over Wisconsin and Great Lakes the 3rd.

Zone 4: Mostly warm and fair. Strong thunderstorms over Montana and the Dakotas on the 2nd and over Wisconsin and western Great Lakes on the 3rd.

Zone 5: Mostly warm and fair. Severe thunderstorms for the Lower Mississippi River Valley the 3rd.

Zone 6: Mostly warm and dry west, yet some showers for the Pacific Northwest on the 1st and thunderstorms and strong winds the 3rd.

Zone 7: Mostly warm and dry west, yet some showers on the 1st. Thunderstorms and strong winds the 3rd.

Zone 8: Alaska: Western and central areas are warm and fair, becoming cool, cloudy, and wet with heavy downpours. Eastern portions start warm and fair. Thunderstorms develop over coastal areas east of Anchorage. Hawaii: Warmer with potentially heavy rainfall.

New Moon July 5–13

Zone 1: Mostly a period of showers and thunderstorms that ends with gusty, erratic winds, thunderstorms, and possible hail.

Zone 2: Mostly a period of showers and thunderstorms that ends with gusty, erratic winds, thunderstorms, and possible hail, strongest over northern areas.

Zone 3: Warm, cloudy, and showery conditions. Some gusty winds. Thunderstorms and possible hail. Great Lakes storms on the 10th.

Zone 4: The west is fair and cool with some showers. Eastern areas are cool and breezy with thunderstorms, hail, gusty winds. Heavy precipitation the 12th.

Zone 5: The west is fair and cool with some showers. Eastern areas are cool and breezy with thunderstorms, hail, gusty winds. Heavy precipitation the 12th.

Zone 6: Scattered thunderstorms form over eastern areas. Breezy conditions become gusty with possible thunderstorms.

Zone 7: Scattered thunderstorms form over eastern areas. Breezy conditions become gusty with possible thunderstorms.

Zone 8: Alaska: Western areas are warm and fair. Cool and clear after the 7th, ending with erratic winds and thunderstorms. Central and eastern areas cloudy and breezy, then cool and fair. Heavy precipitation likely over eastern areas the 11th. Hawaii: The islands experience warm and pleasant conditions.

2nd Quarter July 13–21

Zone 1: Cooler temperatures, then thunderstorms the 16th–18th. Colder with gusty winds and thunderstorms the 20th.

Zone 2: Cooler north. Low pressure over North Carolina and Virginia the 16th. Colder with gusty winds and thunderstorms the 20th.

Zone 3: Intense storms, cooler temperatures north on the 18th. Becoming warm and fair the 21st.

Zone 4: Western and central areas start warm. Strong storms the 14th. Cool, fair, and breezy the 18th, then fair and warmer the 21st. Eastern areas see precipitation and warmer temperatures.

Zone 5: Western and central areas start warm. Strong storms the 14th. Cool, fair, and breezy the 18th, then fair and warmer the 21st. Eastern areas see precipitation and warmer temperatures.

Zone 6: Squally storms push eastward with winds, heavy rain, and lightning.

Zone 7: Squally storms push eastward with winds, heavy rain, and lightning.

Zone 8: Alaska: Fair conditions. Western areas see high winds and possibly dangerous storms the 18th–21st. Low pressure over south-central and eastern coasts through the 18th. Hawaii: Mostly warm and fair conditions.

Full Moon July 21–27

Zone 1: A stormy period. Strong storms over the mid-Atlantic and New England.

Zone 2: A stormy period. Windy conditions north on the 23rd, then thunderstorms over mid-Atlantic and West Virginia the 24th.

Zone 3: Mostly fair and clear. Low pressure over Louisiana and Mississippi the 23rd. Strong storms over eastern Great Lakes through West Virginia the 24th.

Zone 4: Warm conditions and atmospheric disturbances. Afterward, cool and windy weather with thunderstorms east and central. Low pressure over central and southern plains the 27th.

Zone 5: Warm conditions and atmospheric disturbances. Low pressure over Louisiana and Mississippi the 23rd, then cool and fair west and central. Low pressure over the southern plains the 27th.

Zone 6: Stormy west. High pressure over Idaho. Winds increase over the west the 26th, then fair.

Zone 7: Stormy west with high pressure over Southern California. Windy west the 26th. High pressure over Arizona the 27th.

Zone 8: Alaska: Western areas are warm with thunderstorms. Central and eastern portions are fair with possible storms over the south-central coast. Hawaii: Temperatures and dryness increase during the period.

4th Quarter July 27–August 4

Zone 1: Some showers throughout the zone. Ending fair and mild over New England.

Zone 2: Showers for northern and central areas. The south remains fair. Heavy rainfall southeast the 31st, then northwest winds and precipitation north.

Zone 3: Warmth generates thunderstorms zone wide. Ohio Valley sees storms on the 31st. Western Great Lakes are cool and fair the 3rd.

Zone 4: Central and western areas see thunderstorms the 29th and 2nd. Storms likely strongest over northern plains. Northeastern portions see high pressure the 29th. Mississippi Valley sees thunderstorms the 31st. Western Great Lakes are fair the 3rd.

Zone 5: Western area begins with thunderstorms. Fair conditions over southern portions the 28th–1st. Central and eastern showers the 3rd. Thunderstorms develop over Mississippi Valley the 31st.

Zone 6: Fair over the Pacific Northwest the 29th–1st. Possible showers the 3rd. Eastern zone is warm and fair the 28th. Strong storms over Intermountain West the 1st.

Zone 7: Fair conditions over western areas the 29th, and showers the 3rd. The east is fair with strong storms the 1st, especially over Southern California and Arizona.

Zone 8: Alaska: Possible thunderstorms for west and central zones, then becoming warm and dry. South-central coast and western storms the 3rd. Possible rain for central and eastern areas the 31st. Temperatures cool as the period ends. Hawaii: Warm and dry with occasional thunderstorms. The period ends with increasing clouds, cooler temperatures, and some rain.

New Moon August 4–12

Zone 1: A windy and stormy period throughout the zone.

Zone 2: Thunderstorms for northern areas around the 5th, and fair conditions southward by the 7th.

Zone 3: Fair conditions with an increase in temperatures.

Zone 4: The period begins with wind or gusty thunderstorms central and east, and storms return on the 10th. Fair conditions north by the 7th.

Zone 5: The period begins with wind or gusty thunderstorms central and east, and storms return on the 10th.

Zone 6: The zone experiences changing conditions. Periods of high pressure, windy weather, and thunderstorm development are shown throughout the period.

Zone 7: Variable weather conditions are indicated for the zone. Windy conditions along the coast, partly cloudy skies, thunderstorms, and fair conditions are shown throughout the period.

Zone 8: Alaska: Western areas see windy weather, thunderstorms, and precipitation. Fair conditions around the 10th. Central areas see some fair conditions and precipitation. Eastern portions are fair and windy with thunderstorms. Hawaii: The period is warm and windy with thunderstorm potential.

2nd Quarter August 12–19

Zone 1: The period shows cooler temperatures over New England, increased wind velocities, and thunderstorms, possibly from a tropical system.

Zone 2: Seasonal temperatures and precipitation. On the 14th, low pressure develops off the coast of Florida, which may be tropical in nature.

Zone 3: Strong thunderstorms begin the period over the Great Lakes area, and low pressure forms over the central Mississippi Valley. By the 16th, fair conditions for the Great Lakes.

Zone 4: Increasing temperatures, humidity, and rain. Low pressure over the central Mississippi Valley. Central and eastern thunderstorms. Fair conditions for the northern plains on the 19th.

Zone 5: Increasing temperatures, humidity, and rain. Low pressure over the central Mississippi Valley. Central and eastern thunderstorms. Warm and fair conditions for Texas on the 19th.

Zone 6: Strong western and eastern thunderstorms with heavy rain. A West Coast front brings showers on the 15th.

Zone 7: Strong western and eastern thunderstorms with heavy rain. Rain for Arizona on the 14th. Afterward, a West Coast front brings showers.

Zone 8: Alaska: A stormy period and lower temperatures for the zone. Windy conditions are indicated. A possible warmup over southwestern portions. Hawaii: Mostly a mild atmosphere with temperate showers. Stronger storms may develop around the 15th and 19th.

Full Moon August 19–26

Zone 1: Windy conditions are indicated for the zone with periods of thunderstorms and lower temperatures. Slightly warmer temperatures may affect the mid-Atlantic area.

Zone 2: Cooler temperatures and windy, stormy conditions, especially for central and northern areas. A period of high pressure likely after storms.

Zone 3: The area sees some thunderstorm activity and lower

temperatures with increased winds. Clear skies for the Great Lakes the 21st and 25th.

Zone 4: Central and eastern portions of the zone are windy and stormy with below-average temperatures. The Dakotas see thunderstorms the 23rd. Fair conditions over the Front Range the 24th.

Zone 5: Central and eastern portions are windy and stormy with below-average temperatures. Fair conditions over Front Range the 24th. Windy Texas-New Mexico the 25th.

Zone 6: Warmer-than-average temperatures over western areas with a chance of thunderstorms. Pacific Northwest storms push eastward the 22nd. Fair skies for the Pacific Northwest the 25th.

Zone 7: Warmer-than-average temperatures and thunderstorms over western areas. Southern California low pushes eastward the 22nd.

Zone 8: Alaska: Windy and stormy west, ends cool and clear. Central and eastern sections stormy with potentially heavy rain. Eastern areas end with fair conditions. Hawaii: Temperatures and humidity increase, bringing showers and thunderstorms. The period ends with windy conditions.

4th Quarter August 26–September 2

Zone 1: The zone sees breezy and variable conditions, some severe thunderstorms, and falling temperatures. Wind velocities may increase as the period ends.

Zone 2: The zone sees breezy weather, warm and dry conditions, and a chance of thunderstorms. Wind velocities may increase, especially over North Carolina and Virginia.

Zone 3: Low pressure over Illinois and Indiana the 28th, then becoming fair, warm, and dry. Temperatures decline and winds increase, especially over the Great Lakes and Ohio Valley on the 1st.

Zone 4: Rain over Illinois and Indiana the 28th, then becoming warm and breezy. Scattered thunderstorms the 1st with fair conditions for northern Rockies.

Zone 5: Strong thunderstorms over southern Texas the 28th, then becoming warm and breezy. Scattered thunderstorms with fair weather over southern Texas the 30th.

Zone 6: After initial showers the 28th, coastal areas become fair, breezy, and cooler. Storms and heavy rain over the zone through the 2nd.

Zone 7: After initial showers the 28th, coastal areas become fair, breezy, and cooler. Storms and heavy rain over the zone through the 2nd.

Zone 8: Alaska: The west begins cool and clear and ends with intense rain. Central and eastern areas are warm and breezy with thunderstorms and end with heavy rain. The Alaskan Panhandle sees storms and heavy precipitation. Hawaii: Warm with thunderstorms. Winds pick up around the 1st.

New Moon September 2–11

Zone 1: Breezy and variable atmosphere with thunderstorms. The 6th and 9th are key dates.

Zone 2: Warm and breezy north on the 3rd. Windy storms the 6th. Potentially heavy rain over southeast coast. Breezy with thunderstorms for Great Lakes and mid-Atlantic the 9th.

Zone 3: Southern Mississippi Valley is fair the 6th. Windy storms in Ohio Valley the 6th. Eastern Great Lakes is breezy with thunderstorms the 9th.

Zone 4: Western and central areas see thunderstorms the 2nd and 9th. Windy high pressure for western Great Lakes the 3rd. Western area sees thunderstorms 4th–6th. Thunderstorms north-central and east the 10th.

Zone 5: Rising temperatures and showers and thunderstorms. Western and central thunderstorms the 2nd, 6th, and 9th. Southern Mississippi Valley is fair the 6th.

Zone 6: Coastal areas warmer with potentially heavy rain the 3rd. Stormy Idaho. Pacific Northwest storms the 7th. Eastern areas warmer, showers and thunderstorms.

Zone 7: Mild conditions, temperate showers, and thunderstorms. Coastal heavy rain the 3rd. Eastern storms the 6th. Arizona thunderstorms the 9th.

Zone 8: Alaska: Initially storm potential is high. Eastern area fair the 4th. Alaskan Panhandle storms the 2nd and 4th. West is fair the 6th. West and central storms the 10th. Hawaii: Generally fine weather. Strong thunderstorms the 7th. High pressure the 9th.

2nd Quarter September 11–17

Zone 1: Rising temperatures and possible rain, especially around the 14th and 16th.

Zone 2: Rising temperatures and possible rain, especially around the 14th and 16th.

Zone 3: Rising temperatures and possible rain. Mississippi storms the 14th and squally conditions zone wide the 17th.

Zone 4: Central thunderstorms 14th–16th. Western storms from the 15th onward, especially for the Colorado Front Range. Eastern areas are cooler and rainy.

Zone 5: Central thunderstorms 14th–16th. Western storms and lower temperatures after the 14th. Eastern areas cooler with Ark-La-Tex storms.

Zone 6: Coastal areas breezy, cool, and fair. California offshore low brings rain and wind. Sharp winds and electrical disturbances the 17th. The east is showery with strong storms the 17th.

Zone 7: Coastal areas breezy, cool, and fair. California offshore low brings rain and wind. Sharp winds and electrical disturbances the 17th. The east is showery with strong storms the 17th.

Zone 8: Alaska: West is breezy and cool. Thunderstorms after the 14th. Period ends cooler with thunderstorms. Central and east are mild and breezy. Cooler with heavy precipitation the 16th. Alaskan Panhandle is warmer with precipitation. Period ends with squally storms. Hawaii: Initially breezy and cooler, then fair and warm. Period ends with showers.

Autumn

Zone 1 experiences higher-than-normal temperatures throughout the season. Under benign planetary aspects, fair conditions prevail with breezy to windy weather and dry conditions. Adverse aspects suggest atmospheric disturbance, wind damage from destructive storms, and intense precipitation, such as may be expected around November 3. By December a mild, more humid influence with southerly winds that increase temperatures will affect the area.

Zone 2 experiences somewhat elevated temperatures and higher humidity through the month of October. November shows a mild influence with temperate showers affecting the zone.

Zone 3 and eastern portions of Zones 4 and 5 are under a warm and humid influence. Under benign planetary aspects, the atmosphere is warm and fair or sometimes warm and windy. Adverse configurations lead to gusty winds with thunderstorms that bring precipitation and hail.

Western parts of Zones 4 and 5 are subject to balmy ascending air currents accompanied by rising temperatures and stagnant calms. Under adverse planetary configurations, prevailing southerly winds induce heavy precipitation with threats of localized flooding.

The western areas of Zones 6 and 7 experience lower ranges of temperatures and easterly winds along with cloudy but generally fair conditions when benign influences are at work. Adverse aspects incline toward intense general rains, hail, and thunder. Eastern parts of these zones see breezy to windy conditions and cooler temperatures but to a certain extent will also participate in the weather patterns of the western zone.

Western and central reaches of Alaska see mild conditions brought on by southerly winds that induce temperate showers when under favorable planetary influences. Cooler temperatures and variable winds are shown for October. Eastern areas, conversely, experience high pressure and lower temperatures. Under adverse influences, there are erratic winds, chilly rain, sleet and snow, squally storms, and night frosts. The Hawaiian Islands experience mild conditions and fruitful showers. By mid-October, cooler temperatures and variable winds. December brings warm and dry conditions.

Full Moon September 17–24

Zone 1: Fair skies, moderate temperatures the 19th. Windy, potentially heavy rain the 22nd. Fair and pleasant temperatures for New England the 24th.

Zone 2: Fair conditions, lower temperatures the 21st. Potential tropic storm over the Turks and Caicos Islands the 22nd. Cool and fair conditions for southern areas the 24th.

Zone 3: Warm and fair conditions the 19th. Stormy over the Great Lakes the 22nd. Cool and fair zone wide the 24th.

Zone 4: West sees possible showers the 19th. Thunderstorms the 22nd. Cool and fair over the Rockies the 24th. Central has showers the 19th. Thunderstorms central and eastern 21st and 24th. High pressure, however, for the Dakotas. Northeastern sections see stormy conditions. Showers increase the 19th. Central and eastern thunderstorms the 21st. Cool and fair north the 24th.

Zone 5: West sees possible showers the 19th. Thunderstorms the 22nd. Cool and fair over the Rockies the 24th. Central and eastern showers likely on the 19th, 21st, and 24th. Coastal thunderstorms the 24th.

Zone 6: Thunderstorms transit from west to east.

Zone 7: Thunderstorms transit from west to east.

Zone 8: Alaska: West is fair, breezy, and cooler. Potentially heavy precipitation the 22nd. Central and east have cooler temperatures with precipitation and some wind. Period ends fair. Alaskan Panhandle has mostly lower temperatures and damp, rainy weather. Becoming fair the 23rd. Hawaii: High pressure and lower temperatures with breezy conditions.

4th Quarter September 24–October 2

Zone 1: Initially warm and fair. Cloudy and windy weather the 29th.

Zone 2: North Carolina and Virginia see an increased chance of thunderstorms. Southern areas are cloudy and windy the 29th.

Zone 3: Thunderstorms at first. The Great Lakes become fair the 26th. Cloudy and windy zone wide the 29th. Western areas have sharp winds and storms the 1st.

Zone 4: West initially has precipitation and windy weather. Montana and Wyoming see high pressure the 25th, then showers. Period ends rainy. Initially, central has precipitation and windy weather. Rainy and windy the 27th–30th. Rain for the Front Range the 1st, but high pressure for the Dakotas. East sees rain and wind early, then fair for northern areas. Sharp winds and thunderstorms the 1st.

Zone 5: West initially has precipitation and windy weather. Period ends rainy. Initially, central has precipitation and windy weather. Rainy and windy the 27th–30th. Central rain the 1st. East sees rain and wind early, then fair. Sharp winds and thunderstorms the 1st.

Zone 6: West, a period of lower temperatures with cloudy and rainy conditions for the Pacific Northwest. East, temperatures increase with possible showers. Breezy weather for eastern portions the 30th.

Zone 7: West sees cloudy and windy conditions leading to rain the 29th. Temperatures increase in the east with possible showers. Breezy weather is indicated for eastern portions the 30th.

Zone 8: Alaska: West sees southerly winds, mild temperatures. Fair conditions and a spike in temperatures the 1st. Central has mild temperatures and fair conditions with possible showers. East has mild temperatures and showers. Windy and cloudy the 29th. Alaska Peninsula is cool and fair with possible showers the

28th and wind the 30th. Hawaii: Mild temperatures and showers. Warmer around the 1st.

New Moon October 2–10

Zone 1: Increasing temperatures and showers or thunderstorms with periods of high pressure. Generally seasonal temperatures.

Zone 2: Generally seasonal temperatures and dry conditions. Occasional strong winds and possible thunderstorms.

Zone 3: West, initially windy conditions, increasing temperatures, and dryness. The Great Lakes are fair the 5th and 8th. Strong winds, thunderstorms the 6th.

Zone 4: Western and central areas are initially windy with showers. Thunderstorms over the Front Range the 3rd. Northern areas fair the 4th–6th. A chance of rain the 9th, then fair. East is initially windy, warm, and dry. Great Lakes fair the 5th and 8th. Windy with thunderstorms the 6th, then fair.

Zone 5: West sees windy conditions and showers for starters. Front Range thunderstorms the 3rd. Northern areas fair 4th–6th. A chance of rain the 9th, then fair. East is initially windy, warm, and dry. Windy thunderstorms the 6th, then fair.

Zone 6: West has possible thunderstorms the 3rd, then high pressure and lower temperatures. Fair for the Pacific Northwest the 6th, then stormy. East is windy and dry the 6th. Fair the 8th–10th.

Zone 7: West has possible thunderstorms the 3rd, then high pressure and lower temperatures, afterward stormy. East is windy and dry the 6th. Fair the 8th–10th.

Zone 8: Alaska: West is fair and cool the 2nd. Showers and thunderstorms the 4th, then fair. Afterward, coastal precipitation. Central is fair and cool the 2nd. Warm over north-central coast. East is fair and cool the 4th. Warm and fair weather the 8th. Alaskan Panhandle is generally warmer with temperate showers. Fair and cool the 4th. Fair and warm the 6th–8th. Hawaii: Warm with temperate showers. High pressure and lower temperatures the 4th. Warm and fair the 8th.

2nd Quarter October 10–17

Zone 1: Showers and thunderstorms zone wide. Mid-Atlantic atmospheric disturbance 14th and 17th. After the 11th, temperatures increase over New England. Thunderstorms through the 13th. Fair and warm the 17th.

Zone 2: Showers and thunderstorms the 10th. Atmospheric disturbance 14th and 17th.

Zone 3: Warm and dry zone wide. Fair over the Great Lakes area the 15th.

Zone 4: High pressure northeast the 10th. Warm and fair the 13th. Cloudy, possible rain the 15th. High pressure over northern Rockies. Central is gusty, thunderstorms the 13th. Cloudy, possible rain the 15th. Northeastern portions and Great Lakes warm and fair the 15th.

Zone 5: High pressure over New Mexico and western Texas the 13th. Cloudy, possible rain the 15th. Central is gusty, thunderstorms the 13th. Warm and fair over Texas the 17th. Eastern coastal areas fair 11th and 15th.

Zone 6: West sees possible rain. Pacific Northwest coastal showers at first, then storms the 14th. East is fair and pleasant zone wide. Thunderstorms erupt zone wide as the period ends.

Zone 7: West sees possible rain. Coastal areas are cooler and stormy. East is fair and pleasant zone wide. Thunderstorms erupt zone wide as the period ends.

Zone 8: Alaska: Showers or thunderstorms for the west coast the 11th and 13th—heavy rain southwest. Fair weather for coastal areas the 15th. Central thunderstorms on the 13th. Fair for central portions. Stormy over northern parts. East is cooler and rainy 11th–15th. Fair conditions the 13th. Alaskan Panhandle is overcast, cooler, and rainy 11th–15th. Warm and fair the 17th. Hawaii: Cooler temperatures, overcast skies, and precipitation.

Full Moon October 17–24

Zone 1: Mid-Atlantic is stormy. Fair and cool over Great Lakes and mid-Atlantic the 19th. Thunderstorms the 21st and 23rd. Warm and fair over New England. Storms likely around the 22nd.

Zone 2: Rising temperatures and storms.

Zone 3: Great Lakes low pressure the 17th, then fair the 19th. Warm and breezy west on the 20th.

Zone 4: West is warm and fair through the 19th. Showers the 21st around Montana, then high pressure. Central is warm and fair through the 19th. Showers the 21st. Fair over central plains the 22nd. East is initially high pressure around Iowa. Great Lakes fair the 19th, then warm and breezy.

Zone 5: West is warm and fair through the 19th. Showers the 21st, then high pressure. Central is warm and fair through the 19th. Showers the 21st. Fair over central plains the 22nd. East is warm and fair. Becoming breezy the 20th.

Zone 6: West initially has high pressure, then rainy the 20th. Partly cloudy and cooler the 22nd. Pacific Northwest showers the 23rd. East is warm and breezy, then thunderstorms. Fair the 19th. Thunderstorms the 21st.

Zone 7: West initially has high pressure, then rainy the 20th. Partly cloudy and cooler the 22nd. East is warm and breezy, then thunderstorms. Fair the 19th. Thunderstorms the 21st.

Zone 8: Alaska: West and central areas are breezy and cool. Possible rain the 17th, then cooler. Thunderstorms the 22nd, then fair. Alaska Peninsula sees showers. Partly cloudy and cooler the 22nd. Northern coastal areas high pressure the 23rd. East is fair with lower temperatures. Alaskan Panhandle is generally warmer with possible rain. High pressure the 19th. Thunderstorms the 21st. Ending windy and partly cloudy. Hawaii sees breezy conditions, variable winds, and cooler temperatures.

4th Quarter October 24–November 1

Zone 1: Warm conditions with some thunderstorm development.

Zone 2: Lower temperatures with a chance of rain.

Zone 3: Lower temperatures with a chance of rain.

Zone 4: West is warm with fair conditions. Central sees lower temperatures, windy conditions, and thunderstorms. East sees lower temperatures, windy conditions, and thunderstorms. Missouri-Arkansas area has thunderstorms the 28th. Northern areas are under high pressure.

Zone 5: West is warm with fair conditions. Central has lower temperatures, windy conditions, and thunderstorms. East sees lower temperatures, windy conditions, and thunderstorms.

Zone 6: West has lower temperatures and rain the 25th, 27th, and 29th. East sees fair conditions the 24th and 30th. Lower temperatures, variable winds, and thunderstorms.

Zone 7: West has lower temperatures and rain the 25th, 27th, and 29th. East sees fair conditions the 24th and 30th. Lower temperatures, variable winds, and thunderstorms.

Zone 8: Alaska: West sees rising temperatures and fair conditions with storms southwest. Central has lower temperatures, variable winds, and thunderstorms. Fair conditions the 24th and 28th. East has lower temperatures, variable winds, and thunderstorms the 26th, 28th, and 31st. Alaska Peninsula sees thunderstorm activity with lower temperatures the 26th and 30th. Hawaii: Chance of rain, rising temperatures, and fair conditions. Specifically fair conditions the 28th and 31st.

New Moon November 1–9

Zone 1: Fair conditions for New England. Then cooler and stormy the 3rd and 5th.

Zone 2: High pressure and lower temperatures are indicated for the week. Rain on the 2nd. Severe storms over Georgia and Florida the 7th.

Zone 3: West begins warm and fair. Cool and cloudy zone wide the 4th. Stormy Great Lakes and southeast the 7th.

Zone 4: The zone is initially warm and fair. Western showers the 5th. Strong central storms the 3rd. Showers the 5th. Eastern areas see severe thunderstorms over northern plains, Minnesota, and Great Lakes the 3rd. Showers over the Mississippi Valley the 4th.

Zone 5: The zone is initially warm and fair. Western showers the 5th. Strong central storms the 3rd. Showers the 5th. Eastern areas see severe thunderstorms over northern plains, Minnesota, and Great Lakes the 3rd. Showers over the Mississippi Valley the 4th.

Zone 6: Strong low pressure off the Pacific Northwest coast the 2nd. Then partly cloudy and cooler the 4th. The east begins dry and warm. Then cloudy with a chance of thunderstorms the 3rd.

Zone 7: The west becomes partly cloudy and cooler the 4th. The east begins dry and warm. Then cloudy with a chance of thunderstorms the 3rd. Windy and stormy the 5th.

Zone 8: Alaska: Thunderstorms over the west coast area. Central sees clouds and local showers the 3rd. East sees temperatures increase. Low pressure brings the chance of rain. Alaska Peninsula has high pressure and windy conditions the 2nd–5th. Warm, fair, and windy the 8th. Hawaii: Temperatures increase, bringing cloudiness and brief, local showers.

2nd Quarter November 9–15

Zone 1: Easterly winds, cooler temperatures, and rain over New England. Strong low pressure or possible tropical storm the 9th for New England. Stormy conditions for the zone the 12th.

Zone 2: Fair and cool. Substantial rain for northern areas the 12th. Pleasant temperatures zone wide, especially Florida, the 13th.

Zone 3: Heavy rain over central Gulf Coast the 10th. Fair and cool over central and south the 12th, but heavy precipitation for the Great Lakes.

Zone 4: West and central are warmer with heavy rain the 9th. Central sees possible rain the 11th. Warm and fair the 14th. Period ends cold and stormy over northern Rockies. East has fair conditions with a chance of rain. Western Great Lakes see low pressure, cooler temperatures, and considerable precipitation the 12th.

Zone 5: West and central are warmer with heavy rain the 9th. A chance of rain the 11th. Central is warm and fair the 14th. East sees fair conditions with a chance of rain. Heavy rain over central Gulf Coast the 10th.

Zone 6: West is cooler with rainy weather the 10th–14th. East sees moderate temperatures with pleasant breezes the 11th. The period ends fair and somewhat cooler.

Zone 7: West is cooler with rainy weather the 10th–14th. East sees moderate temperatures with pleasant breezes the 11th. The period ends fair and somewhat cooler.

Zone 8: Alaska: West sees variable temperature with generally fair conditions. Southwest thunderstorms the 14th. Central has area-wide lower temperatures, easterly winds, and stormy conditions. East sees increasing temperatures and some heavy precipitation along southern coast. Moderate temperatures with pleasant breezes the 11th. Alaskan Panhandle is mostly cooler with storms likely after the 10th. Hawaii: Lower-than-average temperatures. Some fair conditions, but mostly cloudy and rainy—heavy on the 9th.

Full Moon November 15–22

Zone 1: Gusty storms with precipitation over the zone. Fair conditions with rising temperatures the 21st.

Zone 2: Lower temperatures and high pressure, especially strong over North Carolina and Virginia.

Zone 3: Warmer with a chance of rain for the west the 18th. Strong Mississippi Valley storms the 20th. Particularly strong over the Great Lakes and southward. Fair the 22nd.

Zone 4: West is cooler with precipitation. Northern areas are stormy. Warm and fair 18th–21st. Central showers the 17th. Warm and fair 18th–21st. Cooler with high pressure the 21st, especially over northern areas. East sees temperatures increase with a chance of rain the 18th. Strong Mississippi Valley storms the 20th. Cool with high pressure the 22nd, especially over Minnesota.

Zone 5: West is cooler with precipitation. Northern areas are stormy. Warm and fair 18th–21st. Central sees showers the 17th, then warm and fair 18th–21st. Cooler with high pressure the 21st. East is warmer with a chance of rain the 18th. Strong Mississippi Valley storms the 20th. Cool with high pressure the 22nd.

Zone 6: West is rainy and cool. Warmer with high pressure over the Pacific Northwest the 21st. East sees a chance of rain the 17th. Windy conditions and varying temperatures the 20th.

Zone 7: West is rainy and cool. Storm center over Southern California coast. Warmer temperatures and high pressure the 21st. East sees a chance of rain the 17th. Windy conditions and varying temperatures the 20th.

Zone 8: Alaska: West sees fair conditions and pleasant temperatures. Possible showers and thunderstorms the 17th. Central has cool, high pressure over the south-central coast the 19th. Lower temperatures and showers the 22nd. Robust storms are indicated throughout the forecast period in the east. Alaskan Panhandle: Cold, damp, and windy weather. A warmup the 18th–21st, then cooler. Hawaii: Generally warm conditions. Cooler temperatures with high pressure the 21st.

4th Quarter November 22–December 1

Zone 1: The zone experiences a chance of showers throughout the period.

Zone 2: Warmer temperatures and higher humidity for the zone. A chance of showers over the zone the 26th.

Zone 3: Southern areas experience showers and thunderstorms. Fair conditions for the Ohio Valley and Great Lakes the 24th. A chance of showers over eastern sections the 26th.

Zone 4: Wind and rain for the Montana area the 24th. Windy conditions and some rain over the Rockies the 25th. Cool, cloudy, and low pressure for central and eastern areas. Wind and rain for the Dakotas the 24th. Fair conditions for eastern areas the 25th and 30th.

Zone 5: West, wind velocities increase on the 25th, then a chance of rain. Cool, cloudy, and low pressure for central and eastern areas. Fair conditions for eastern areas the 25th and 30th.

Zone 6: Windy over the Pacific Northwest with cool and fair conditions. East, increased wind velocities the 25th. A chance of rain for the area and fair, cool, and windy conditions the 30th.

Zone 7: West, initially declining temperatures and fair conditions. Southeastern regions are windy and stormy. Wind velocities increase the 25th. A chance of rain with fair, cool, and windy conditions the 30th.

Zone 8: Alaska: West sees showers and thunderstorms. Dry and windy weather southwest the 29th. Fair conditions the 30th. Central sees lower temperatures, fair conditions, and wind over south-central coastal areas the 24th. East sees a warmer period with thunderstorms. Fair and cool after the 23rd. Alaskan Panhandle is dry and windy. Cold and dry the 29th. Hawaii: Increasing temperatures and showers. Pleasant conditions the 24th. Dry and windy the 26th.

New Moon December 1–8

Zone 1: Gusty thunderstorms increase over the New England area the 1st, 6th, and 7th. The mid-Atlantic is fair and cooler. Warmer temperatures and shower potential the 6th.

Zone 2: Higher-than-average temperatures and showers. Southern zone showers the 1st. The mid-Atlantic is fair and cooler. Rain the 4th–6th.

Zone 3: Windy and stormy, and lower-than-average temperatures, especially the 5th and 6th. Deep South rain the 1st. Great Lakes storms on the 3rd.

Zone 4: West, showers the 2nd. Calm and warm the 5th. Fair the 7th. Low pressure afterward. A stormy period for the northern plains. Calm the 5th. Low pressure after the 7th.

Zone 5: West, showers the 2nd. Calm and warm the 5th. Fair the 7th. Low pressure afterward. Central is calm the 5th. Low pressure after the 7th. East sees lower-than-average temperatures with an increased chance of rain.

Zone 6: West is breezy with possible rain the 2nd. Sharp wind and rain the 4th, then cold and stormy. Temperatures remain lower than average. East sees lower-than-average temperatures. Thunderstorms with gusty winds the 1st. Breezy to windy the 4th.

Zone 7: West, mild and breezy along the coast on the 2nd with possible rain. Rainy with sharp winds the 5th, then a strong low over Southern California. Temperatures remain lower than average. East sees lower-than-average temperatures. Thunderstorms with gusty winds the 1st. Breezy to windy the 4th.

Zone 8: Alaska: West is windy and stormy with possible heavy precipitation the 5th, especially over the Alaska Peninsula. Central sees high pressure on the 1st. Sharp winds and possible thunderstorms the 5th. The eastern area is under clear skies and lower temperatures the 2nd. Alaskan Panhandle: Clear skies and lower temperatures throughout the period. Hawaii: Generally warm and dry. Sharp winds with possible thunderstorms the 5th. From the 6th on, increasing temperatures, dryness, and westerly winds.

2nd Quarter December 8–15

Zone 1: The mid-Atlantic sees strong thunderstorms. New England sees increasing temperatures, cloudy weather, and showers and thunderstorms.

Zone 2: A period of strong thunderstorms for northern and central areas. Fair conditions the 10th.

Zone 3: Fair conditions the 10th. Severe thunderstorms in Tennessee and southward the 12th. Stormy over the eastern Great Lakes area the 13th.

Zone 4: Initially, area showers west and central. Low pressure for the central plains the 11th. Thunderstorm activity likely the 13th.

East sees fair conditions the 10th, especially over the Minnesota-Wisconsin area.

Zone 5: Initially, area showers west and central. Rain over Oklahoma the 11th. Thunderstorms likely over the zone. East, fair conditions the 10th. High pressure in and around Minnesota the 13th.

Zone 6: The Pacific Northwest is cool and windy. A cold front on the 14th. Stormy the 15th. East is warmer with breezy conditions the 12th. Cooler and windy with possible rain the 14th. Area thunderstorms most intense over Idaho, Utah (13th), and Arizona (15th).

Zone 7: West has southerly winds and cloudy weather. Passing cold front on the 14th. Storms break out over the zone the 15th. Southern California and Arizona are fair the 9th. Area thunderstorms most likely intense over Idaho and Utah (13th), and Arizona (15th).

Zone 8: Alaska: West sees increasing temperatures, cloudiness, and possible precipitation on the 1st. Stormy over the Alaska Peninsula the 11th. Thunderstorm the 15th. Central sees fair conditions around the 12th. Eastern areas are cool and damp. Fair but cooler conditions the 13th. Alaskan Panhandle sees fair and cool conditions. Colder, possibly rainy, and windy the 15th. Hawaii: Increasing temperatures and cloudy weather. Showers and thunderstorms the 12th and 15th.

Full Moon December 15–22

Zone 1: Possible thunderstorms the 17th. Lower temperatures and fair conditions as the period ends.

Zone 2: Initially windy. Stormy Appalachians the 18th. General storms the 21st. Cooler and fair as the period ends.

Zone 3: The Great Lakes and eastern zone stormy and windy 15th and 18th. Area thunderstorms the 21st.

Zone 4: West and central see showers the 15th. Warmer, windy, and rainy the 19th. Possible fog. Period ends warm and dry. Fair conditions for northeastern sections the 18th. Mild with temperate showers as the period ends.

Zone 5: West and central see showers the 15th. Warmer, windy, and rainy the 19th. Possible fog. Period ends warm and dry. East is mild with temperate showers as the period ends. However, strong storms develop over the Louisiana area.

Zone 6: Storm systems zone wide. Cloudy, cooler, and higher-than-average precipitation. Fair 17th and 19th. Storm formation over the Great Basin the 22nd.

Zone 7: Storm systems zone wide. Cloudy, cooler, and higher-than-average precipitation. Fair 17th and 19th. Storm formation over the Great Basin the 22nd.

Zone 8: Alaska: Area-wide, low-pressure systems west. Clear and mild the 20th. Period ends cloudy, cooler with heavy rain. Central is stormy and windy, especially the upper Alaska Peninsula. Period ends cloudy, cooler with heavy rain. East sees a stormy and cooler period, which ends warm and rainy or foggy. Alaskan Panhandle: Colder and windy with precipitation. Clear skies the 16th. More precipitation the 18th. Hawaii: Mild temperatures and possible showers during the lunar phase. Initially windy. The period ends with higher-than-average precipitation.

4th Quarter December 22–31

Zone 1: Strong thunderstorms and cooler temperatures for the mid-Atlantic. Cloudy, cooler, windy, and rainy zone wide the 27th.

Zone 2: Southeastern US sees strong thunderstorms and cooler temperatures. Stormy and windy the 27th.

Zone 3: Cooler, cloudy, windy, and rainy the 27th. Intense storms around Wisconsin, Illinois, and western Great Lakes areas as they push eastward.

Zone 4: Thunderstorms over the central Rockies and plains. Strongest storms the 25th and 27th. Central and east see a stormy period, especially over the Colorado Front Range. Strong winter thunderstorms around Wisconsin, Illinois, and western Great Lakes areas as they push eastward the 27th.

Zone 5: Thunderstorms over the central Rockies and plains. Strongest storms the 25th and 27th. Central and east see a stormy period, especially over the Colorado Front Range and Oklahoma.

Zone 6: Storms over western coastal areas push eastward. Low pressure over the Pacific Northwest the 25th.

Zone 7: A stormy period for California. Storms then push eastward. Low pressure over Southern California and Arizona the 25th.

Zone 8: Alaska: Cooler with higher-than-average precipitation for western and central areas. East sees winter storm conditions the 24th. Storms intensify over eastern coastal areas the 27th. More precipitation the 29th. Alaskan Panhandle: Warmer with windy storms from the 27th on. Hawaii: Generally cloudy with below-normal temperatures and higher-than-average precipitation.

Economic Forecast for 2024

Christeen Skinner

You may know of an average 11.2-year solar cycle. Solar Cycle 25 began in December 2019 and is expected to peak with a maximum number of sunspots in July 2025. Though unconfirmed, it is entirely possible that the distribution of planets around the Sun affects this rhythm.

Stock markets tend to rise and fall to the beat of this solar rhythm. If the past indicates the future, as the number of sunspots increases through 2024 toward the expected maximum in 2025, then indices should increase.

Yet other factors are at work, and although the year should finish relatively well, it may not exceed the expectations associated with earlier peak sunspot activity. Sunspot activity is entirely separate from the position of the Sun on the ecliptic.

Earth's year is divided into the twelve signs of the zodiac, with research showing that indices do better when the Sun is traveling through certain parts of the ecliptic (divided into the signs of the zodiac) and less well at others. For example, the Dow Jones Industrial Average (DJI—and for which we have over one hundred and twenty years of data) tends to do best when the Sun moves through Capricorn and least well as the Sun moves through Virgo.

The S&P Index, for which we have data from 1950, similarly shows Virgo to be the weakest sign and Aries to bring the best results. This is unsurprising given that the S&P Index is made up of very different sectors—usually much younger (Aries is associated with youth) companies than the DJI. The Australian All Ordinaries Index also makes most gains as the Sun moves through Aries, but makes fewest gains as the Sun moves through Scorpio.

This is not dissimilar to Hong Kong's Hang Seng Index, which again does best at the start of the astrological year when the Sun moves through Aries but tends to lose value when the Sun passes through either Leo or Pisces.

The London FTSE Index can also be shown to gain with the Sun in Aries and fares least well with the Sun in either Virgo or Pisces. (Please note that whilst this information is interesting—and perhaps even valuable—it is insufficient information on which to trade).

The outstanding "winner" for Moon sign position is Leo for the DJI, Australian, and Hang Seng, Taurus for the London market, and Aries for the S&P. (Again, this is noteworthy but does not offer a trading system.)

From the above information, we might then deduce that 2024 will find all markets doing best in the first quarter of the year (the Sun moving through Capricorn and Aries) but declining in the fourth quarter of the year before a possible rise in the days leading into the Sun's move into Capricorn on December 22, 2023, where it conjoins Mercury in that same sign.

The chart for the December 2023 solstice shows this conjunction, which is within orb of opposition between Venus and Uranus whilst Vesta is inconjunct (150°) Pluto (completing its transit of Capricorn). Together this suggests a surprise ending to a financially chaotic year: the unexpected being a slight lift in the last ten days of the year but insufficient to bring indices back to the position held at its start.

Discontinuity

Pluto's entry into Aquarius on January 20 at 19:50 EST should mark the start of significant global financial turbulence. Pluto last visited this area of the zodiac between 1778 and 1798: years which covered the better part of the American Revolution. (Will that eventually go down in history as the first American Revolution as the world now witnesses its second?)

Within that period, the Coinage Act of 1792 brought the US dollar into existence. No single planet denotes a currency, but it is generally agreed that Pluto is a planet of wealth and taxation. As Pluto returns to the position it held on April 2, 1792, we should expect the US to experience a wealth crisis and for its currency, the US dollar, to have its position on the world stage usurped. Although Pluto does not reach this position (22° Aquarius) until 2038, in 2024, it should be clear that its days as a globally dominant currency are over.

The demise of the US dollar amongst other fiat currencies as cryptocurrency trading develops is understandable given that so many of the slow-moving planets are moving into air signs where the emphasis is on intellectual rather than physical property. History tells us that Pluto's passage through the last degrees of Capricorn in the eighteenth century, followed by Aquarius ingress, coincided with financial discontinuity.

The United States of America (USA) as we now know it was not the only area of the world to experience political upheaval in the late eighteenth century. Across the globe, those years saw widespread dissatisfaction with the ruling classes and their eventual replacement. Discontent grew, culminating in the French Revolution (1789) and the Irish Rebellion (1798) as Pluto left Aquarius. Both countries witnessed financial stress as those in power—and usually wealthy—struggled against rising tides of political change.

In 2024, indications of shifts in financial power should be felt as early as January 21. It is striking that Pluto makes Aquarius ingress as the Sun also crosses into that sign. This suggests spotlight (Sun) on Aquarian activity (political groups) and the likely dawn of a new era for governments across the world. We should anticipate that this will bring turmoil to financial markets.

Clues as to just how affected stock markets will be should be apparent in newspaper headlines the day after the alignment and three months later as the Sun moves into Taurus, then later into Leo, and three months after that into Scorpio. These fixed signs of the zodiac form a financial axis. We are likely to see headlines focused on power struggles (Pluto) between the heads of existing corporations and governments and the people they seek to serve, with a major issue being taxation (Pluto). We should also anticipate increased volatility in foreign exchange markets.

It is the transition period covering Pluto's moves from Capricorn to Aquarius that should make clear discontinuity. As a slow-moving planet crosses from one sign to another it seems that altered forces give rise to discontent. Pluto retrogrades and then returns to Capricorn between September 1 and October 11 before making final Aquarius ingress on November 19.

As Pluto returns to Capricorn, those who have been clinging to power (CEOs as well as heads of government) should be very challenged. Financial markets, which often give negative response when there is lack of certainty, are likely to move sharply. When lunar and other planetary phases are taken into account, the potential for sharp moves to the downside (which also present buying opportunity) is great.

Since the major planetary alignment of January 2020, the concept of decentralised banking has gathered momentum. We should expect this to accelerate as Pluto moves into air (ideas) sign Aquarius. We should also anticipate upheaval (Pluto) within the mutual fund (Aquarius) sectors and for there to be reduction in the apparent power of the seemingly rich, who may find it increasingly hard to hide their assets and to protect these from governmental interference. Positively, this planetary energy should also see simultaneous growth in systems built using block-chains whose power is in decentralisation.

Turmoil

The dwarf planet Haumea made final Scorpio ingress on October 3, 2023, and by the close of 2024 will have covered just 2° of that sign. Scorpio is deemed one of the more financially oriented signs of the zodiac, and key words for Haumea center on a theme of awe. These can be *awesome, awful, overwhelming, astounding, horrible, fearsome,* or *tremendous.*

With Haumea (in Scorpio) in near-exact square (90°) aspect to Pluto (in Aquarius) first on March 20 and again on August 19, we should expect crisis and a probable total rethink of financial systems—most likely through trade dispute or war. Pluto has a reputation for bringing transformation and sometimes ruthless change. The Haumea factor indicates sudden and even terrifying upheaval. Value systems should be turned upside down, with what was once deemed precious becoming worthless.

Haumea's orbit exceeds that of Pluto by just thirty-five years and, as has been described by Sue Kientz in her excellent work *More Plutos*, the two appear to be "playing tag" (2015, 30). They form a series of conjunctions over a few centuries and then spend the better part of a millennium and a half in loose opposition to one another.

The last exact squares between the two took place in the fifth century CE: encompassing the fall of the Roman Empire (Kientz 2015, n.p.). We might reasonably deduce that the square between these two planetary bodies coincides with great shifts in power base. This does not have to be violent, but will surely be distressing to those left with little as the "values crisis" takes hold.

The potential for this crisis is increased by the square aspect between another planetary pairing: the two dwarf planets Makemake and Quaoar, which reach their geocentric (as viewed from Earth) square on March 20 (coinciding with Pluto square Haumea) and July 9. They each then move on to form right angle with the Moon's nodes in early August.

Research shows that not all degrees of the zodiac are equal, with some often highlighted at times of financial stress (notably 8° and 19° of the cardinal signs of Aries, Cancer, Libra, or Capricorn).

In early August 2024, the lunar node is at 8° of Aries, with Makemake opposing this degree at 8° Libra and Quaoar at 8° Capricorn. Please note that precise dates are not available, as this would open up a discussion about mean or true node! That said, it seems reasonable to anticipate extreme volatility in the first week of August. The combination of lunar node (destiny), Makemake (environmental wisdom), and Quaoar (discovery) may be thought of as a firework display that lasts for moments but leaves lasting memories. Positively, it promises an explosion of creativity but, in the world of commerce, the announcement of several mergers and acquisitions (Aries-Libra axis), which might not be welcomed by all. (Commercial lawyers should be especially busy.)

Confusion

Neptune does not move from Pisces to Aries until 2025 but, during 2024 in late degrees of Pisces, is quincunx (150°) aspect to Haumea. Neptune is often linked with deception, confusion, idealism, fantasy, and fraud. If Haumea really does bring "a terrible gift," then it may be that the exposure of manipulation of funds (perhaps initially intended for humanitarian aid) will simultaneously expose terrible suffering and the need to have new—and safer—methods for charitable transactions.

Alarming levels of corruption will surely coincide with calls for constraints to be applied. Blame may be aimed at those working with cryptocurrencies, which a large section of the public might still think of as "emperor's new clothes." Misunderstandings, misinformation, and lack of education or access to crypto trading would leave many people vulnerable and out in the trading cold. Even experienced traders could be caught out with those who have relied solely on technical analysis, finding 2024 an exceedingly testing time.

The planetary patterns created by Neptune, Pluto, and Haumea have not been experienced in present-day traders' lifetimes. These uncharted trading waters will be alien, causing a large number of traders to at least contemplate moving to other industries whilst some trading houses collapse. The likelihood of this happening is strengthened by the influence of another planet: Uranus.

Chaos

After the Voyager 2 spaceship flew past Saturn, the brilliant NASA scientists watched the spaceship move past Uranus in 1986—at the time moving to conjoin Saturn. Astrologers across the world anticipated discoveries that would amaze astronomers. They were correct, as Uranus's poles were found to lie "off centre" and not directly opposite one another. The planet held other surprises: it spins on its axis in precisely the opposite direction to that of the other planets, fulfilling its astrological reputation for "doing things differently."

Throughout 2024, Uranus continues its transit of Taurus: a sign associated with money. Uranus's entry into Taurus in 2019 coincided with major advances in the development of cryptocurrencies and the move away from fiat currencies.

On April 20, and just after the Sun moves into that sign, Jupiter and Uranus conjoin at 21° Taurus. This planetary pairing brings sudden breakthroughs. We should anticipate exciting developments in the world of finance. That this conjunction takes place as Vesta (the asteroid often prominent in the charts of traders) is out of bounds (beyond the Sun's maximum declination) accentuates the probability of newsworthy trading activity.

Banking Crisis?

The Jupiter-Saturn conjunction of December 2020 marked the opening phase of a twenty-year business cycle. For the last two centuries, the pulse of this cycle has been regular (i.e., peaks and troughs have occurred on schedule as the two planets formed major aspect: square, trine, or opposition). There is no reason to suppose that this new cycle will be any different *except* for the fact that this latest alignment was the first of a series of Jupiter-Saturn conjunctions in air signs: a series that does not complete until 2219.

Whereas the former was an earth sign–dominated series, with the focus on tangible ownership (mainly property), this new "air sign" series brings emphasis to intellectual property and ideas.

Within financial markets, an increasing number of alternative currencies and non-fungible tokens (NFTs) have become available, mystifying many but rapidly becoming trading tools for individuals, companies, and even governments. At the time of writing, many major companies accept cryptocurrencies at point of sale. Acceleration in their use is to be expected.

In 2024, Jupiter moves through Gemini as Saturn moves through Pisces: signs at right angle to one another. Most notable is the exact square (90°) between the two planets on August 19 at 17:46 EDT. It is not abnormal for hard aspects between these two planets to coincide with bank drama. What is interesting about this square is that it is at 17° of Gemini and Pisces. In the chart for the New York Stock Exchange (NYSE), Mars lies at 17° Virgo— another of the mutable signs. Saturn will oppose the NYSE Mars as Jupiter forms square to it. The NYSE Mars has long been noted as a sensitive point (i.e., when major planets conjoin or oppose this degree, the NYSE reacts by moving sharply). (Direction determined by the planet involved.)

Analysis of Southeast Asian markets shows them tending to turn downward as Saturn moves through a mutable sign. It may be that events on the other side of the world drive US markets lower mid-August 2024. As this Jupiter-Saturn square follows on from the aforementioned lunar node, MakeMake, and Quaoar aspects, at the very least we should anticipate financial turbulence.

Cryptocurrencies

There are now thousands of crypto, digital, and alternative currencies, and it is impossible to monitor the charts of all. What can confidently be predicted is that these currencies are here to stay. Their accelerated development and expansion has correlated with major phases of the Saturn-Uranus cycle. By the next Saturn-Uranus conjunction in 2032, they will be considered the norm. Children born in 2024 will surely grow up to be amazed that paper currency was ever in operation!

Bitcoin, usually viewed as the foremost cryptocurrency, was launched in January 2009. Pluto crosses Jupiter's position in Bitcoin's chart in late December 2023. If Washington, DC is used as the location for Bitcoin's launch, then Pluto simultaneously crosses the midheaven of Bitcoin's chart.

The effect of a Pluto transit is to upend everything: exposing weaknesses and often leaving destruction in its wake. That this transit coincides with Pluto reaching another—and vital—position in Bitcoin's progressed chart suggests that Bitcoin will be in the news and that it will need to fight to keep its place as the foremost cryptocurrency. Remembering that Pluto is moving in square aspect to Haumea, any effect is likely to be headline grabbing.

Bitcoin's fifteenth birthday chart is notable for the conjunction of asteroid Hygiea with Bitcoin's natal Venus, suggesting review of Bitcoin's health and value. It may be thought by some people to have moved to "asset class." This transit follows on from Saturn (think cosmic headmaster) crossing Venus's position: usually acting as a restraining or confining influence. Were this the chart of an individual, one would wonder about difficulties with cash flow.

Bitcoin's identity is that it is a "proof of work" coin (i.e., its starting value was based on the work done to create it). Its value has grown with demand, which Saturn's transit should limit.

The majority of Bitcoin transactions come through centralized exchanges where "know-your-customer" protocols have been put into place. The net effect is that Bitcoin trades are now traceable, bringing the potential for governments to place trading restrictions on its users. Far from being an "alternative" or "open access" currency, Bitcoin traders will likely continue to lose anonymity, and by early 2024, it could be thought of as similar to the currencies we have been using. It might no longer be a "people's currency." Should this be the case, then its value would surely soar but be available to few people.

Eclipses

The two solar eclipses in 2024 are in the cardinal signs of Aries (April 8 with the Sun on the financially sensitive 19° of that sign) and Libra (October 2 with the eclipse at 10° Libra—within orb of another "super-sensitive financial degree"). These factors alone suggest that 2024 will eventually go down in annals of financial history as highly significant.

That may, in part, be due to how these two eclipses are experienced in the Americas. The arc of the April eclipse cuts through Mexico and part of the Eastern Seaboard of the United States. An interesting feature of the geodetic chart for this event is Mercury's presence on the ascendant through New York. Mercury is the planet of commerce. That planet will be retrograde on the day of the eclipse, suggesting that the effect of the eclipse may be felt before the eclipse itself. A key date is March 21, when Mercury reaches the degree of the approaching solar eclipse on April 8 Mercury—especially in Aries—suggests fast and furious trading. Coming within a day of the equinox, it is not unreasonable to think that March 20 and 21 will prove days of dramatic market activity. This won't necessarily be to the downside, though there may be many people keen to liquidate equities, which then results in falling prices. Just as the "Great American total solar eclipse" of 2017 heralded a period of political upheaval and divide in the US, so might this next eclipse: this time with Mexico playing a significant role.

A strong possibility, given that the US will be completing Pluto's return to the position it held in 1776, is that there will be trade disputes (hopefully not actual war) and that events in the political arena—and likely linked to taxation—will be a key factor in any drama.

The second eclipse will be visible in South America and prominent in Chile and Argentina. Significantly, the geodetic chart for this October eclipse places Mars on the IC through New York (Wall Street) and not far from Washington, DC. It is entirely possible that a dispute involving a company working in South America will be a factor in volatile stock market movement on Wall Street.

First Quarter

The first New Moon of 2024, on January 11, is special for two reasons: first, both the Sun and Moon are exactly square the nodes, and second, because Mercury, conjoining the Galactic Center, opposes asteroid Vesta.

We should anticipate financial drama within twenty-four hours of this lunation. The general rule is that in the twenty-four hours following the Sun squaring the nodal position, there is a short decline (buying opportunity). That the aspect is so tight indicates the likely sharpness of market moves. Given that this is the Capricorn New Moon, it is reasonable to expect that banking stocks will be in the eye of this planetary storm and that if there is a decline in stock value that it will be down to lack of investor confidence in this sector.

At the Full Moon on January 25 (12:54 EST), Jupiter (in fixed sign Taurus) is positioned midway between the Sun and Moon.

By that date, Pluto will have made Aquarius ingress which, as explained earlier, offers a very different financial background to Pluto's Capricorn transit. Where subprime mortgages were the rogues as Pluto entered Capricorn, this time it is likely to be loss of investor confidence in Aquarius sectors. These will surely include enterprises built on algorithmic analysis (including digital currencies). These sectors should move to the downside.

Jupiter has a reputation for moving sectors to the upside. Market moves that day, especially in Taurus sectors (building, land, and farming), should make the business headlines. To be clear: it is reasonable to expect that the creation of energy-efficient homes and developing bioenergetics to improve food supplies will put companies working in these areas into the spotlight. At this Full Moon, they could reach peak value.

However, the planetary picture at this Full Moon draws attention to the pending first square of the Jupiter-Pluto cycle that began in January 2020 at the dawn of the pandemic. Not only might echoes of that earlier time be heard—with possible lockdowns suggested—but the burden of taxation will likely cause much anguish to companies and individuals.

Meanwhile, with Pluto moving toward its square with Haumea (and that dwarf planet opposing Jupiter) there is very real risk of war and possible food shortage. The price of raw foods—especially cereals—is likely to rise. It is interesting to note that historically the price of sugar has reached a high as Jupiter moves through Taurus.

Just how volatile these shares are should be apparent at the next New Moon on February 9 at 17:59 EST when the Sun-Uranus aspect reaches its last quarter phase. This cycle began on May 9, 2023, reached first quarter on August 6, and reached opposition on November 13, 2023. Companies that were in the news on those few dates should be so again at this February New Moon.

Attention then moves to metaverse activity at the Full Moon on February 24 at 07:30 EST With the Pisces Sun then at the midpoint of Mercury and Saturn, talk of regulatory activity could compromise the value of major companies working in this field.

The Pisces New Moon of March 10, 2024 (05:00 EST), contains a kite formation with Saturn, also in Pisces, at its apex. Saturn can be thought of as the "cosmic headmaster": likely giving a warning signal of what lies ahead. This, together with Mercury's position at the world axis, suggests a major shift in thinking. With Pluto in Aquarius, this should be revolutionary.

Analysis shows that Asian markets tend to do least well when Saturn passes through one of the mutable signs. Investors should be prepared for turbulence in these markets especially and for the period between this New Moon and the accompanying Full Moon on March 25 (03:00 EDT) to be markedly so, as this Full Moon is also a lunar eclipse.

Mercury crosses the degree of the solar eclipse on March 21, and it may be that there is considerable movement across all indices from the equinox on March 19. When the chart for this lunar eclipse is set for London, Saturn is near exact on the descendant whilst Chiron is within orb of a critical finance degree (19° Aries)—the planetary picture suggesting a correction notably affecting the London markets on March 25.

Note that throughout the twentieth century, whenever a slow-moving planet moved across 19° of Aries, Cancer, Libra, or Capricorn, markets reacted by losing value—sometimes dramatically. With Chiron approaching the sensitive degree of 19° Aries at this lunar eclipse, correction seems more likely than not.

The conclusion of this quarter, then, could be worrying for many—especially for those in the process of purchasing annuities. Returns may not be as expected.

Second Quarter

The solar eclipse of April 8 should be another critical date for markets worldwide. Chiron is then in exact conjunction with

the Sun and Moon at 19° Aries. This echoes of the 1929 crash through the square aspect to the position held by Pluto through late October 1929. Adding to the pressure, Mars and Saturn are conjoined (within a degree of exactitude). It is reasonable to expect brakes to be applied and for indices across the world to decline.

The planetary picture is not much improved at the Full Moon later that month (April 23 at 19:49 EDT). As in February, Pluto lies midway between the Sun and Moon where it once again accents the financial axis of the zodiac. This planetary picture is indicative of large-scale moves.

With Jupiter and Uranus—both in Taurus—separated by only 1 degree at this Full Moon, a possibility is financial collaboration involving a major bank and one of the emerging alternative currencies.

The theme continues at the next New Moon, which is in Taurus on May 7 at 23.22 EDT when Uranus is positioned at the midpoint of the New Moon and Jupiter whilst Mercury is exactly aligned with Chiron. The Sun-Jupiter-Uranus combination is generally thought to bring sudden good fortune or breakthroughs whilst Mercury and Chiron in Aries allude to quick, commercial problem-solving. Investors should be on alert for companies offering alternative and fast-trading systems.

The accompanying Full Moon on May 23 at 09:53 EDT warrants especial focus. This chart, set for London, UK, shows Neptune conjoined with the Vertex—a pattern that may be indicative of fraud, whilst Venus and Jupiter are also conjoined as Mercury transits a degree held by Uranus at the Saturn-Uranus square in 2022. It is quite possible that facts will come to light exposing gross manipulation of funds.

The next New Moon on June 6 shows Venus in tight conjunction with the Sun. Investors should note which companies are launched on that date or, better still, are listed on stock markets that day, as this is a most fortunate aspect promising great wealth and success.

If those businesses relate to Gemini (travel and communications), it is likely that they will experience fast growth and deliver excellent and quick reward.

The chart for the Full Moon on June 21 at 21:08 EDT following this burst of positive stock market activity returns emphasis to currency markets and to global taxation: global because the Full Moon is within a degree of the world axis, taxation as Pluto is involved, and currencies through the opposition of Pluto to Vesta.

Third Quarter

Focus on a declining US dollar and increased volatility in currency markets is indicated at the New Moon on July 5 (18:57 EDT) when Mercury and Vesta are closely aligned. This should prove an exciting time for day (Mercury) traders (Vesta) working in either foreign exchange or the developing alternative currency markets. Other traders will likely steer clear of this volatility and turn instead to physical gold—pushing its price up temporarily.

This theme continues at the Full Moon on July 21 when it is Venus's turn to align with Vesta—again in Leo. Popular astrological thinking assumes that gold does well when Venus is traveling through Leo. However, research shows that this is not the case. (Gold does best when Venus passes through geocentric Gemini.) The alignment with Vesta in fixed sign Leo, however, may be indicative of interest in physical wealth as opposed to cryptos or non-fungible tokens (NFTs), again suggesting that the price of gold might rise, if only for a few days.

As outlined at the start of this forecast, financial drama is to be expected around the August 4 New Moon (07:13 EDT) when the lunar nodes reach 8° of cardinal signs Libra and Aries (the north node is in Libra). The spotlight then might turn to precious metals as an apparently promising safe haven for cash.

Two weeks later at the Full Moon on August 19 (14:26 EDT), asteroid Vesta is prominent again—this time conjoined with the Sun and opposing the Moon. This is an apt description of the tug-of-war between physical and digital currencies.

Then, at the next New Moon (September 2 21:56 EDT), Saturn opposes the position of Mars in the NYSE chart. We can learn much by turning back three decades to when Saturn was last moving across this degree. What we find is that this coincided with decline across all markets.

Just how aggressive the decline might be is shown in the chart for the Full Moon on September 17 at 22:34 EDT, when Mars is at right angle to the nodal axis as that planet moves through Cancer. Though Mars will also be "out of bounds," with analysis suggesting that indices tend to rise as Mars reaches maximum declination, many may feel that their assets (Cancer accumulates) are under threat and decide to liquidate holdings. This in turn would drive down prices.

Fourth Quarter

The planetary picture at the Libra solar eclipse New Moon on October 2, 14:49 EDT coincides with a grand trine formed between Mars (15° Cancer), Venus (11° Scorpio), and Saturn (16° Pisces). The blend of air (Libra) with these water signs conjures an image of a brewing storm. Mercury configures with the eclipse degree. A possibility is that trading sanctions with extreme economic penalty will be at the very least mooted if not implemented.

Two weeks later at the Full Moon on October 17 (07:26 EDT), the Sun is exactly conjoined with asteroid Juno as Chiron comes within a few degrees of the Moon. Juno is thought of as the "marriage" asteroid, and Chiron is sometimes viewed as a company doctor or auditor. A strong possibility is the active merger of a bank with a digital trading platform.

Further evidence pointing to a shake-up in the banking sector comes at the next New Moon (November 1 at 08:47 EDT) when Mars opposes Pluto exactly at 29° Cancer-Capricorn. This may be considered a "last gasp" aspect, as from then on, when Mars

opposes Pluto, it will be across the Leo-Aquarius axis. Mars versus Pluto suggests a boxing match to the finish which, coinciding as it does with Venus opposing Uranus, will likely bring unexpected consequences. That could take the form of a shock or sudden market correction at the accompanying Full Moon (November 15 at 16:28 EST), which once again has Uranus conjoined with the Moon and Chiron crossing the financially sensitive 19° of Aries.

Chiron is still on this degree at the Sagittarius New Moon on December 1 at 01:21 EST as Mars, then in Leo, is within orb of opposition to Pluto. As by this time Pluto will have made its final Aquarius ingress, it should be clear that we are entering a brave new financial world—most likely dominated by emerging currencies. Though markets may still be depressed, there should be signs of fresh shoots: enough, perhaps, to encourage previously disillusioned investors to show interest.

Mercury is stationary and turning direct at the final Full Moon of 2024 on December 15 at 04:02 EST, and this should prove the trigger moment for markets advancing into an end-of-year bull run: likely insufficient for indices to return to the position held at the start of the year but enough to tantalise with investment opportunities in 2025.

Reference

Kientz, Sue. *More Plutos*. Indianapolis, IN: Dog Ear Publishing, 2015.

New and Full Moon Forecasts for 2024

Sally Cragin

I love watching the Moon wax and wane. "There's nothing there," one thinks. But that's incorrect. In the last sixty plus years, there has actually been tons of stuff left up there—more than 400,000 pounds of "Moon junk," starting with the Soviet Union's space probe Luna 2. This 860-pound device crashed soundlessly on September 14, 1959, onto the Palus Putredinis region (Latin for "marsh of decay"), a small lunar mare (flat area) in the basin of the larger Mare Imbrium. You can't see the probe, but you can definitely discern the Mare Imbrium in the top quarter of the Moon, near the center when the Moon is full. (To be accurate, a chunk of the rocket detached, and if anyone knows where that landed, they're not telling). But Luna 2 is not the only item.

During the next decade and change, we Americans discarded seventy space vehicles, bags of trash, six American flags, two of Alan Shepard's golf balls, and, of course, dozens if not hundreds of footprints made by the twelve men who jumped, skipped, hopped, and trotted along the surface. However, consider this: despite those relatively recent visits, the Moon is the one object that every human being who has ever lived on this planet has in common.

Yes, everyone. From King Tut, to Sophocles, to Jesus and the Virgin Mary, to Genghis Khan, to George Washington, to Jane Austen, to Harriet Tubman, to your parents, and now you. All of us have gazed at the Moon in awe and admiration. And every generation does its best to interpret what it means when the Moon gets a shadow across its surface or when it's fully lit.

An easy method for considering what you should do and what you should plan is this: the New Moon to Full Moon is for growth; the Full Moon to New Moon is for releasing. And for those who enjoy a closer examination, consider the following: During the time of the New Moon to first quarter, look to build, emerge, or grow a project. Next is the first quarter to Full Moon. That's when you want to accelerate, expand, enlarge into things. During the Full Moon to the last quarter, focusing, narrowing, and consolidating should become easier. And then the last quarter to New Moon is a time of increasing quiet and diminution of stimuli. Think about simplifying, removing, refining.

The New and Full Moons at a Glance for 2024

For each entry, all signs are mentioned, with a focus on the sign who is the subject of the New or Full Moon. Remember that the New Moon is always in the same sign as the Sun, and the Full Moon is in the opposite sign. So, Sun in Capricorn means Full Moon in Cancer; Sun in Aquarius means Full Moon in Leo, and so on.

Thursday, January 11, New Moon in Capricorn

With Mars also in Capricorn (January 4 through February 13), everyone is likely to be a little more defensive—and just plain stubborn—than usual. Pay attention to details, including those regarding finance, as well as the parts of your body that move (knees, elbows, and wrists). Capricorn: you have begun a six-week interval in which others seek you out—not just because you know how to do something, but because you're a rock star! Look back to midsummer 2023. Have you moved along a challenge that emerged then? Aries, Libra, Leo, Gemini, and Cancer: others may try to rile you up, or money problems could be an unwelcome distraction. Scorpio, Sagittarius, Aquarius, Pisces, Taurus, and Virgo: a slower pace gets you where you need to be faster.

Thursday, January 25, Full Moon in Leo

This Full Moon says, "Lighten up." You may crave food you loved when you were a child (does that mean bowls of sugar cereal while binge-watching a favorite TV show?). In any event, serving our appetites takes precedence. Leo rules—and fuels—the fifth house of children, fabulous hairstyles, the heart, laughter, and public relations, and this Full Moon should temporarily banish winter blahs. Leo: it's time to shine and to be listened to. Behave with dignity rather than fury, and you'll get everything you want. Capricorn, Pisces, Taurus, Scorpio, and Aquarius: it's easy to misstep and misspeak. What you hear may not be the whole story. Gemini, Cancer, Virgo, Libra, Sagittarius, and Aries: your social side must be indulged—a great time for friend-making and improving.

Friday, February 9, New Moon in Aquarius

Spirituality and innovation beckon. If you do a task the way it's always been done, frustration can occur through the weekend. Aquarius: ask for what you want; you're sure to get it—even if it wasn't the color or style you thought you adored. Be patient with others—your mind is moving faster than those of the rest of us. Cancer, Virgo, Taurus, Scorpio, and Leo: this Moon may find you ambivalent about everything but spending money on whims. Sagittarius, Capricorn, Pisces, Aries, Libra, and Gemini: if you need to reverse course, do so. Ditto if you need to simplify your life by removing someone (or something) from your daily interactions.

Saturday, February 24, Full Moon in Virgo

Health, work, and service to others is the virgin's terrain, and this Full Moon finds Virgo at peak capability. Questioning systems (or having insights into more efficient and healthy habits) makes sense right now. However, Saturn, the planet of limitations, is far from this Moon, which could bring an unwelcome feeling of thwartedness. Your focus should be on what others need (to help you along). Virgo: reflect on your previous New Moon (September 2023). What moved forward or improved? Think about taking things to the next level. Taurus, Capricorn, Leo, Libra, Cancer, and Scorpio: be exacting about what you want and what you need. It's a fine time to improve a health practice (extra reps, miles, or veggies!). Sagittarius, Pisces, Gemini, Aries, and Aquarius: your temper could flare, which could put you in the position of needing to "beg pardon." Better to isolate from others than let them push your buttons.

Sunday, March 10, New Moon in Pisces

Indecisiveness or heavy feelings could erupt during this New Moon. Do not rush into anything new. The sign of the fish rules the twelfth house (endings, hidden places, the emotionally satisfying arts of music, photography, and dance), so you may want to waltz with yourself (Pisces rules the feet) in a darkened room—or in a darkened room with hundreds of others. Pisces: resist "pleasing others" right now, especially if you're feeling more sensitive than usual. It's okay to isolate. And as of March 22, you embark on a six-week interval in which Mars conjuncts your Sun sign, making you irresistible to others who need a leader, lover, or confidant. Scorpio, Cancer, Aries, Taurus, Aquarius, and Capricorn: start a project that could have alternate outcomes—this is not the time for a "straight shot"; rather, the "long and winding road." Gemini, Virgo, Sagittarius, Leo, and Libra: your insight into others could lead you into thinking you know what's best.

Monday, March 25, Full Moon in Libra

The sign of partnerships plus spring fever finds us wanting to connect deeply with one another. Venus has moved into sensitive Pisces, which transforms casual conversations into enjoyable but emotional interactions. This Full Moon brings social urges. If there are friends or family members you haven't seen for a long time, check in now. Libra: reflect on mid-September 2023. What person or project emerged in your life, and where is that relationship or endeavor now? This Full Moon brings needed clarity and simplicity. Gemini Aquarius, Scorpio, Virgo, Sagittarius, and Leo: finding the middle ground, which isn't usually your jam, comes

more easily than usual. Capricorn, Aries, Cancer, Pisces, and Taurus: talk is cheap, and you may be impatient with those less articulate than yourself. And then you'll miss some vital information. Take time to listen.

Monday, April 8, New Moon in Aries

You have to adore the nimble-footed ram who trots fearlessly up the hill, full of confidence. Though New Moons can bring tentative feelings, this Aries Moon can bring a fanfare of "look at me!" behavior from folks in touch with their "inner child." With Mercury continuing its retrograde (through April 24), technology might not function as well as one would like. Hold off on firm decisions until later in the month. Aries: that desire for new stimulation or comrades is strong. The folks you meet now or the projects you begin could teach you a lot in the next six months. But what do you want to learn? Leo, Sagittarius, Taurus, Gemini, Aquarius, and Pisces: take big chances and trust your gut. Capricorn, Libra, Cancer, Virgo, and Scorpio: irritability is close to the surface—don't get caught in other folks' cross fire.

Tuesday, April 23, Full Moon in Scorpio

Scorpio rules the sex organs, death, and "other people's money." Secrets, intrigue, and romantic heat coming to a boil are likely with this Full Moon. With Jupiter (generosity) opposing the Moon, others might be petty, particularly about financial matters. Scorpio: no one can say no to you, but are you asking the right questions? Reflect back on the month of your birthday in 2023. Who turned up with new opportunities? Now ask yourself, "Did they pan out?" Cancer, Pisces, Sagittarius, Capricorn, Libra, and Virgo: your sharp eyes (and sharper comments) take others aback. Taurus, Leo, Aquarius, Gemini, and Aries: gullibility could be a danger. Don't be taken in.

Tuesday, May 7, New Moon in Taurus

The sign of the bull is easy to underestimate. Tauruses are always more complicated than they seem, and their preoccupations involving security, loyalty, and fiduciary partnerships are strong. This New Moon brings excellent astrological aspects for all kinds of investments or home beautification. With Jupiter (the planet of generosity and taking a chance) also in Taurus, the urge for luxury is strong. Taurus: if last November and December was a period of soul-searching, the answers you hoped for then should be close at hand. Virgo, Capricorn, Gemini, Cancer, Aries, and Pisces: make a point to appreciate beauty—in a garden center or on a gallery wall. Libra, Scorpio, Leo, Aquarius, and Sagittarius: you could be annoyed by others who are strong willed. Don't think you need to say something just because another is provocative.

Thursday, May 23, Full Moon in Sagittarius

Social excitement is in the works as Mars (planet of action) is in fiery Aries and Jupiter moves into Gemini (more on that in the next entry). Friendships among folks who are very different at first glance find traction. As Sagittarius rules education, beneficence, philosophy, and justice, stick with folks who can teach you things. Sagittarius: look back in your calendar (if you bother to keep one!) as this Full Moon brings a project or relationship that began in your birth month to a culmination. Leo, Aries, Libra, Scorpio, Capricorn, and Aquarius: exercise and laughter will keep you in tune with the Moon. Gemini, Virgo, Pisces, Cancer, and Taurus: if others are "loosey-goosey" about promptness or other work matters, be careful you don't overreact.

Thursday, June 6, New Moon in Gemini

Jupiter rules "benevolent patriarchy" along with "extended education," which is appropriate for the month celebrating dads and grads, as Jupiter got into alignment with the Gemini sun recently. (The last time Jupiter was in the sign of the twins was 2012 to

2013.) If you've just collapsed on the academic finishing line, diploma in hand, congratulations, but current planetary alignments suggest that more education will seek you out! Gemini: few people can resist your intensity and forward thinking—this is your time to shine. Aquarius, Libra, Taurus, Aries, Cancer, and Leo: you may be at a low ebb with energy, but networking pays off big during this lunar phase. Sagittarius, Virgo, Pisces, Capricorn, and Scorpio: you may have difficulty getting "the whole story." Ask folks to repeat themselves so you understand.

Friday, June 21, Full Moon in Capricorn

You know how goats are always pictured clambering atop rocks in an intimidating terrain? Difficult paths could be the story for many folks this month, and particularly Capricorn. Doing things "the hard way" is an easy choice for too many folks. Capricorn: we depend on you to be, well, dependable, but this Full Moon could find you darting in different directions. Usually, you identify with the relentlessly dedicated Wile E. Coyote, but the Road Runner is your animal spirit this month. (Beep! Beep! And off you go!) Leo, Aries, Libra, Scorpio, Sagittarius, and Aquarius: Do a little more research if there's some matter that's emerged in the past six months. Virgo, Pisces, Gemini, Taurus, and Cancer: self-righteousness or "bossiness" from others could spark your irritability. Don't stay in the same place for long. Do: focus on exercise that uses your legs or tools that take you places quickly (the shortcut you found, for example). Don't: move too quickly or think those cool new shoes are designed for running—Capricorn Moons are for putting one foot (carefully) in front of another.

Friday, July 5, New Moon in Cancer

Water sign Moons bring deep feelings welling up, which artists can use as fuel but that may leave the rest of us with a trembling lower lip. Recommended activities include cooking (particularly tried-and-true favorite dishes) and gardening (no, it's not too

late). Cancer: July 12–15 is a good time to improve your professional skills—or to request privileges you deserve. Look ahead to
December 2024. What can you do now to improve your position
then? Scorpio, Pisces, Gemini, Taurus, Leo, and Virgo: your loyalty
matters right now, and you may be surprised by how fondly others
feel about you. Libra, Capricorn, Aries, Sagittarius, and Aquarius:
be cautious about how you speak to others who may be in a
subordinate social or business position—feeling "dissed" is like a
virus going around.

Sunday, July 21, Full Moon in Capricorn

Warm-weather Full Moons coupled with late sunsets can be
romantic as well as a great time for family bonding. And Capricorn, which rules over joints and structures for our lunar phase,
could prompt all of us to look more carefully at our own atti-
tudes about routine—if you like a "tight ship," this phase is your
heaven. Capricorn: look back to last December and see whether
problematic situations resolved themselves naturally. If the gam-
ble you took paid off, take another one this month. Taurus, Virgo,

Aquarius, Pisces, Sagittarius, and Scorpio: A slow and stately pace is indicated—so is planning ahead. Homebodies might look at the bumper crop of berries and wonder how hard it is to set up fruit for canning. Libra, Cancer, Aries, Leo, and Gemini: Usually you have such lovely people skills, but you could find your inner brat leaping to the table.

Sunday, August 4, New Moon in Leo

What a cheerful and good-natured New Moon we have—a Moon that tells you to dig deep into joys that charmed you as a kid. From now through the Full Moon on August 19, Mars and Jupiter are in harmony in Gemini, so it's an excellent time for eloquence in all kinds of writing (from poetry, to code, to memos). However, Mercury retrograde means you better buff up your proofreading skills! Leo: your persuasive abilities are never better—others look to you to lead. Sagittarius, Aries, Virgo, Libra, Gemini, and Cancer: if you're having a difficult time "fixing" on one activity, relationship, or project, it's because this New Moon is telling you to entertain more options. Scorpio, Aquarius, Taurus, Capricorn, and Pisces: resentments could come easily—too easily, especially through miscommunication.

Monday, August 19, Full Moon in Aquarius

The sign of the water carrier asks us all to look outside of ourselves. What behavior or companion makes you a better person? Since this is our third Full Moon of four in the summer season, it is also known as a "Blue Moon." Activities you might do "once in a Blue Moon" include prioritizing your hopes, dreams, and concerns for humanity. This Full Moon can illuminate "angels among us," along with the space cadets who fell to Earth. Aquarius: with Mars now conjunct with Jupiter in Gemini, you can persuade anyone of anything. Libra, Gemini, Capricorn, Sagittarius, Pisces, and Aries: nostalgia has no place in your day—look to new technology to make you more efficient. Taurus, Scorpio, Leo, Virgo, and Cancer: are you feeling tetchy around others who don't share your steady dependability? Ask yourself, "Are they annoying me because they mean to, or am I annoyed because I can't accept how different they are from me?"

Monday, September 2, New Moon in Virgo

If you've had a good summer but are itchy to return to your routine at work, this phase of the Moon will focus you on business and best practices. Although a nagging perfectionism could accompany this New Moon, it's survivable, particularly if you discover more efficient methods of doing simple tasks. Virgo rules the lower digestion, so take no chances on fancy food or fussy ingredients. Virgo: the spring equinox brought some changes; are things improving now? This lunar phase is not a time to be shy—speak your piece, and if you have ideas for efficiency or innovation, share with confidence. Libra, Leo, Cancer, Scorpio, Capricorn, and Taurus: this is a fine time to look for a new position, particularly one involving short projects accomplished quickly. Sagittarius, Pisces, Gemini, Aries, and Aquarius: words meant kindly could be heard as petty—use a soft voice.

Tuesday, September 17, Full Moon in Pisces

This is our fourth Full Moon of the season, and since Pisces rules the feet, you may want to stroll under this beautiful big Moon (a Supermoon!). From now through the end of the month, many planets in water signs suggests that soul-searching and secret-sharing will be an urge indulged by many. However, this Moon might also afflict those who are depressed or anxious—be patient. Pisces: you may have difficulties focusing because others desire your attention (and approval). Retreat from codependence and make time for yourself by reflecting on spring events, projects, or relationships that eased your life. Did you start a healthy habit? Does it continue? Scorpio, Cancer, Aquarius, Capricorn, Aries, and Taurus: your insights into others—including your willingness to work hard right now—will bring a career boost. Virgo, Sagittarius, Gemini, Libra, and Leo: anxiety and paranoia may be on the menu with this Moon for you—none of these feelings are permanent.

Wednesday, October 2, New Moon in Libra

The scales keep everything "even Stephen," and Libra's occupation of the seventh house governs partnerships and public relations. Is there someone new arriving at your workplace? Or are you the new person? Libra helps us all to be diplomats if we listen to its guidance. Libra: from now through early November, others may try to dissuade you from a path you've chosen. Don't let them, and if you need to spend a little more money this month to make your life more comfortable, please do. Aquarius, Gemini, Leo, Virgo, Scorpio, and Sagittarius: others want to hear your opinion, so if you're on the fence about an important matter, use friends as a sounding board. Capricorn, Cancer, Aries, Pisces, and Taurus: getting swept away by something that looks pretty good (but needs closer scrutiny) is a hazard.

Thursday, October 17, Full Moon in Aries

September can be leisurely, but this Aries Full Moon that comes when the Sun is in Libra reminds us that the sands in the annual hourglass are running out and that the seriousness of autumn (back to school, elections imminent) is at hand. Since Aries symbolizes the head, you may need a new haircut, hat, striking new hair band, or even a fascinator! Aries: you will want to do it all—I mean everything—and this Full Moon can help you achieve those goals. Leo, Sagittarius, Taurus, Gemini, Pisces, and Aquarius: look for new relationships and projects, especially those that are targeted to last for six months. Libra, Cancer, Capricorn, Virgo, and Scorpio: "impulse control" is your friend, because others are irksome. Make sure you eat sensibly to keep your body in equilibrium!

Friday, November 1, New Moon in Scorpio

After Libra's emphasis on partnership last month, this Scorpio Moon challenges you to think about your self-sufficiency. Partnerships that had been sailing smoothly may hit rough winds. And with Mercury retrograde, missed communication could be a factor. Some folks will be able to stand up for themselves, but later in the month, their comments could come off as arrogant or misinformed. Scorpio: Mars in Leo is putting roadblocks in your forward motion. Be very cautious this month about legal matters or those involving children and public relations. How can you improve on matters that emerged in May 2024? Cancer, Pisces, Virgo, Libra, Sagittarius, and Capricorn: this Full Moon could turn you into a detective, able to ask the right questions. Taurus, Leo, Aquarius, Aries, and Gemini: social awkwardness could be a danger. Find out whether business casual or semiformal is required.

Friday, November 15, Full Moon in Taurus

Acquisition is the theme with this lunar phase, and with the holidays looming, you may consider deep-sixing that charge card and cancelling the Amazon app. Taurus rules the throat, so singing (or enjoying vocal music) could bring joy (plus there are plenty of amazing Taurus singers—from James Brown to Kelly Clarkson). Taurus: you can speak soothingly to the most riled-up folks in your circle, and your new ideas are worth pursuing. Just take a look back to your birthday and ask yourself, "Am I where I need to be?" Virgo, Capricorn, Pisces, Aries, Gemini, and Cancer: home beautification brings enormous joy. Leo, Scorpio, Aquarius, Libra, and Sagittarius: others may perceive judgment or criticism in what comes out of your mouth. Cultivate your smile instead.

Sunday, December 1, New Moon in Sagittarius

This New Moon could find you attracted to someone with an exciting life, hobby, or profession. Sagittarius New Moons also

prompt our sense of "fairness," as the ninth house oversees higher education, philosophy, and long-distance travel. Sagittarius: this is a fortunate time for you, despite the ups and downs of 2024. Mars (planet of taking action) in fiery Leo will make childish pursuits more appealing to many of us. Scorpio, Libra, Virgo, Capricorn, Pisces, and Cancer: deep feelings need to be explored—now's the time. Taurus, Aries, Gemini, Leo, and Aquarius: foot in mouth is a danger. No one needs to know everything you think right now.

Sunday, December 15, Full Moon in Gemini

Jupiter, the planet of generosity, is halfway through its orbit in Gemini, and now that it is syncing up with the Full Moon, pretty much everyone is going to feel like "I have to write my memoirs!" Communication is intoxicating, but remember, those "twins" are staring in two directions. Are you feeling torn about which way to turn? Don't let others underestimate your ability to multitask. Gemini: if your career or personal life took a turn in June, this Full Moon should illuminate how successful decisions you made then have turned out to be. Make sure the people who need to know how fabulous you are hear about how fabulous you are! Aquarius, Libra, Taurus, Aries, Cancer, and Leo: step lightly, and push yourself to the max. Sagittarius, Pisces, Virgo, Scorpio, and Capricorn: situations could get complicated—not by you, but by individuals or circumstances that arise in this interval. Hold off on taking action.

Monday, December 30, New Moon in Capricorn

Party people would prefer a Full Moon at the year's end, but this New Moon in Capricorn is excellent for tending to tenth house matters such as careers, responsibility, dependability, and structures. Over the generations, the glorious fish tail that originally adorned Capricornus has disappeared, but it's still there in spirit! Capricorn: leap with all your might, and start enormous projects—the stars are with you. Taurus, Virgo, Aquarius, Sagittarius, Scorpio, and Pisces: if you've had enough of the holiday, jump back into your favorite preoccupations. Libra, Cancer, Aries, Leo, and Gemini: you might get a touch of the blues or strike others as upset over some matter that is truly trifling. If you need to hole up to rest up, get to it.

References

"Luna 2." NASA Space Sience Data Coordinated Archive. NASA. Accessed October 12, 2022. https://nssdc.gsfc.nasa.gov/nmc /spacecraft/display.action?id=1959-014A#:~:text=Luna%202%20 was%20the%20second,%2C%20Archimedes%2C%20and%20 Autolycus%20craters.

"Luna 02." NASA. Updated September 13, 2021. Accessed October 11, 2022. https://solarsystem.nasa.gov/missions/luna-02/in-depth/ (page discontinued).

"What Do You Wonder?" NASA. Accessed October 12, 2022. https:// moon.nasa.gov/inside-and-out/top-moon-questions/.

Zeidan, Adam. "What Have We Left on the Moon?" Encyclopedia Britannica. Accessed October 12, 2022. https://www.britannica.com /story/what-have-we-left-on-the-moon.

2024
Moon Sign Book
Articles

Inviting Invertebrates

Lupa

If you consider yourself a nature lover, what first comes to mind when you're extolling the virtues of the natural world? Maybe the first thing you think of is adorable baby mammals and birds in springtime, or perhaps it's the deep, green world of plants that captures your imagination. These are certainly easy for us to love and appreciate, but they aren't the whole of nature by far.

Now think about parts of nature you may be less thrilled with. If you've ever had a run-in with poison oak, poison sumac, or poison ivy, the urushiol oil on their leaves may have left you with a nasty rash. Venomous snakes may be difficult for some people to feel comfortable around, especially if they happen to show up in your yard. And while charismatic "bugs" like bumblebees, butterflies, and dragonflies have their fans, it's harder to find cheerleaders for ants, spiders, or ticks.

Yet from an ecological perspective, every single one of the living beings on this planet is important, regardless of our personal feelings about them. Each species may have evolved with its ecosystem for millions of years, carving out a niche complete with many interdependencies with other species of animal, plant, fungus, and microbe. As humanity has spent the past few centuries in particular wreaking ever-growing devastation upon the planet, these relationships within ecosystems have been severed, sometimes permanently.

The result? Everything from trophic cascades that cause an entire food web to collapse when key species go extinct, to migration of remaining species into new lands where they may not fit as well, to habitat loss that can cause further extinctions. We ourselves are increasingly at risk as ecological degradation tied to ecosystem collapse threatens our water, food, and even air. And we could find ourselves facing more pandemics of zoonotic diseases as wildlife carrying them venture closer to humans because they have nowhere to go.

What are we to do about all this? There are many people around the world seeking to solve ecological problems locally, regionally, or even globally using a variety of tools and tactics. From planting more native plants to pushing for stronger pollution laws, these nature lovers are putting their love into action on behalf of every species on the planet—not just our own.

The Importance of "Creepy-Crawlies"

"Every species" includes the millions of species of insects, arachnids, crustaceans, and other invertebrates still found on Earth. Though most are quite small, they outnumber us many times over. And they are absolutely crucial to the continuation of life both on the land and in fresh- and saltwater ecosystems. Without invertebrates, life as we know it would cease to exist and would likely collapse back into largely unicellular forms. No more mammals, birds, or plants, and no more mosquitoes, copperheads, or tarantulas.

This often comes as a shock to many people. But invertebrates fill an immense number of ecological roles in every ecosystem they're in. Some species are pollinators, making sure that four out of every five flowering plants—including over a third of our food plants—continue to exist. Others are detritivores that help to break down carrion, feces, and other decaying matter, recycling the nutrients therein and minimizing the risk of disease transmission to other beings. Invertebrates aerate and even create our soil.

Perhaps most importantly, invertebrates are (ironically) the backbone of the food web. Many, many mammals, birds, reptiles, amphibians, and fish would starve to death if there were no invertebrates to eat. Invertebrates are also important predators on their own, either of animals (usually other invertebrates) or of plants, and in doing so they keep their prey species from overpopulating.

Let's take a good example promoted most famously by ecologist Douglas Tallamy. He points out that 96 percent of terrestrial bird species in North America need substantial amounts of insects to feed their young (Tallamy 2007, 24). And the best source of insect protein is a nice, soft caterpillar. Not only is that caterpillar chowing down on its host plants and keeping them from overgrowing, but if a bird manages to snatch it up to feed to its young, it's transferring the nutrients in the plant to the baby bird through its own body. The birds wouldn't be able to just eat the same plants directly, and even if they could eat the same weight in berries, they'd be missing those nutritional components that the caterpillar has. (We'll revisit caterpillars later on, so remember this story.)

Eek! A Bug!

Okay, so maybe you can find a fat, colorful caterpillar to be cute in its own way, and you're a little more inclined to tolerate its presence because even if it doesn't feed those adorable baby birds you like so much, it will eventually turn into a beautiful butterfly or a mysterious moth. But think about your reaction when you see a spider, centipede, or fly. For a lot of people, the first response is to smash the little critter even if it's not doing anyone any harm.

This even includes people who understand the ecological importance of invertebrates. To an extent, we can't help it. Deep in our ancestry there have been so many experiences where a human encountered a spider or other "bug" and got bitten or otherwise harmed; the same, incidentally, goes for snakes even though they have backbones. It's not necessarily a voluntary reaction, and it can cause alarm bells to go off in our brains. In extreme cases, this can even manifest as phobias associated with certain animals.

Does that mean we're stuck with that reaction forever? Nope. With time and effort, it is possible to override it. For myself, I've found it's a combination of consciously replacing fear with curiosity whenever I see an invertebrate that sparks that panic in me, and continuing to learn more of the cool facts and natural history about these little animals so that I see them as whole beings who are as worthy of being on this planet as I am. I deliberately look for invertebrates during the warm months, and I try to catalog every one I see through my account on iNaturalist, a free app on my phone. Through this constant desensitization, I've gotten to the point where I only very, very rarely ever react with fear, and that's usually because I've suddenly found an unexpected "guest" on my skin. Once I realize what's happened, I simply escort my guest to a more appropriate place in or around my home.

Mind that I say "appropriate." Any invertebrate that you put outside on a cold night is going to freeze to death. Their counterparts that are hibernating found a safe shelter to do so when it was warmer, and the one you put outside isn't going to have enough time to find a similar niche before it dies. If you don't want them in your living quarters, consider a quiet corner of the basement or garage instead, perhaps under a sheltered area. It's still a big risk of them dying, but they have a better chance at least. Also, most of the spiders you find in your home are specifically adapted to indoor settings; they don't just come inside when it's cold. Putting them outside at any time could mean death because they aren't able to handle significant temperature changes, being more suited for the constant temperatures found indoors.

Making the Ecological More Important Than the Personal

And this is one way to start learning to shift your priorities. Whether someone is squashing a bug because they don't want it in their house or relocating one to a place likely to kill them just a little slower or spraying a garden with pesticides, most of our interactions with invertebrates place our preferences over theirs at the cost of their lives. In fact, most of the damage we've done to the planet has been for our convenience and without any consideration for the impact on other beings (to include our fellow humans).

When I decide to let spiders take up long-term residence in my windowsills, I'm not just thinking about the benefit to me in terms of them keeping flies and other insects in control. I am also deliberately thinking about what the spiders need, weighing that against any minor discomfort I may feel at their presence, and determining that their need is more important. It is a conscious act to factor in other living beings in my decisions, especially those that are often ignored or even openly persecuted by other humans. It benefits them, it benefits me, and it benefits the local ecosystem in a variety of ways.

The more times I make this conscious choice, the more automatic it becomes in my decision-making in the future. Do I always put other beings first? Of course not. I am working to transform my yard into a native plant garden, so the non-native grasses, the sheep sorrel, and the bittercress have to go (though I keep a small number of purple foxglove because the native bumblebees love the flowers.) I will kill ticks I find on me, partly out of reflex. And I've probably eaten more than a few teensy spiders and other invertebrates as I've grazed raspberries and blueberries off the bushes.

Still, the very act of considering other beings is seemingly radical in the Western world. And why not start with some of the ones that are considered hardest to love, especially when we increasingly understand just how intrinsically valuable they are, both as individual beings and as members of their ecological community?

Ways to Help Invertebrates

If I've done my job well, by now you're wondering what you can do to aid these misunderstood little animals. None of us can save the world on our own, but we can make some changes that will at least help our corner of it a bit more.

First and foremost, keep educating yourself about invertebrates and why they're important. A great place to get started is the Xerces Society for Invertebrate Conservation. Based in Portland, Oregon, but working globally, they have a wealth of articles and other resources on their website at http://www.xerces.org. While they certainly advocate for charismatic butterflies, bees, and other pollinators because they're easier to get support for, they also focus on ways that help other invertebrates too, both terrestrial and aquatic.

For instance, one of the leading threats to invertebrates after habitat loss is the overuse of pesticides. Between the 1980s when I was a kid happily exploring the invertebrate biodiversity in my backyard and now, the use of pesticides has grown exponentially. The numbers of invertebrates have dropped in the same time period. These chemicals don't discriminate against the target insects and other invertebrates, and other lawn and agricultural chemicals are a problem too. Not only can some of them directly kill terrestrial invertebrates, they can harm or kill aquatic invertebrates when rain washes them into storm drains and waterways. And that, of course, affects whatever preys on those invertebrates. (If you've noticed a drop in fireflies, by the way, you can thank lawn chemicals for killing the invertebrates that firefly larvae eat while living their first two years underground.)

By stopping the use of these products and urging others to do the same, you can make a big positive impact on your local invertebrates. You also model a way of living that respects these living beings and takes your ecological community into account. That way it's not just you who's being educated about invertebrates, but those you share this information with as well.

Creating an Invertebrate Oasis

If you want to go a step further, you can deliberately create invertebrate habitat! Even if you have a very small yard, if you're able to make changes to it, you can make an important living space for insects, spiders, and more.

The most low-effort addition you can make is adding native plants to your yard and garden. An increasing number of nurseries carry or even specialize in ready-to-plant species that are native to your area. While some people may find planting from seeds challenging, adding in some starts that are already well-established in their nursery pots is an easier option. Just pick a suitable area of your yard where they'll get the right amount of sun or shade and won't get trampled on, and get them planted in! Don't worry about tilling or turning the soil; that actually does more damage by upsetting the many delicate layers of soil microbiomes. If you want, keep the non-native plants around your natives trimmed short so they're less competitive.

If you have more time, energy, and other resources, you may consider a more extensive habitat restoration. For instance, if you have a patch of grass lawn you'd like to convert, cover it over with black plastic or layers of cardboard for at least a couple of seasons—the longer, the better. That will kill off the grass underneath and keep seeds from sprouting back. You may need to research the best time to uncover it and add in your native plants; seeds are often best in fall, but starts in spring. If you have a county extension office or a Master Gardeners group in your area, they may be able to give you more advice.

If all you have is a tiny garden bed or a balcony with some pots, that's okay! You can still help your local invertebrates with some native plants! Winged pollinators may fly by for a sip of nectar, and spiders can catch flies in the gaps between leaves and branches. And the more people who create these little native gardens, especially in urban areas, the more the patchwork quilt of microhabitats comes together—what Tallamy refers to as "Home-grown National Park" (Tallamy 2020, 62).

If you are in the United States and want to know what native plants will help the most butterflies and moths in particular, check out the Native Plant Finder at https://www.nwf.org/NativePlantFinder. Created by the National Wildlife Federation and based on Tallamy's research, it allows you to find the most pollinator-supportive plants in your zip code.

Remember our caterpillar earlier? While adult pollinators may be able to visit many species of flower, most herbivorous insects—including caterpillars—can only eat a very narrow range of plants, in some cases as few as one or two species. This is because every plant has its own chemical composition, and some of those chemicals are designed to keep them from being eaten. Capsaicin, which makes hot peppers hot, and our beloved caffeine are two examples of these chemicals; while we super-omnivore humans have adapted to eat these and many more, most of our insect neighbors have only been able to work their way around a few chemicals in native plants that they've evolved alongside for millennia. By replacing inedible non-native plants with native ones, we make a little more food and shelter for our local invertebrates, and for the other animals, plants, and living beings that they have interrelationships with.

And that, to me, is a wonderful reason to break out of our self-centered approach to nature, embrace the creepy-crawlies to the best of our abilities, and invite invertebrates into our lives.

References

Tallamy, Douglas W. *Bringing Nature Home: How You Can Sustain Wildlife with Native Plants*. Portland, OR: Timber Press, 2007.

Tallamy, Douglas W. *Nature's Best Hope: A New Approach to Conservation That Starts in Your Yard*. Portland, OR: Timber Press, 2020.

The Perpetual Grocery Store

Penny Kelly

There is nothing that gives you a greater sense of security and self-sufficiency than planting a garden and growing some of your own food. Even if you've never planted anything in your life, you will be surprised at how successful you can be with a garden. Given the rising prices of food, anything you can grow will not only help your wallet, but you will also find that homegrown foods taste much better and last much longer than store-bought.

In 1970, depending on where you lived, a loaf of bread cost $0.22, hamburger was $0.70 per pound, and coffee was about $1.25 per pound. Today a decent loaf of bread runs from $4.50–$6.00 a loaf, hamburger is about $7.00–$8.00 per pound, and a bag of coffee is going for $8.00–$9.00 at the supermarket. Although it's not possible for many people to raise wheat, beef, or coffee, anything you can do to add nutrition to your diet and reduce the bill at the grocery store is a good idea. One of the best ways to do this is to plant a garden.

Getting Organized

Start with a list of what you'd like to grow and a survey of how much space you have. If space is limited, plan to train your plants *up* by using trellising. Be sure to choose a spot that gets an absolute minimum of eight hours of sun every day—ten to twelve hours is much better. If you live where there are lots of rabbits and deer, think about how to protect your plants from these friendly raiders, who will take the attitude that you have just served up a delicious smorgasbord of tasty greens for their dining pleasure!

Once you have settled on a spot, it's time to get your seeds and seedling plants. Back in the 1940s, a packet of seeds cost $0.10 and might have one hundred to two hundred seeds in it. Fifty cents might have gotten you a two-pound bag of seeds! Today, seeds cost $3.50–$5.50 for a packet that might have only forty seeds in it. Depending on the type of seeds, there might be only twelve or fifteen seeds in the packet! With germination rates at 50 percent to 80 percent, clearly seeds are some of the most expensive garden supplies you will buy.

Think about Seeds for Next Year

Given the cost of seeds, it would be a good idea to make a serious effort to collect seeds from what you grow. Before you plant, there are a couple things to consider if you undertake such an effort. The first thing to be aware of is that a seed is an intelligent, living system. When you put it in the soil, it assesses not only the mineral and carbon composition of the soil, but also the amount of water available, how much sun there is, how much carbon dioxide is available, the range of temperatures it must cope with, the amount of fungus and bacteria in the soil, how much electrical energy is moving through the topsoil, and how loose or tightly packed the soil is. It is responding to all of this information, and, when the mother plant begins to produce its progeny, those seeds will have been encoded with all of the information collected in order to give her offspring the absolute best chance for survival when it is their turn to grow and produce.

The less time and energy a seed has to spend coping with its environment, the faster it will germinate. Not only that, the root mass will be bigger, it will cope with bacteria and fungus much more successfully, its fruits will be more nutritious and flavorful, and the crop it produces will be earlier—sometimes as much as two weeks—as well as considerably more abundant. It doesn't matter whether you are talking about lettuce, radishes, and carrots, or beans, corn, and melon. The difference is quite amazing.

While it's easy to let a few zucchinis get overgrown and produce excellent seeds, it's a little trickier to get viable seeds from plants that are densely nutritious and promote excellent health like cabbage, kohlrabi, carrots, beets, onions, and garlic. The cabbage, kohlrabi, carrots, beets, and onions are biennials, which means they have to stay in the ground, unpicked, for the entire gardening season and winter. The next spring, when it warms up, they will send out flowers and begin the process of making seeds. This will take most of that second gardening season.

Over many years of gardening, I have tried many different garden layouts in my attempts to set aside this or that plant in order to collect seeds from it. Sometimes I would start out well: the plants would come up, and I would note the ones I wanted to save, but then a couple weeks later, I would forget which ones I had targeted! Other times, someone else would be working in the garden who had no idea that I had my eye on one or two special plants and had deliberately left these unpicked. They would pick what I was saving and throw it aside as overgrown and no longer edible. Other times, rabbits or deer would come along and make a meal of what I was trying to save. One year, my husband decided to till the garden early when I was away on a business trip. I came home to find shredded cabbage, beets, and carrots where my precious seeds had been anticipated. Another year, I managed to be out there when the tilling was happening, but it was clear that trying to go around this or that plant was a nightmare for my neighbor who was driving the tractor and trying to follow my directions.

The bottom line for seed collecting began to be clear. First, mark the plants from which you want to collect seeds. If it's a big plant putting out lots of produce, like a cucumber, mark the actual cucumbers you intend to collect seeds from. Second, mark it in such a way that family, friends, or helpers will understand why there's a yellow ribbon on that cucumber or lettuce plant. Third, protect the plant from wildlife. One fine spring day, I went into the garden to see if my carrots were beginning to come to life after the long winter. What I found was a neat row of long, narrow, empty holes that looked like they had been excavated with a drill! Not a single carrot remained.

Protecting Your Bounty

Whether you are growing for something to eat or collecting seeds to plant, you will have to come up with some way to protect your garden or you won't get any veggies or seeds. For several years, I used a V-shaped "tent" made of chicken wire that I folded in half and then placed over the plants. The sides were held in place by long tent staples, and the ends were sort of woven together, resulting in lots of poked, scratched, and injured fingers. The wire tent helped, but hungry rabbits eventually found their way inside and deer learned to push it aside and get at the kale or beets underneath.

I ended up spending the better part of three days designing and building ten chicken wire cages using 1" × 2" × 8' lumber. The finished cages were 2' high × 2' wide × 8' long. My garden

rows were 40' long, so five cages covered two entire rows in which I planted all the delicacies that deer and rabbits love! The cages were also lightweight and easy to remove and set aside when tilling or weeding.

I placed the cages over the seedlings in the spring and used them again to protect overwintering plants that I was saving for seed production. They also served as excellent little greenhouses over which I stretched plastic or frost cloth if there was an untimely frost in spring, or to prevent cantaloupes from giving up when they were almost ripe but the weather was turning colder. They were worth every bit of the time, energy, and money that went into building them!

Harvest Time!

Be forewarned that getting your garden set up and planted is not even half the work. Keeping it tilled and weeded adds time and energy to the task of growing food. Harvesting is an almost continuous job once things reach maturity, especially if you have beans, peas, and cucumbers.

The following are some general guidelines for picking what you've grown. I've separated them into 2 groups: annuals and biennials.

Guidelines for annual plants:
- Pick beans every three days when they are pencil-sized and before they get lumpy.
- Pick peas every other day, especially if they are edible pods like sugar snap or Sugar Ann.
- Pick cucumbers when they get 2" in diameter, before they get seedy and begin turning yellow.
- Pick pickling cucumbers every other day when they are about 1" in diameter and 3" long.
- Pick zucchini daily when it is 1–1½" in diameter.
- Pick summer squash every other day when the fat end is about 2–2½" in diameter.
- Pick green peppers when they are 3–4" in diameter. If they are yellow or red peppers, wait until the color change is completed and then pick.
- Pick corn when the silk coming out of the top of the ear turns brown and looks dried.
- Pull radishes when they are about 1–1½" in diameter before they get woody.
- Harvest tomatoes as they ripen and turn to the color you planted (red, yellow, etc.).
- Harvest leaf lettuce every 2–3 days by picking the largest leaves, which allows the plant to keep producing.
- Harvest romaine lettuce when the head is about 8–10" tall.
- Harvest head lettuce when the head is small, compact, and well-formed, about 5–6" in diameter.
- Harvest kale only after the first frost, unless you like bitter kale.
- Harvest collards and Swiss chard like leaf lettuce.

- Dig potatoes and sweet potatoes only after the entire plant above ground has died and turned brown.
- Pick eggplant when it is smallish and the diameter of the large end is about 4".
- Pick pumpkins when they turn a clear orange.
- Pick butternut squash when all tinges of green are gone and the skin is a nut-colored beige.
- Pick acorn squash when the skin is completely black and has an orange area where the squash was sitting on the ground.
- Pick okra when the pods are 3" long.
- Pick cantaloupe when the skin between and under the "netting" loses its greenish tinge and turns a creamy beige.
- Pick watermelon when the belly touching the earth turns a creamy white.
- Harvest most herbs in the morning, after the dew has dried but before the heat of the day.

Guidelines for harvesting biennial plants that don't produce seeds until the year *after* they're planted:

- Harvest broccoli when the heads are still very tightly closed, then continue to check for smaller shoots after the main head has been harvested.
- Harvest kohlrabi when they are 1½–2" in diameter, before they get woody.
- Harvest cabbage when the heads are about 5–6" in diameter.
- Harvest cauliflower when the heads are anywhere from 4–6" in diameter and still tightly closed.
- Harvest beets when they are 2–2½" in diameter.
- Harvest carrots when the top of the carrot measures about 1" from shoulder to shoulder.
- Pick brussels sprouts after the first frost or the weather cools significantly and the sprout heads are 1–1½" in diameter.

- Pick onions when they are young and you want green onions; or let them grow until 2½–3" in diameter.
- Harvest leeks when they are about 1½–2" in diameter.

Seed Collection and Storage Tips

Annuals produce seed the first year and biennials produce seed the second year. If you pick and eat everything your garden produces, you won't be able to collect any seeds for next year. If you rototill under everything at the end of the season, you'll destroy the biennial plants that do not produce seed until the second year.

To collect seeds from any of the veggies that produce seeds the same year they're planted, you just avoid picking whatever it is you want seeds from. Let the veggie keep growing long past the time when it becomes tough or woody and is no longer suitable for eating. During this time, it will focus on building seeds that are overflowing with the germ, oils, and moisture that form the store of nutrition the seed will use to feed itself from the time it germinates until the time it gets enough root mass to begin feeding itself from the soil.

Once you collect the seeds, letting them dry out completely is a Goldilocks effort. They have to be dried just right and stored just right. Don't try to dry them in an oven, microwave, or the sun, and don't store them in paper envelopes. The oven and microwave will destroy them, and the sun will dry out their oils and moisture to the point that they won't germinate. Don't be in too big a hurry to put them away because if they are not dried enough, they will develop mold or mildew and, again, won't germinate.

Don't store your seeds in paper envelopes. If there are mice around, they will find those seeds in a hot second and in one evening will enjoy what would have fed you for months. The paper also tends to wick moisture away from the seeds, and if the paper then turns moldy, it will allow molds to destroy them. Store your precious seeds in small glass jars with tight-fitting lids. Baby food jars or small jelly jars are just right, but, again, be sure they are dry enough to avoid molds and mildews once confined to the jar.

Label with the kind of seed, the year it was grown, and especially the specific name. For example, Nantes carrots or Bolero carrots, Brandywine tomatoes or Amish Paste tomatoes. Store in a cool, dark place until it's time to plant next year.

Gardens Are a Good Deal for All!

Be aware that gardening is like having a perpetual grocery store. It's also a way of life that helps to keep you in good shape physically, improves nutrition, and anchors your food security to an extraordinary degree. The Ball canning book of fifty years ago claimed that gardens tend to increase your initial investment in seeds by 400 percent. Even if those numbers have changed over the years, when you consider the food security that a garden brings, it's a good deal by any measure!

2024 Solar and Lunar Eclipses Through the Houses

Alice DeVille

Eclipses have always been a favorite topic I cover when I'm analyzing a client's astrological chart. A minimum of four eclipses occur each year, two solar eclipses (New Moon) and two lunar eclipses (Full Moon). Sometimes as many as six eclipses take place. Their presence creates intense periods that often start to manifest a few months before the eclipses actually occur.

Eclipses unfold in cycles involving all twelve signs of the zodiac and usually manifest in pairs about two weeks apart. In 2024, the first eclipse pair is a lunar eclipse in Libra on March 25 at 5° ♎ 07' at 3:00 a.m. EDT, and in the opposite sign Aries on April 8, a solar eclipse at 19° ♈ 24' at 2:21 p.m. EDT. The remaining 2024 eclipses are the final lunar eclipse on September 17 in Pisces at

25° ♓ 41' at 7:34 p.m. EDT, and the final solar eclipse on October 2 in Libra at 10° ♎ 04' at 2:49 p.m. EDT.

Eclipses Through the Zodiac

The featured article examines possible outcomes or meanings for the eclipses through the houses, using the natural wheel of the zodiac beginning with Aries and ending with Pisces. Your natal chart drives the actual houses where these eclipses occur. Natal planets in those houses affect the intensity of the eclipse; the closer to a conjunction, the more powerful the effect.

First House

Solar eclipses that occur in this house tend to make a strong statement about self-esteem and a desire for personal growth. Dealing with setbacks results in a lack of self-confidence that you'll want to shed in order to succeed. Image is important, along with acknowledgment of strengths that you would like to show the world. If they are lacking, you are likely to enroll in seminars or workshops to develop them. This house represents what you show the world. When a solar eclipse falls here, you often land in the spotlight headed toward a promotion, a status change via an engagement or marriage, or notoriety related to a significant accomplishment. A solar eclipse occurs here this year in Aries on April 8, allowing the Sun to warm your spirit and help dreams come true.

If a lunar eclipse were to occur here in 2024 in Aries, you would be motivated to explore your inner desires, develop passion and incentive for your goals, and eliminate a tendency to put off asking questions or taking charge of your life purpose. The solar eclipse will have sign polarity with your seventh house of partners since two Libra eclipses will occur in 2024.

Second House

When a solar eclipse occurs in your second house, the focus is on your financial picture, which includes assets, income, personal possessions, resources, and what you would like to do to increase prosperity and your buying power. It also reflects how you like to spend your money, what you value, and how you feel about saving. If you feel that an important skill is missing from your portfolio, you usually enroll in classes to make sure you are qualified for future advancement.

A lunar eclipse in the second house has you looking at any situations that may contribute to emotional or financial instability, such as difficulty finding work, not enough money to pay bills, too much emphasis on material values, or marrying for fiscal security rather than love. Self-doubt in earning capacity is at the root of the anxiety. The lunar eclipse motivates you to open retirement and savings accounts to build financial security for the future.

Third House

Communication is at the core of the impact a solar eclipse has in your third house. You could have a profession where verbal expression is key, such as teaching, instructing, developing guidelines, or writing. Your mental capacity plays a role in how curious you are to stretch your mind, improve your memory, or educate yourself in numerous disciplines via formal or online classes.

Lunar eclipses drive your mental state and how you perceive the world around you. You stretch your intellect via reading, studying languages, using your intuitive mind to solve problems, expanding your imagination, and writing expressive material. You could be an over-talker or a bookworm. You get to the heart of the matter through your feelings. Humor becomes you.

Fourth House

The domestic scene in your home dominates the landscape when a solar eclipse occurs in your fourth house. From the type of home you choose to live in to the people who live with you—family, friends, or roommates—you'll be aware of what needs attention in your household. This might be safety and security, improvements to the interior of the home, the outer facade including landscaping and gardening, and the pride you feel in showcasing your unique residence. Often, a residential move takes place when a fourth house eclipse occurs.

A lunar eclipse in the ruled-by-the-Moon fourth house is sure to involve concerns about family matters, parents, emotional satisfaction, and a home that gives you a feeling of security. When an eclipse lands here, disruptions occur, and you'll soon know about any secrets hiding in the woodwork that will have to be addressed, ranging from physical repairs to healing of the heart and people who are coming and going. Temporary residents often show up.

Fifth House

Here's your chance to bond with dear ones when an eclipse lands here. The natural ruler of this house is the Sun, bursting with creative energy, passion, and affection that is ready to embrace children, romantic partners, and your love of entertainment and fun. Individuals grow closer to parents, children, students, and people they coach. An eclipse may bring out your entrepreneurial side.

A lunar eclipse shows you what makes your children tick and how you can achieve nirvana in perfecting these relationships so that no alienation exists. Learn to listen rather than judge. An eclipse here can lead you to the trip of a lifetime like your bucket list cruise, an amazing yet unexpected career, or the love of your life.

Sixth House

A number of events may occur when a solar eclipse connects to this house and makes you aware of responsibilities to yourself and others. Illness makes you aware of the state of your health or the health of others around you, prompting you to seek medical advice and correct the physical problems. The health of your work environment may be plucking your nerves when you notice the lack of organization and the impact it has on delivering the finished product.

If a lunar eclipse shows up, it can get emotional if your mental state feels the strain of unsuitable work relationships and chaotic conditions. Cohesiveness and a sense of belonging are your preferences as you seek compatible workmates. Orderliness motivates performance and accelerates the rate of accomplishment. You cherish a secure relationship with your boss.

Seventh House

This year two eclipses fall in the natural seventh house. A Libra lunar eclipse occurs on March 25, highlighting personal or professional relationships. Everything you love about intimate partnerships surrounds you when this eclipse appears. Happiness with partners blossoms, giving you a sense of fulfillment. You could meet someone new, get engaged, or tie the knot. Knock your socks off with joy. Business partnerships could be in the works. Sit down at the table with these important cooperators and work out an agreeable deal.

A solar eclipse in Libra occurs here on October 2. Quite the opposite occurs when you're trying to hold on to emotionally empty relationships. If you are experiencing aching disappointment, it's time to explore the reasons. Remember the adage "happy wife, happy life," and get to work on restoring unity. It's not unusual for partners to drift out of your life, and divorce can be the outcome. Business associations could start falling apart over differences in goals, daily operations, and staff employment. Heed warning signs and consider interventions using a neutral management consultant.

Eighth House

This complex house covers all facets of joint financial holdings: savings, debts, mortgages, and retirement funds as well as how you use your mutual income to fund the goals you agreed on as

partners. An eclipse here can announce a big raise or inheritance for you or your partner. The house represents intimacy too, and an eclipse might reawaken the sexy spark between you and draw you closer depending on what is going on in the relationship.

When the eclipse is lunar, one emphasis may be on your money and how you will protect it via wills and legal documents related to disposition of goods. It can also be a wake-up call when the assets arrive to make sure your plans for the future are in pristine working order. Your motivation to succeed intensifies, and you might consider new employment or education that qualifies you for a higher salary. The Full Moon aspect draws you closer to your psychic insight and the spiritual realm. Individuals may find themselves soul traveling between the worlds when their deep intuitive vibe is receptive.

Ninth House

When a solar eclipse contacts this house, your higher mind awakens, and you seek answers to explain practices, codes, theories, ethical and moral standards, and political positions. Individuals often experience a change in outlook or a religious conversion, enroll in a university, study languages, travel, and spend time with people from other countries to experience new cultures. You might become an activist and separate philosophically and spatially from your family in your search for the truth. Writers develop material and often publish books, articles, or journals.

If the lunar eclipse occurs here, you may be more restless than usual. Travel holds considerable appeal. You could go on the honeymoon of a lifetime or fulfill a bucket list wish, like a multicountry cruise or tour. Eclipses here stretch your intellect, and you crave learning experiences. You may enroll in online seminars or attend classes on topics that interest you. Check good chart dates for travel plans to avoid getting stranded in undesirable locations.

Tenth House

When eclipses drop by this house, you'll be concerned with career matters, ambition, and your status in the world. Opportunities crop up and offers come in to improve your profile in the work organization. Expect promotions, awards, bonuses, or transfers. Bosses praise your performance and could offer you a leadership position. Show your stuff if you supervise others by building a talented team, making sure all members get the recognition they deserve. Your family situation could be in high focus now as well, especially if you are dealing with parents' health and family matters.

If a lunar eclipse arrives in your tenth house, you are probably in the midst of evaluating how much your work is providing you with emotional satisfaction. "Is this the right job for me?" could be the refrain going through your mind if it has been lacking, and you could be looking for a new job. If you have gone as far as you can in the current organization, the eclipse hit may be the source of your search for new employment. Instead of dwelling on what isn't working, focus on your accomplishments and how they may strengthen your resume for future employment. Sometimes the lunar eclipse leads to layoffs, transfers, or getting you fired. Take heart. A better option is behind the next door.

Eleventh House

A solar eclipse in this gregarious house aligns you with group interests and how your humanitarian attitude helps you interact with associates, friendships, goals, and members of professional organizations. These groups participate in endeavors that look for the betterment of conditions that improve the stability of the world population. You'll be genuinely concerned about how humanity survives challenges, overcomes poverty, rebuilds structures damaged by storms, and receives much-needed health care coverage where it has been lacking. You'll tap your best networks to find work that meets goals to lift the human spirit, such as with charities, medical facilities, and training institutions. Politics is another field that draws you to seek new employment.

When a lunar eclipse occurs in the eleventh house, you may be doing an about-face regarding your attitude to support humanitarian causes, which you may have previously thought were too boring. Suddenly, an aha moment captures your curiosity, and you start researching current local or global dilemmas, feeling the pull deep inside to join forces with those who are busy creating awareness that gives these circumstances attention. Your altruistic nature finds a home in a rewarding passion that motivates you to expand your worldview and brings you the emotional satisfaction you desire.

Twelfth House

The psychological and spiritual sides of your life get a wake-up call when a solar eclipse visits your twelfth house. You may feel in the pit of your stomach that something is giving you an uneasy, queasy feeling—one that you ordinarily just blow off. Not this time, though, because your subconscious mind is turning out visions of what is off-kilter and needs attention to bring your spiritual core into balance. One aspect could be that you need more sleep, and quality rest is one of this eclipse's gifts. If you seem confused more than usual, you have work to do. Start with identifying phobias that keep you from performing your best work while you hide in the shadows taking too many days off from work. Identify the fears that drive you to a standstill instead of confronting what is in the way of success and a positive mindset. Keeping too many secrets may cause them to come out unexpectedly. Seek help from qualified advisors and bare your soul.

This year a lunar eclipse in Pisces occurs in this house, awakening your subconscious mind and your psychic senses, while deeply stirring the spiritual instincts that drive your soul. At the same time you are craving emotional support, this powerful eclipse is awakening your creative mind and generating ideas that help you turn out beautiful, original work. Your mind becomes more receptive to assimilating better health care practices and showing compassion for those who are suffering. That body-mind connection leads to improvements in relationships with children, entrepreneurs, romantic partners, authority figures, and teachers. By staying in an unsatisfactory personal relationship, you will either seek a way to improve it or leave it altogether, especially in a year like this one where two eclipses may have appeared in the natal seventh house. Under this lunar eclipse, individuals sometimes merge with their psychic powers and embrace mediumship.

Plant-Based Benefits for the Whole Body and Mind

Mireille Blacke, MA, LADC, RD, CD-N

As a registered dietitian and certified dietitian nutritionist, I'm aware of the reputations certain foods have as nutritional powerhouses or "superfoods," though it's also clear that the media's agenda in making such claims is often to target your wallet more than your well-being. Always take statements about "miracle foods" and "magic bullets" with many grains of salt and a lot of skepticism. Even nutrition professionals get overwhelmed with all of the contradictory information flying around online and in print!

However, there's a general consensus—backed by long-term, evidence-based research—that certain plant-based "superfoods" are considered legitimately beneficial to your overall physical health and well-being and an easy enhancement to your regular nutritional intake.

Superfoods

Some plant-based foods are common, accessible, and readily available nutritional powerhouses that positively impact brain health (memory and cognitive functioning) and other bodily functions (cardiovascular, eye health, immunity, digestion, inflammation, blood sugar regulation, and skin, hair, and nails). Even if you're not interested in becoming a vegetarian or vegan full-time, adding plant-based meals to your menu a few days per week can lead to some significant health benefits and possibly save you some money over time. In this article, I'll review the highlights of several plant-based "nutrition powerhouses" that you can easily add to your regular dietary intake, even if you're on a budget. I've also provided a more comprehensive list of Health Benefits of Common Plant-Based Food Sources at the end of this article for easy reference.

As always, before making any concentrated nutrition or lifestyle changes, consult with your healthcare provider(s) about potential safety, risks, medication and supplement interactions, and effects on your current conditions and treatments.

Powerhouse Properties Abbreviations:
- AI= anti-inflammatory
- AOX= high in antioxidants (compounds that protect your cells from damage)
- BHM= brain health/memory
- BSR= blood sugar regulation
- CVD= cardiovascular/heart healthy
- DIG= digestion
- EYE= eye health/vision related
- IMM= immunity
- SHN= skin/hair/nails

Blueberries

Powerhouse properties: AI, AOX, CVD, EYE, IMM

Blueberries are one of the highest-rated foods in terms of anti-oxidant power and are exceptionally high in proanthocyanidins (powerful and health-promoting plant compounds), which prevent degenerative diseases. The blueberry's high antioxidant capacity translates to strong protection for the cardiovascular system and reduced inflammation and oxidative stress in the body. Such conditions have been connected to Alzheimer's disease, Parkinson's disease, diabetes, heart disease, and various forms of arthritis.

I use the acronym "BLUEMAN" to recall the benefits of blueberries:

Brain food
Lipid-lowering ability
Urinary tract health
Enhancement of vision
Memory protection
Antioxidant powerhouse
Neuron signaling

Simply put, blueberries are brain food. The same anthocyanin compounds that create the distinctive color of the blueberry also increase brain function. (The more vivid the color, the more of these compounds the fruit contains.) Blueberries are considered a memory-protecting food and somewhat of a buffer against mental deterioration, loss of coordination, and loss of balance. Blueberries also help to increase neuron communication ("signaling") in the brain.

The compounds in blueberries have also been shown to lower serum cholesterol, positively impact vision, guard against macular degeneration, and promote urinary tract health (move over, cranberry). One particular compound, pterostilbene, aids in fatty acid metabolism, reducing lipids in the blood and plaque deposits in your arteries. In addition, blueberries contain the cancer-fighter ellagic acid (more on that with strawberries).

The blueberry's skin is its primary source of beneficial antioxidants. One half cup of fresh or frozen blueberries is enough to provide significant health benefits. All forms of the fruit have proanthocyanins, so view fresh and frozen blueberries as equivalent. Most of us are budget-conscious, and frozen blueberries are generally less expensive and are readily available in most grocery store freezer sections. One half cup of blueberries equals one serving.

Strawberries

Powerhouse Properties: AI, AOX, BHM, CVD, EYE, IMM

One cup of unsweetened strawberries provides fifty calories and three grams of fiber, making strawberries a filling, low-calorie snack option. Strawberries have no saturated fat or cholesterol and are low in sodium. Strawberries are also a good source of vitamin C, folic acid, potassium, and manganese. Vitamin C acts as an antioxidant in the body, helping to boost immunity and fight infection, counter inflammation, prevent heart disease, and protect against cancer. B-complex vitamins (such as folic acid) in strawberries help the body with carbohydrate, protein, and fat metabolism. Potassium is a mineral involved in the body's cell and fluid regulation, heart rate control, and blood pressure stability. The mineral manganese acts as a cofactor for enzymes needed in fat and protein metabolism and antioxidant utilization. Strawberries, along with blueberries, rank among the top food sources in antioxidant content.

What's the big deal about antioxidants like those found in strawberries and blueberries? The longitudinal research on humans is clear: antioxidants and proanthocyanidins (as noted with blueberries) offer us protection against degenerative diseases, cancer, heart disease, inflammation, and diabetes. Specifically, ellagic acid in strawberries has been shown to be anticarcinogenic and antimutagenic, meaning it promotes cellular death of cancer cells without changing healthy, normal cells. Ellagic acid has also been shown to inhibit tumor growth in liver cancer cells and protect against cervical and breast cancers. Other compounds in strawberries have been shown to improve brain function and memory, decrease macular degeneration, and prompt increased short-term memory, faster learning, and increased motor skills. Strawberries also contain fisetin, which possesses antioxidant properties shown to fight Alzheimer's disease and diabetes-related kidney failure.

That *sounds* great, but what's the catch? Well, like anything else involving nutrition and long-term behavior change, there are guidelines and recommendations to follow, and if we're talking about strawberries, blueberries, raspberries, and cherries in particular, I'm not talking about getting your servings from milkshakes, sugary fruit juices, or Pop-Tarts. The USDA's *Dietary Guidelines for Americans, 2020–2025* recommends 2 cups of fruits and 2.5 cups of vegetables daily, and most Americans fall far short of this goal. (Confused about portions and serving sizes? For more specifics, use the link to the USDA's MyPlatePlan in References and Resources at the end of the article.) The best way to get the most nutrients from your strawberries or blueberries is to eat them raw as a between-meal snack, or in salads, cereals, oatmeal, yogurt, and smoothies. Avoid calorie overload from excessive fruit and vegetable juices. Keep in mind that whole fresh fruit and vegetables will always have the lowest calorie count.

"Whole and fresh" doesn't always equal boring. Consider serving strawberries over frozen yogurt with some additionally heart-healthy walnuts, sliced almonds, or macadamia nuts, or get creative and design a "strawberry fruit pizza." Soak strawberries in balsamic vinegar and black pepper to invigorate traditional green or fruit salads, dairy-based desserts, or low-calorie angel food cake. Note: In general, eight medium-sized strawberries equal one serving.

Cayenne Pepper

Powerhouse Properties: AI, AOX, CVD, IMM

The greatest health benefits of cayenne stem from its high concentration of capsaicin, which inhibits a neuropeptide associated with inflammatory processes and the transport of pain messages to the brain. Capsaicin is effective in treating cluster headaches, osteoarthritis pain, and diabetic neuropathy. Cayenne and capsaicin are also helpful in fighting inflammation, promoting cardiovascular benefits, and boosting immunity. Despite a reputation to the contrary, chili peppers like cayenne are associated with a reduced risk of stomach ulcers by helping to kill certain ingested bacteria and stimulating protective gastric juices which prevent the formation of ulcers.

Add a pinch of cayenne to existing recipes to enhance many of your basic meals. Introduce some kick to your standard salad dressings, soups, or snacks by slicing, chopping, or frying whole peppers. Dry and soak them in oil for a spicy infusion. Consider using cayenne in Cajun deviled eggs for some extra heat or to mask strong flavors in certain foods that some may find bitter (e.g., mustard greens). At the other end of the spectrum, add cayenne to chocolate baked goods and confections to incorporate the pepper's health properties into them.

For those who are sensitive to hot spices, bell peppers may be a better option.

Sweet Potato

Powerhouse Properties: AI, AOX, BHM, BSR, CVD, EYE, SHN

Sweet potatoes are excellent sources of vitamin A in the form of beta-carotene, a potent antioxidant that helps to prevent sun damage and fight premature aging. Sweet potatoes with dark orange flesh are richest in carotenoid pigments and bioavailable beta-carotene. Eating sweet potato (and pumpkin) with small amounts of "healthy" fat (like olive oil) will increase the absorption of beta-carotene and its associated health benefits. Toss sweet potato spears with olive oil, roast at 400°F for thirty minutes, and enjoy healthier fries.

Sweet potatoes offer numerous additional health benefits, such as blood sugar regulation, anti-inflammatory properties, and assisting with successful blood clotting. As starchy root vegetables, you might expect sweet potatoes to elevate blood sugar levels, since concentrated starches are easily converted by the digestive tract into simple sugars. However, the sweet potato's dietary fiber (four grams per medium potato) helps to modify insulin metabolism and improve glucose regulation, even in people with type 2 diabetes. The slow breakdown of these root vegetables in the body leads to more stable blood sugar and insulin levels, and also offers low calories and high nutrient content (specifically when eaten with the skin), benefiting people with diabetes in particular. Boiling sweet potatoes seems to favorably impact blood sugar regulation more than roasting or baking.

Reduced inflammation after eating sweet potatoes has been linked to vitamins A and C specifically, especially in purple sweet potatoes. These anti-inflammatory properties are due to the phytochemical and antioxidant anthocyanin and other color-related pigments; like the blueberry, the purple sweet potato owes its rich color to anthocyanin and other polyphenols. In addition to reducing inflammation, these substances help to reduce cardiovascular disease, improve vision, and enhance memory.

Vitamin B6 in sweet potatoes is responsible for platelet aggregation and blood clotting impact. It's important for individuals taking medications for clotting issues to keep this in mind and consult with healthcare providers, particularly if sweet potato consumption is high.

Sweet potatoes are an easy substitute for white potatoes in most recipes, including baking, mashing, roasting, and frying. Add layers of flavor with peppers (black, white, cayenne, or chili), onion, or cloves. Remember to include the skins for maximum nutritional benefit!

Watermelon

Powerhouse Properties: AOX, CVD, EYE, IMM, SHN

Plant-based, antioxidant-rich food sources high in the nutrients lutein and zeaxanthin can help reduce the risk of vision loss from cataracts and macular degeneration. Cooked, dark green, leafy vegetables such as collard greens, kale, and spinach provide the highest amounts of lutein and zeaxanthin, but "eat the rainbow" of colorful fruits and vegetables to ensure your daily intake of vision-protecting carotenoids, flavonoids, and vitamin C. One such carotenoid is lycopene, and it's found in watermelon.

Watermelon is classified as both a fruit and a vegetable and is a low-calorie source of vitamins A, B6, C, and lycopene. Vitamin A boosts immunity and maximizes eye health, and B6 assists with

immunity, nerve functioning, and red blood cell formation. Vitamin C offers antioxidant protection and assists the body in tissue growth and maintenance. Lycopene, noticeable in the red color of the edible portion of the watermelon, has been shown to lower the risk of macular degeneration, heart disease, and several types of cancer. In addition, because watermelon is over 90 percent water and provides so much hydration, it's beneficial to the skin. Watermelon also contains a phytonutrient called citrulline, which aids blood flow to the scalp, promoting hair growth. One cup of cubed watermelon equals one serving.

Chickpeas

Powerhouse Properties: AOX, BHM, BSR, CVD, IMM

Chickpeas (aka garbanzo beans) are relatively well-known as the primary ingredient in hummus, but currently chickpea pasta and flour options are becoming more commonplace in grocery stores and in online recipes. Generally, chickpeas have been considered a heart-healthy, plant-based food due to low sodium, lack of cholesterol, and being a healthy source of polyunsaturated fats, all of which reduce the risk of abnormal cholesterol profiles and the risk of developing cardiovascular disease. As far as legumes go, chickpeas are second only to lentils in terms of antioxidant content. There may also be an association between increased chickpea intake and reduced risk of colon and other cancers.

Each one-cup serving of chickpeas provides fifteen grams of non-animal protein, about twelve grams of dietary fiber, seven of the nine essential amino acids, and choline for a healthy brain and nervous system. Because chickpeas are high in fiber and low on the glycemic index, they may be beneficial to individuals with problems regulating blood sugar. As chickpeas are naturally gluten-free, using them as a lower-sugar flour substitute for cookies and desserts is a great option for those who need or choose to avoid gluten.

Another interesting fact about canned chickpeas is that the residual "juice" or "water" left in the chickpea can, known to many as *aquafaba*, also has culinary uses, typically as a substitute for egg whites. You'll probably have to try it for yourself to believe it, as I did, but you can successfully (and deliciously) make everything from banana bread to chocolate mousse to whisky sours with the leftover "chickpea juice" that most of us would just toss down the drain!

Eggplant

Powerhouse Properties: AI, AOX, BHM, BSR, CVD, DIG, IMM, SHN

Eggplant is low in calories (about 20 calories per cup), saturated fat, cholesterol, and sodium, and provides a healthy and tasty option for active weight loss, weight loss management, and heart-healthy dietary needs. It also has compounds that benefit the brain, blood sugar regulation, digestion, inflammation, immunity, and skin and hair.

One such compound is nasunin, a powerful antioxidant and phytochemical that fights inflammation, lowers cholesterol levels, and strengthens the cardiovascular system. Another compound found in eggplant is chlorogenic acid, an anti-inflammatory with links to tumor growth inhibition. Eggplant is high in soluble fiber, which increases feelings of fullness, aids digestion and weight loss, and also assists in blood sugar regulation and the stabilization of glucose levels. The presence of scopoletin in eggplant assists brain health by boosting serotonin and facilitating better mood and sleep. Eggplant is also rich in B vitamins, which aid in stress management. The iron, potassium, and folate in eggplant increase blood flow to the scalp to promote growth of new hair follicles, and vitamin C assists in protecting the skin from free radical damage.

In terms of preparation, eggplant contains nicotinoid alkaloids, which makes it somewhat bitter. Try degorging to address this: salt, rinse, and drain the eggplant to reduce overall bitterness. Salting your eggplant will also reduce the amount of oil absorbed from cooking.

The eggplant's low calories and saturated fat make it an excellent substitute for meat in weight loss efforts. I've found the eggplant's bulk and texture easy and almost imperceptible as a meat substitute in vegetarian or vegan meals. Just be careful not to negate these benefits by adding extra cheese, oils, and other calorie-laden ingredients to your eggplant dishes!

For multicultural versatility, consider dishes one can make from eggplant: ratatouille (France), moussaka (Greece), baingan bharta (North India), baba ghanoush and hummus (Middle East), and caponata (Sicily). Talk about global diversity!

In the United States, eggplant is available year-round, with peak season in August through October. Store fresh eggplant at room temperature to maintain better texture and flavor, and use within a few days to avoid softening and wrinkling. Don't consume eggplant leaves, as they're toxic! But do add this diverse plant to your recipe arsenal for better health!

Health Benefits of Common Plant-Based Food Sources

- **Anti-inflammatory:** Basil, beets, bell and chili pepper (e.g., cayenne), black beans, blueberry, broccoli, cardamom, cinnamon, eggplant, garlic, ginger, green leafy vegetables, oats, olive oil, onion, raspberry, spinach, strawberry, sweet potato (purple), turmeric.
- **Blood sugar regulation:** Cinnamon, chickpeas, collards, eggplant, ginger, ginseng, kale, oats, spinach, sweet potato, Swiss chard.

- **Brain health:** Avocado, beets, blueberry, broccoli, chickpeas, eggplant, garlic, green tea, pumpkin seeds, rosemary, sage, strawberry, sweet potato, tomato, turmeric, walnut.
- **Cardiovascular:** Asparagus, beans, blueberry, broccoli, chia seeds, chickpeas, eggplant, flax seeds, garlic, green tea, lentils, oatmeal, onion, spinach, strawberry, sweet potato, tomato, watermelon.
- **Digestion:** Beets, black pepper, broccoli, brussels sprouts, cardamom, chia seeds, dill, eggplant, fennel, ginger, kale, lemon balm, papaya, peppermint, soybeans (miso soup, natto, tofu), spinach, whole grains (oats, quinoa, farro).
- **Eye health:** Bell and cayenne pepper, blueberry, broccoli, butternut squash, cantaloupe, carrot, chia seeds, citrus, collards, flax seeds, kale, kiwi, papaya, peas, rosemary, turnip greens, spinach, strawberry, sweet potato, walnuts, watermelon, yellow squash.
- **Immunity:** Blueberry, cardamom, cayenne pepper, cherry, chickpeas, cinnamon, eggplant, garlic, onion, oregano, paprika, raspberry, strawberry, watermelon.
- **Skin/hair/nails:** Avocado, beans, blueberry, carrot, collards, eggplant, kale, oatmeal, pumpkin, spinach, strawberry, sweet potato, tomato, watermelon.

References and Resources

For additional nutritional and consumer information, as well as countless exceptional sweet potato recipes, please refer to http://www.sweetpotato.org.

"MyPlate." USDA. Accessed July 18, 2022. https://www.myplate.gov/eat-healthy/what-is-myplate.

US Department of Agriculture and US Department of Health and Human Services. *Dietary Guidelines for Americans, 2020–2025.* Ninth Edition. December 2020. https://www.dietaryguidelines.gov/sites/default/files/2020-12/Dietary_Guidelines_for_Americans_2020-2025.pdf.

Lunar Mansions

Charlie Rainbow Wolf

Sun signs have become a rather mainstream interest, with forecasts printed in daily newspapers and horoscope interpretations readily available from many sources. For the armchair astrologer, the long and tedious calculation of the planets (which was how I learned astrology back in the 1970s) has been replaced by free websites who do the math in seconds. Astrology may be more accessible now than it ever has been.

The seasons are marked by solar astrology. The longest day is midsummer, around the twenty-first of June when the Sun moves into Cancer, and the longest night is midwinter, six months later around the twenty-first of December when the Sun moves into Capricorn. The halfway points are the equinoxes; the spring equinox is approximately the twenty-first of March when the Sun moves into Aries, and the autumn equinox is half a year later, generally the twenty-first of September and marking the Sun's entry into Libra.

Throughout history, the human race has been fascinated by the skies. In addition to what is now accepted as astrology (which is vastly different from astronomy), every culture has origin stories about the Sun and the Moon and the stars. Many of them have unique calendars marking the passing of time through the study of the movement of the lights and planets through the night sky. Western astrology is just one way of marking the Sun's passage through the skies.

The early calendars were not just based on the Sun, either. Many of them focused on the journey of the Moon, which makes sense, given that it is the earth's own satellite and something that is easily seen and tracked. Today, such celebrations as the Hebrew Passover or the Chinese New Year are fairly mainstream, but those are only the most well-known ones. Other lunar calendars include, but are not limited to, the Pagan Wheel of the Year, the Cherokee "sacred calendar," and the Islamic calendar (Hail 2000, n.p.).

What Are the Lunar Mansions?

Some may be familiar with this term while others might never have previously heard of it. The lunar mansions—also referred to as the "mansions of the Moon" or the "stations of the Moon"—are a form of timekeeping dating back centuries. Just as the Sun passes through the constellations on its orbit through the year, the Moon passes through fixed points on its journey around the earth. These are called the lunar mansions.

The lunar mansions are different from the waxing and waning phases of the Moon. The former looks at the Moon's journey through the fixed points in the sky, where the latter looks at the

Moon's relationship between the earth and the Sun. The phases of the Moon through the mansions will vary because the time spent in each mansion is different to the time spent in each phase. It's quite heavy astrology when you start looking closely!

The origins of the lunar mansions are unclear, although there is evidence that they have been used in India (Vedic astrology), China, Arabia, and more. The Moon's orbit is approximately 27.3 days. Some systems of lunar astrology use 27 days, and some use 28. For example, the Vedic system uses 27 mansions, while the Chinese and Arabic ones use 28. Because Arabic astrology was the foundation of European astrology, a system of 28 mansions has been widely adopted (Warnock 2019, 7).

Using the lunar mansions often seems complicated because of the precise locations and somewhat outdated meanings. There's also some contradiction from one interpretation to the next. They're quite hard taskmasters and often misunderstood because some of the descriptions are quite archaic. Like advanced planetary positions and interpretations of the astrological signs, the lunar mansions include full and also partial degrees (called minutes) of the signs as the Moon passes through them. This means the Moon can be in more than one mansion on a given day—although it will not be in two mansions simultaneously. Fortunately, today there are websites like astroseek.com, lunarium .co.uk, sunsigns.org, and more to do the calculations very quickly!

Today's astrology is not just divination based; its psychological nature is also frequently used as a character analysis or to assist when doing shadow work. Astrology used to be more forecasting and foretelling than understanding, and it is with this in mind that we explore the lunar mansions. They tell a very predictive story.

Talismans

Each lunar mansion is also associated with a magical symbol. This means that if someone were to carve the image associated with the mansion into a talisman, then they would draw to them the energies of that mansion. Timing is vital when doing this kind of work. Not only does the Moon need to be in the right mansion, it also needs to be in the correct phase, in the right relationship with the Sun, and not making challenging aspects to vital planets.

Lastly but by no means least, check the ephemeris and make sure the time zone is correct. Because there are some vastly different interpretations of the meanings of the mansions, it's imperative that when doing this kind of talismanic work, the intent is absolutely clear.

The Meaning of the Mansions

Below are my versions of the lunar mansions; it's kind of a combination of the meanings according to Ibn 'Arabī, a Sufi mystic, and also Christopher Warnock's interpretation (Warnock 2019, n.p.). Over the years I've seen several different versions of the lunar mansions, but it has been my experience that Warnock's meanings are the most popular and the ones that are used the most frequently. I stress, though, that these are not the *only* interpretations. Do some exploring and see what resonates on a personal level.

Mansion 1: Al Sharatain (The Two Signs)

This mansion is measured from 0° Aries to 12° Aries. It's good for starting a journey, purchasing livestock, or taking remedies. It is not good for marriages or partnerships of any kind.

Mansion 2: Al Butain (The Little Belly)

This mansion goes from 12° Aries to 25° Aries. It's also good for journeys as well as for sowing seeds, but it is not good for marriages or employment issues.

Mansion 3: Al Thurayya (The Pleiades)

This mansion goes from 25° Aries to 8° Taurus. This is another time when it is fortunate to purchase animals, for hunting, and for land travel. It's not good for marriage or partnerships, or for planting seeds of any kind.

Mansion 4: Aldebaran (The Follower)

This mansion goes from 8° Taurus to 21° Taurus. It's a good time for building and investing, for employing others, but not for partnering with them. Marriage is not advised and traveling could be risky.

Mansion 5: Al Haqqah (A Crown on a Horse)

This mansion goes from 21° Taurus to 4° Gemini and is very focused on matters concerning the head—including dreams and even haircuts! It's a good time for romantic partnerships, but not so hot for marriage. Education, travel, and career are also favored.

Mansion 6: Al Hanah (A Brand, or a Scar)

This mansion goes from 4° Gemini to 17° Gemini. It's a good time for seeking fairness and pursuing justice, for invading (although that's *not* recommended by this author!), and for partnerships. Financially it's not particularly positive, and it is not the time for growing things either. Injuries and illnesses are ill-favored too.

Mansion 7: Al Dhira (The Forearm)

This mansion goes from 17° Gemini to 0° Cancer. It's very good for anything to do with planting or gardening, also anything that deals with purification. Mediation and reconciliation are highlighted, but it's not favorable for conveyancing or any curatives.

Mansion 8: Al Nathra (The Tip of the Nose)

This mansion goes from 0° Cancer to 12° Cancer. It's a very good time for healing, for making purchases or receiving gifts, and for travel. Any kind of partnership is ill-advised, and it's not particularly favorable for anything to do with jobs or career.

Mansion 9: Al Tarf (The Eye)

This mansion goes from 12° Cancer to 25° Cancer. It's really not a good time for planting anything or trying to achieve something. Partnerships could be deceitful and journeys perilous. This is a time to build up the defenses, but the general essence is one of disappointment and discord.

Mansion 10: Al Jabha (The Forehead)

This mansion goes from 25° Cancer to 8° Leo. It's very good for partnerships of all sorts and for any kind of building, whether it is a metaphor or physical construction. Not very favorable when it comes to finances, though, and extra caution should be taken when traveling. It's a good time for recuperation too.

Mansion 11: Al Zubra (The Lion's Mane)

This mansion goes from 8° Leo to 21° Leo. It's very good for planting seeds of all sorts, whether they're physical or metaphorical. Partnerships are favored, as is building something new or working on something started. It's neutral when it comes to commerce and travel.

Mansion 12: Al Sarfah (The Change)

This mansion goes from 21° Leo to 4° Virgo. It's very advantageous for anything to do with building, renting, property, farming, or partnerships. Even new clothing is favored here! However, travel and employment are negatively aspected.

Mansion 13: Al Awwa (The Barker)

This mansion goes from 4° Virgo to 17° Virgo and is a generally beneficial energy. It's good for anything to do with gardening, marriage and travel, healing, employment, and appealing to those in authority over you. It's even an appropriate time for a haircut! The only negative here is to avoid overindulging.

Mansion 14: Al Simak (The Uplifted)

This mansion goes from 17° Virgo to 0° Libra. Like Al Awwa, this mansion is generally positive for most things, including health, relationships and partnerships, contracts (personal or business), and traveling by sea. Travel by land is the only thing not particularly favored.

Mansion 15: Al Ghafr (The Covering)

This mansion goes from 0° Libra to 12° Libra and is a mixed bag of energy. Well digging and building canals is favored, employment and house moves look positive, and trade (buying and selling) looks good. The downside of this mansion involves any kind of journey and any kind of partnership.

Mansion 16: Al Zubana (The Claws)

This mansion goes from 12° Libra to 25° Libra, and it's not the most favorable of mansions. Healing, travel, any kind of deals or contracts, anything planted or grown, and any kind of partnerships are not well aspected. The only bright spark here, really, is

it's good for employment and things leading to increased wealth or prosperity.

Mansion 17: Al-Iklil (The Crown)

This mansion goes from 25° Libra to 8° Scorpio. Newness is highlighted here, as this is a good time for new livestock, new clothing, new buildings, new love, and new remedies. Travel is also favored, even though there's a worrisome energy that things might go wrong on the journey. Partnerships and employment are troublesome.

Mansion 18: Al Qalb (The Heart)

This mansion goes from 8° Scorpio to 21° Scorpio. This is quite a positive mansion for all things dealing with buildings: constructing them, buying them, or renting them. Land purchases are favored, as is getting promoted at work, gardening, and trying new medications. Travel is highlighted, but only to the east! Partnerships and employment issues are best left for another time.

Mansion 19: Al Shaulah (The Sting)

This mansion goes from 21° Scorpio to 4° Sagittarius. Litigation, planting trees, childbirth, and journeying by land are favored. Partnerships of all kinds, travel by sea, and anything to do with employment is best avoided.

Mansion 20: Al Naaim (The Ostriches, sometimes called the Dragon's Head)

This mansion goes from 4° Sagittarius to 17° Sagittarius. The focus here is on livestock or animals (purchasing, breeding, or hunting) and also construction. It's rather neutral when it comes to travel plans. Partnerships of any kind are ill-favored.

Mansion 21: Al Balda (The Place, sometimes the City)

This mansion goes from 17° Sagittarius to 0° Capricorn. Like the previous mansion, it's good for building, also planting and investing or making big-ticket purchases. Travel is neutral to slightly favored. It's not good for career moves or employment.

Mansion 22: Sa'd al-Dhabih (The Lucky Slayer or Assassin)

This mansion goes from 0° Capricorn to 12° Capricorn and is quite a favorable mansion for most things. Healing, fixing things, journeys, and partnerships are positively highlighted, also escape routes! It's not good for romantic partnerships, marriage, or anything to do with employment.

Mansion 23: Sa'd Bula (The Luck of the Swallower, sometimes the Lucky Aviator)

This mansion goes from 12° Capricorn to 25° Capricorn. This is another challenging mansion, full of conflict. It's a time for trying on new clothes and exploring new partnerships. New medicines and escape routes are also highlighted again. It's not good for marriages, as bad behavior might ensue. Journeys, keeping secrets, and trust are also disadvantageous.

Mansion 24: Sa'd al Su'ud (Luck of the Lucks, and also Wretched of the Wretched)

This mansion goes from 25° Capricorn to 8° Aquarius. It's another mansion where escape and freedom are highlighted, as are medicinal treatments and anything to do with employment. It's neutral for travel and not good at all for marriage or partnerships of any kind.

Mansion 25: Sa'd al-Akhbiyah (Luck of the Tents)

This mansion goes from 8° Aquarius to 21° Aquarius. It's good for picking fights, revenge, and making castles stronger, whether they're buildings or metaphorical structures. Delay in travel is indicated. This is not a good mansion for marriage, employment, partnerships of any kind, or dealing with animals and livestock.

Mansion 26: Al-Fargh al Muqaddam (The Preceding or First Spout)

This mansion goes from 21° Aquarius to 4° Pisces. It's good for travel, reinforcing buildings and employment positions, but not much else! Relationships of all kinds are ill-favored, but the positive note here is the seeds of reconciliation may be sown at this time.

Mansion 27: Al-Fargh al Muakhkhar (The Following Spout)

This mansion goes from 4° Pisces to 17° Pisces. It's good for growing things (ideas or business) and also for marriage. Travel is not favored, and lending or borrowing money should be avoided.

Mansion 28: Batn al-Hut (The Belly of the Fish)

This mansion goes from 17° Pisces to 0° Aries. It's good for anything concerning planting, growing, healing, and existing partnerships, particularly marriage. However, relationships that start here could be joyful at first, then soon come to a rocky end. This is not a good time for lending or borrowing anything. Travel is neutral.

Other Interpretations

One of the earliest resources regarding the lunar mansions is most probably *The Picatrix*, which has been translated many times, as perusing an online bookseller will reveal. I'm rather partial to *The Mansions of the Moon* by Christopher Warnock, as he has examined different interpretations and the history of the lunar mansions and presents them in a very easy-to-read style. Another book for further reading is Alexandre Volguine's *Lunar Astrology*. Volgine examines many different sources in his work. Some of them contradict each other, which is why the lunar mansions are sometimes so hard to understand! Llewellyn published an annotated version of Agrippa's *Three Books of Occult Philosophy*, which is a good interpretation of sixteenth-century astrology and magic. This book gives descriptions of the lunar mansions, as well as explaining how they are used in magic.

A quick trip through any search engine reveals just how many people over the years have written about and tried to understand the lunar mansions, so it is no wonder there are so many different interpretations. It's not that some are wrong and others are right; it's just a case of perception. As in all types of divination and mysticism, it's important to find what resonates, and then stick with that so as not to muddy the energy.

Conclusion

I've tried to simplify this as much as possible to make it easier to understand, but the truth is that the lunar mansions are *complicated*, and—as mentioned above—there isn't any one hard and fast way of interpreting them. When doing any forecasting, including interpreting signs and portents, find the method that resonates with you and stick with it. My own take on the lunar mansions is that they are a great peek back through historical interpretations, but they have to be allowed to evolve into how life is lived today. Take them with a pinch of salt, and use them as a seasoning for other astrological calculations and forecasts.

References

Agrippa, Henry Cornelius. *Three Books of Occult Philosophy*. Edited by Donald Tyson. Translated by James Freake. Woodbury, MN: Llewellyn Publications, 2018.

Butler, Ryhan. "The Mansions of the Moon." Medieval Astrology Guide. Accessed October 14, 2022. https://www.medieval astrologyguide.com/lunar-mansions.

Greer, John Michael, and Christopher Warnock, trans. *The Complete Picatrix: The Occult Classic of Astrological Magic Liber Atratus Edition*. Iowa City, IA: Adocentyn Press, 2010.

Hail, Raven. *The Cherokee Sacred Calendar: A Handbook of the Ancient Native American Tradition*. Rochester, VT: Destiny Books, 2000.

"Ibn Al-'Arabī (1165–1240)." Encyclopedia.com." Accessed May 5, 2022. https://www.encyclopedia.com/humanities/encyclopedias-almanacs-transcripts-and-maps/ibn-al-arabi-1165-1240.

Kolesnikov, Alexander. "The Mansions of the Moon." Lunarium. Accessed January 31, 2023. https://www.lunarium.co.uk/articles/lunar-mansions/.

Volguine, Alexandre. *Lunar Astrology: An Attempt at a Reconstruction of the Ancient Astrological System*. New York: ASI Publishers, 1974.

Warnock, Christopher. *The Mansions of the Moon: A Lunar Zodiac for Astrology & Magic*. 2nd ed. with 2019–2033 Mansion Ephemeris. Renaissance Astrology. 2019.

How the Moon Speaks

Bernadette Evans

The word *communication* means different things to people. Of course, it's how a person speaks to another, but it's also how you interpret and relate to others. Are you someone who enjoys making light conversation with many individuals? Are you more comfortable engaging in one-to-one discussions? Everyone has their own comfort zone and style. Each day brings with it a different mood that affects all of us uniquely. Let's have fun exploring how a transiting Moon feels (and therefore communicates) in each of the zodiac signs.

Aries Moon

Aries is a fire sign. Fire is hot and can burn rather quickly. When the Moon is traveling through the sign of Aries your thoughts and speech may be quicker, possibly even louder. You may feel impatient and want things and people to get to the point, which may cause you to blurt things out. This in itself can be a problem—you can never unsay something. Using some forethought, thinking before you speak, is always good advice but not always easy to do.

It's easy to initiate projects or to promote yourself with an Aries Moon. You could be more confident and assured, which makes selling yourself or a product less painful. Maybe you can project your voice more. This would be a great time to give a presentation.

An Aries Moon is ruled by the planet Mars, which is about action. Speak up and share your thoughts with friends, coworkers, and your boss. This energy can come off as pushy or aggressive at times. Be secure in your abilities and assertive without running someone else over.

Taurus Moon

Taurus is an earth sign. This energy moves slower, so you may be more careful and take your time when speaking with others. I always think of Ferdinand the Bull, and maybe that's because the symbol for the sign of Taurus is the bull. Ferdinand was gentle and took things at a leisurely pace. You may feel more grounded and proceed deliberately and calmly. Taurus also gets the label of being stubborn. There could be certain issues where you refuse to budge. Don't dig in your heels before hearing all sides.

Taurus is ruled by the planet Venus. This planet appreciates beauty and art. They say music can soothe the savage beast. (Congreve 1797, 13). When the Moon is transiting Taurus, put on your favorite music and sing along. You could also put on a soothing meditation or hypnosis track to ground you and get you into your body. When the Moon is here, maybe you'd like some quiet time—silence, just the sound of your own breath. Taurus likes to manifest and acquire worldly goods. There is also a concern around finances. Have an honest discussion about how to balance your budget with yourself or your significant other.

Gemini Moon

Gemini is an air sign, and air, like fire, moves fast. Thoughts and communication are coming and going quickly. In fact, you may not even have time to process everything before you become restless and feel the need to move on to something else. When the Moon is here, you'll be more than happy to share what you've learned with others; after all, this sign is ruled by Mercury, the "winged messenger."

When the Moon is in Gemini, there's a good chance you're socializing. It can be a light and friendly energy, and you communicate easily. Maybe you're keeping everyone laughing with your humorous anecdotes. You may discover you enjoy being the center of attention while regaling others with your stories. Remember to come up for air once in a while and leave space for others to respond.

Have fun learning, communicating, and playing with this energy. Enjoy the moment before you become distracted and move on to the next thing that grabs your attention.

Cancer Moon

Cancer is a water sign and, like earth, moves slowly. The sign of Cancer is ruled by the Moon, which means it feels at home in this sign. When the Moon is here, you may feel the need to withdraw from other people, even if it's for half an hour. Sometimes that peace and quiet are just what you need to recharge your batteries. Then, at other times, surrounding yourself with the people you love is also in keeping with this energy. It's whatever nurtures you. Pay attention to your intuition and follow what feels right for you.

When the Moon is here, you could verbally express your love for others. You may find that you speak words of love, gratitude, or praise to your loved ones. Its also nice to show them you care by doing something that would make them happy.

This Moon is sensitive and intuitive. You may want to feel your way, just as if you're in a pool and feeling for the bottom before it drops off. Your conversations and speech may be slower; maybe you're protecting yourself. Feeling safe is important when the Moon is in Cancer. Do what feels right for you, tune in to the energy, and go from there.

Leo Moon

Leo is a fire sign, and you already know fire is fast. Did you know that the sign of Leo is ruled by the Sun? You could feel more energetic and enthusiastic when the Moon is here. Maybe you're bubblier and more outgoing! When tuning in to this energy, remember the activities you loved as a child. As adults, it's easy to get caught up in all the work you need to do everyday to keep the household running smoothly. Set some time aside to connect with your inner child and laugh. Laughing, smiling, and playing are good for your spirit.

A Leo Moon can amplify your generous and affectionate nature. Call up a friend and do something exciting. It's easy to be swept up in this energy, especially when you have a partner in crime!

Expressing yourself is a must. Singing, acting, or creating are essential for this energy to be happy and fulfilled. Maybe you can't see yourself getting up in front of people to sing or act; you can still sing to your heart's content at home. Have fun reciting lines from a movie you love. It doesn't matter what you do as long as it lights you up!

Virgo Moon

Virgo is an earth sign just like Taurus. Earth moves slowly. When the Moon is here, you may not communicate at all unless you are 110 percent sure of what you have to say. You could find you're critical and hard on yourself and sometimes others. It's not helpful to criticize yourself—or anyone, for that matter. Do the best you can and move on.

This sign is also ruled by the planet Mercury, the sign of the communicator. Learning and talking with people fills you up. You don't just want to spout theories, though. There's a need for the knowledge to be practical and useful. Otherwise, you may think, "What's the point?"

Use this energy wisely by creating some order. Maybe now is the time to dissect whether or not that sofa is in its optimum place. You may be able to analyze situations through a more objective lens. Having order could bring you peace of mind. You're not as willing to go into your feelings (or express them); you probably want to sit above them and focus on practical applications instead. Tune in to the energy and follow it. There will always be another time to connect with your feelings.

Libra Moon

Libra is an air sign, and just like the other air signs—Gemini and Aquarius—it moves quickly. When you speak, your words are transmitted through the air. Libra is the sign of balance and fairness. These themes usually play out in your relationships with other people.

Libra is ruled by the planet Venus. The planet Venus's focus is on love and relationships. Maybe you need to have a conversation with your partner about sharing the workload or how to make things easier for each other. Take time to listen to what your partner wants and needs.

Its not all about balance and fairness—there's also romance. Why not put on some beautiful music and dance around the living room? Maybe reciting poetry is more your style. Reading something to your partner can be an aphrodisiac. You'll know what works best for you and in your relationships.

Scorpio Moon

Scorpio is a water sign. When the Moon is here, your emotions may be amplified. As you know, water moves slowly. Scorpio has a reputation for being sexual as well as being possessive. This sign is also one that enjoys meaningful conversations, talking about subjects that other people may shy away from.

Scorpio has two rulers: the traditional one is the planet Mars, and the modern ruler is Pluto. Mars likes to take action. Pluto does too, but something has to die to be reborn. This brings us to the theme of transformation. Scorpio is known for death and rebirth, being transformed in the process.

When the Moon is transiting through Scorpio, your discussions could be of a more serious nature. You may not say a lot, but you'll be sure to get your point across when you need to. While the Moon is here, make time for the conversations that matter to you and your partner. Expressing yourself through lovemaking is also a beautiful use of the energy. Have fun exploring the Scorpionic side of your nature.

Sagittarius Moon

Sagittarius is the last of the fast-moving fire signs. This sign is known for being an explorer, being interested in education, and embracing other cultures and philosophies. The world is their playground. Freedom is important for Sagittarius, so you could find yourself dreaming about travel and getting away from it all.

Sagittarius is ruled by the planet of Jupiter. Jupiter is often called the "great benefic." Everyone loves Jupiter's optimism and generous spirit. It's the planet that does everything in a big way. It expands whatever it touches.

When the Moon is in Sagittarius, you may feel called to explore a different subject, maybe with a focus on religion or philosophy. Conversations could be quite interesting and varied. Since this is a fire sign, you may find yourself talking more quickly. Be conscious of talking over someone or sticking your foot in your mouth. Have fun and play while leaving room for others to join in the fun too.

Capricorn Moon

Capricorn is the last of the slow-moving earth signs. This sign has a reputation for being a hard worker. All earth signs are diligent and like order and stability, but Capricorn is also known as a leader. It sets itself apart from the pack.

Capricorn is ruled by the planet Saturn. This planet often doesn't get a lot of love, being called the "great malefic"; it's also called the "great timekeeper" or the "taskmaster." This energy says, "Work first, then you get to play." If it wasn't for Saturn kicking you in the butt, you wouldn't finish anything! Don't worry; in the end, you'll be recognized and rewarded for your hard work.

Communicating when the Moon is here could be challenging for you. Like everything, it will depend on your chart, your personality, and how you process. If you're someone who thrives on creating order, you may find it easy to say what you need. If not, you could feel restricted when the Moon is in Capricorn, unsure how to get your needs met. There's also the possibility you don't want to talk to anyone. You just want to do your work…alone. Figure out the best way to utilize this energy for you.

Aquarius Moon

The Aquarius Moon is the last of the quick-moving air signs. This sign is often thought of as the humanitarian. It thinks of what's best for everyone. Aquarius is also renowned for thinking outside of the box. You may receive sudden inspiration to solve a problem that's been plaguing you for ages.

This sign also has two rulers: Saturn, the traditional ruler, and Uranus, the modern ruler. As described above, Saturn can be a worker bee while Uranus thinks up unusual ways of doing things. Imagine what you can accomplish if you tap into the energy of both planets!

When the Moon is in the sign of Aquarius, you could suddenly be inspired to start a project. A new idea sparks something within, and you're off and running. Thoughts of how it could assist the collective are first and foremost in your mind. You may just spout off ideas. When the Moon is here, you may want to get together with friends to discuss interesting topics (not your usual run-of-the-mill convos). Everyone's contributions make the discussions rich.

Pisces Moon

Pisces is the last sign of the zodiac, as well as the last of the slow-moving water signs. As you already know, water is sensitive and impressionable. This sign is also known for being intuitive and psychic, as well as imaginative.

This sign has two rulers assigned to it too. The traditional ruler is Jupiter, and the modern-day ruler is Neptune. Jupiter is optimistic and generous while Neptune can be creative and a dreamer. It's a lovely energy, if you put it to work. You could create something beautiful, just relax and watch a movie, or stroll through an art gallery.

Conversations could be dreamy, or they could be confusing. When the Moon's in Pisces, your intuition can be heightened. You may decide to sit quietly and either communicate with yourself or with spirit. There's also the possibility of getting your wires crossed when speaking with others. Make sure you're clear on what they mean and vice versa.

Final Thoughts

The Moon plays a big part in your everyday life. Whenever it changes signs, the energy shifts. Of course, it's not the only player in the universe; it's interacting with the other planets all the time. You choose how your day plays out as you interact with the planetary energies and the world around you. Have fun molding your unique creation. As always, have fun surfing the cosmic waves.

Reference

Congreve, William. *The Mourning Bride: A Tragedy*. In *Bell's British Theatre*. Vol. 19. Compiled by George Cawthorn. London: British Library, Strand, 1797.

About the Contributors

Mireille Blacke, MA, LADC, RD, CD-N, is a registered dietitian, certified dietitian-nutritionist, and licensed alcohol and drug counselor residing in Connecticut. She has written numerous articles for Llewellyn's annuals series since 2014 and has also been published in *Today's Dietitian*. Mireille worked in rock radio and the music business for two decades before shifting her career focus to behavioral health nutrition and addiction counseling. She spends considerable time renovating her Victorian home, pining for the city of New Orleans, and entertaining her beloved Bengal cats. Someday, Mireille plans to complete a doctorate in behavioral health nutrition when such a program actually exists. She can be reached at mireilleblacke@gmail.com.

Pam Ciampi was a professional astrologer from 1975 until her passing in 2019. She served as president of the San Diego Astrological Society and was President Emeritus of the San Diego Chapter of NCGR. Pam was the author of the Weekly Forecasts for Llewellyn's best-selling *Daily Planetary Guide* since 2007. Her latest contribution was an astrological gardening guide titled *Gardening by the Light of the Moon*. In its fourth printed edition, it is now available in a calendar format.

Sally Cragin is an award-winning writer living in Massachusetts. She teaches history, writing, theater, and other subjects at Fitchburg State University, and her books include *The Astrological Elements* and *Astrology on the Cusp*, both with Llewellyn Worldwide. These have been translated and sold overseas. She is also a city councilor at large for the Fitchburg (MA) City Council and is the only professional astrologer serving in public office in the Commonwealth. For an astrological forecast or tarot reading, visit "Sally Cragin Astrology & TaroT" on Facebook or text: 978-320-1335. Email sallycragin@gmail.com.

Vincent Decker, a native New Yorker, has been actively studying planetary influences on the weather for over thirty years. His forecast method relies on the work of the main modern and ancient contributors to the field of astrometeorology. At the same time, Vincent has incorporated many new techniques discovered from his own rewarding and fruitful study of planetary influence on weather patterns. His analyses of important past weather patterns have appeared in several astrological magazines. His forecasts and their results are available on his blog at www.theweather alternative.blogspot.com.

Shelby Deering is a lifestyle writer from Madison, Wisconsin. She specializes in writing about home décor, natural wellness, and mental health, contributing to publications like *Better Homes & Gardens*, *The Pioneer Woman*, *Naturally, Danny Seo*, and more. When she's not writing, you'll find her hiking Wisconsin's many trails, shopping flea markets, or going on road trips around the country.

Alice DeVille has been writing articles for Llewellyn annuals since 1998. Her contributions have appeared in the *Sun Sign Book*, *Moon Sign Book*, *Starview Almanac*, and *Herbal Almanac*. She is the principal author of four *Sun Sign Book* annuals from 2021–2024. Alice discovered astrology in her late teens when browsing the book section of a discount department store and found a book that piqued her interest in astrology. Alice is known internationally as an astrologer, consultant, and writer. She specializes in relationships of all types that call for spot-on, problem-solving advice to get to the core of issues and give clients options for meeting critical needs. Numerous websites and publications have featured Alice's work, such as StarIQ, Astral Hearts, Llewellyn, Meta Arts, Inner Self, ShareItLiveIt, world-famous quotes lists, Oprah's website, and Twitter. Contact Alice at DeVilleAA@aol.com or alice.deville27 @gmail.com.

Bernadette Evans has worn many hats—or toques (she's from Canada)—over the years, from daughter and sister to mother and now grandmother, as well as being a clinical counselor, astrologer, hypnotherapist, and writer. Her daily and monthly forecasts were a mainstay on Conscious Community Magazine's website for four years. When she is not working with clients or writing, you can find her with her nose in a book, going to the movies, singing around the house, or taking a class to gain more knowledge. Her new love is playing with her grandson. She hopes to travel more and soak up some sun. You can contact her at bernadetteevansastrology.com or email her at bbevans001@gmail.com. You can also follow her on Facebook and Instagram.

Penny Kelly is a writer, teacher of intuition, author, publisher, consultant, and naturopathic physician. After purchasing Lily Hill Farm in southwest Michigan in 1987, she raised grapes for Welch Foods for a dozen years and established Lily Hill Learning Center. Today, she teaches online, posts regularly on Patreon, Bitchute, Odyssey, YouTube, Spotify, Google Podcasts, and Apple Podcasts. She is the mother of four children, has co-written twenty-three books with others, and has written twelve books of her own. Penny lives, gardens, and writes in Lawton, Michigan.

Lupa is an author, artist, and nature lover in the Pacific Northwest. She has written several books on nature-based Paganism and is the creator of the Tarot of Bones. More about her work may be found at http://www.thegreenwolf.com.

Kim Rogers-Gallagher has been a professional astrologer, writer, and lecturer for over twenty years. Based in Florida, Kim is the author of *Astrology for the Light Side of the Brain* and *Astrology for the Light Side of the Future*. Her monthly, weekly, and daily columns appear in *Dell Horoscope* and other astrological websites. She served on the board and edited the quarterly journal for the

International Society for Astrological Research and was a Steering Committee Member of AFAN (Association for Astrological Networking).

Christeen Skinner, D.F.Astrol.S., FRSA, is a director of Cityscopes London Ltd., a future casting company based in the UK. She is author of several books, including *Exploring the Financial Universe*, *The Beginner's Guide to the Financial Universe*, and *Navigating the Financial Universe*. The latter was published in 2019 and correctly forecasted the pandemic of 2020. She is a trustee of the Urania Trust and a director of the Alexandria iBase project, which, together with the Urania Trust, seeks to preserve material that might otherwise be lost. A free monthly newsletter is published and available at www.financialuniverse.co.uk.

Charlie Rainbow Wolf is an old hippie who's been studying the weird ways of the world for over fifty years. She's happiest when she's got her hands in mud, either making pottery in the "artbox" or tending to things in the yarden (yard + garden = yarden). Astrology, tarot, and herbs are her greatest interests, but she's dabbled in most metaphysical topics in the last four decades because life always has something new to offer. She enjoys cooking WFPB recipes and knitting traditional cables and patterns, and she makes a wicked batch of fudge. She lives in central Illinois with her very patient husband and her beloved Great Danes.

Moon Sign Book Resources
Weekly Tips provided by Penny Kelly, Shelby Deering, and Lupa
"The Methods of the *Moon Sign Book*" by Penny Kelly
"Gardening by the Moon" by Pam Ciampi

Notes

Notes